Samuel C. Cronwrigth-Schreiner

The Angora Goat

Published under the auspices of the South African Angora Goat Breeders'

Association and a paper on the ostrich, reprinted from the Zoologist for March,

1897

Samuel C. Cronwrigth-Schreiner

The Angora Goat
Published under the auspices of the South African Angora Goat Breeders' Association and a paper on the ostrich, reprinted from the Zoologist for March, 1897

ISBN/EAN: 9783337308353

Printed in Europe, USA, Canada, Australia, Japan

Cover: Foto ©ninafisch / pixelio.de

More available books at **www.hansebooks.com**

THE ANGORA GOAT

(PUBLISHED UNDER THE AUSPICES OF
THE SOUTH AFRICAN ANGORA GOAT BREEDERS' ASSOCIATION)

AND

A PAPER

ON

THE OSTRICH

(REPRINTED FROM THE *ZOOLOGIST* FOR MARCH, 1897)

BY

S. C. CRONWRIGHT SCHREINER

WITH ILLUSTRATIONS

LONGMANS, GREEN, AND CO.
39 PATERNOSTER ROW, LONDON
NEW YORK AND BOMBAY
1898

Dedicated

TO

MY FRIEND,

DUNCAN HUTCHEON,

COLONIAL VETERINARY SURGEON;

THE SAVIOUR OF

THE ANGORA GOAT INDUSTRY

IN 1881,

AND THE TRUE FRIEND

OF THE SOUTH AFRICAN FARMER.

CONTENTS.

CHAPTER I.
                                                   PAGE

THE DESCENT OF THE ANGORA FROM THE WILD GOAT . . 1

    Differentiation of wild species—Ibexes and goats proper—Horn differences—*Capra Aegagrus* and *Capra Falconeri*—*Capra Aegagrus* the wild parent stock—Authorities—Note on supposed relationship of Angora to sheep and their hybrid progeny—Theory of descent of Angora from *Capra Falconeri*—Dr. Hayes' book.

CHAPTER II.

EARLY RECORDS 21

    The goat in heathen mythology—Of the Swiss lake cities—Fleece-bearing goats among the Egyptians, Greeks and Romans—Curious ideas—Biblical and classical references—The celebrated goats of Phrygia and Cilicia—Mediæval and modern references—Theory of recent introduction of the Angora into Asia Minor.

CHAPTER III.

THE EVOLUTION OF THE ANGORA 32

    Variation under domestication—Influence of climatic and pastoral conditions—Man's controlling influence—Development of fleece—Choice of sires—Tendency of country about Angora to produce long fine hair—Mohair goat gradually localised and perfected there—Eventually confined to that neighbourhood—Origin of kemp and of mohair—Theory of albinism.

CHAPTER IV.

THE PROVINCE OF ANGORA 38

    The ancient Ancyra—History of town—Description of province—Resemblance to Cape Colony—Rainfall—Population—Number of goats—Compared with Cape Angoras—Superiority of Turkish mohair—Farming in Angora—Poverty of peasant farmer—System of partnership—The Turkish peasant—His limitations as a breeder.

CHAPTER V.

THE ORIGINAL PURE ANGORA GOAT 51

Authorities—Delicacy of constitution—Stamina regained and losses repaired by crossing with the Kurd goat—Summary—Description of original Angora—One kid at a birth—In-breeding—Antiquity of fixed characteristics—Its prepotency.

CHAPTER VI.

THE LOCALISATION OF THE ORIGINAL PURE-BRED ANGORA . 60

The goats of Phrygia and Celænæ—Strabo, Tournefort, Conolly, Tchikatcheff—Boundaries of the part to which the Angora was confined—Its size—Deterioration of this goat when removed to other districts—Detailed description of region—Essentials to production of best fleeces.

CHAPTER VII.

THE CROSSING OF THE PURE ANGORA WITH THE COMMON OR KURD GOAT 69

Why and when crossing became general—Three varieties of goat—Description of the Cashmere-like goat and the Kurd—First mention of a cross-bred flock—Turkish ideas as to fifth in-bred cross—Early American breeders' opinions of "full bloods"—The bulldog-greyhound cross—Other references to the general crossing—Tradition about the spread of the white Angora—Binns—General indiscriminate crossing—Nearly all flocks still tainted—Cessation of general crossing—Summary—How "oil" came into vogue.

CHAPTER VIII.

EFFECTS OF THE CROSSING 91

Kemp—Difference between kemp and mohair—Pure Angora kempless—Crossing produces kemp—Atavism—Kemp mainly due to Kurd goat—Kemp common in Turkey—Horned and hornless Angoras—Fine undergrowth in some Angoras—Beardless ewes—Shape and size of horns—And ears—Number of kids at a birth—Summary—Effects of the crossing.

CHAPTER IX.

THE MOHAIR AREA OF TURKEY. 108

Provinces of Angora and Kastamouni—Boundaries and extent of present mohair area—Description of veld and climate—Table of goat districts—Each district characterised by its own variety of mohair—Naming of clips—Origination of different varieties of Angora goat—Effect of food on fleece—Description of sundry goat districts, and mohair typical of each—Peculiar variety found at Koniah—The Van goat—Summary—Best goats all of one general type.

CHAPTER X.

THE FARMING OF THE ANGORA GOAT IN TURKEY . . . 127

Size of flocks—Tameness of the goats—The "evil eye"—Bells—Winter shelter—Effect of severe winter on the clip—Pleuro-pneumonia—Feeding in winter—No scientific breeding—Size of rams' horns—Fleece with parting on belly—The Koran on in-breeding—Weights of fleeces—The "evil eye"—A secretly used ram—Purity of blood unknown—Shearing and shedding—Prices of goats between Turks—Prices paid by exporters—How to buy from the Turk—A good trait.

CHAPTER XI.

THE TURKISH MOHAIR TRADE 141

Early days—Mohair yarn in Europe—Turkish prohibition against exportation of unmanufactured mohair—Levant Trading Co.—Conolly's account of spinning at Angora—First export of unmanufactured mohair—Rapid decline of manufacture at Angora—Introduction of cheap machine-made fabrics—First spinning of mohair in England—Last export of mohair yarn from Turkey—Angora's loss Turkey's gain—First separate account of mohair imported into England—The 1851 Exhibition—Progressive imports of mohair into England—Salt's mills—Export of Angoras to the Cape—The Cape's rivalry of Turkey—Diehl's account of spinning at Angora—Comparative prices of mohair—England's monopoly—Collapse in the mohair trade—Turkish prohibition against export of Angoras—Figures showing import of Turkish mohair to England—Variation in yearly quantity exported from Turkey—The world's mohair clip.

CHAPTER XII.

IMPORTATIONS TO THE CAPE COLONY—THE FIRST IMPORTATION **166**

"Cashmeres or Angoras"—The Cashmere goat—Importations of Cashmeres—First importation of Angoras—Impotency of the twelve rams—The Boer goats—Their effect on the Angora industry—Spread of the Angora blood—Effect on constitution of Boer goat.

CHAPTER XIII.

IMPORTATIONS TO THE CAPE COLONY (*continued*)—THE 1856, 1857 AND 1858 IMPORTATIONS **180**

Efforts of the Swellendam Agricultural Society—The second importation—Mosenthal's account—Sale at Graaff Reinet—First pure Angoras seen there—The third importation—Located in Swellendam—Foundation stock of pure Angoras in Western Province—And Midlands—Importation of Alpacas—Fourth importation of Angoras—Niland's and Holland's flocks—General remarks on first four importations.

CHAPTER XIV.

IMPORTATIONS TO THE CAPE COLONY (*continued*)—THE FIFTH AND SUBSEQUENT IMPORTATIONS UP TO 1880 . . . **194**

Blaine & Co.'s large importations—In what goat districts of Turkey the Angoras were purchased—Stewart's importations—Featherstone's and Cawood's flocks—Blaine & Co.'s further importations—Mosenthal's—J. B. Evans's 1879 importation—The sale—Record prices for rams—The 1880 importations—Pleuropneumonia—Some details of the sales—Record average prices for ewes—The importations as a whole—Many very inferior animals—Black kids—The Sultan's prohibitory edict.

CHAPTER XV.

IMPORTATIONS TO THE CAPE COLONY (*continued*)—THE 1895 AND 1896 IMPORTATIONS **209**

Meeting of Angora goat farmers—The 1895 lot—Gatheral's account of the purchase—Quality of the goats—The sale—The 1896 lot —The sale—Record prices for single ewes—World's records— Quality of the goats—No special distinct breeds imported— Prospect of Cape mohair surpassing Turkish—Fixing the type.

CONTENTS. xiii

CHAPTER XVI.

THE PLEURO-PNEUMONIA EPIDEMIC IN THE CAPE COLONY . 219

PAGE

The Mount Stewart outbreak—Evans's rams—J. H. Cawood's flock—His compensation—The Bedford outbreak—Rapid spread and deadly nature—Mr. Hutcheon—Inoculation—Slaughter of infected flocks—Total loss of goats—Total cost of eradication—Description of the disease—Criticism as to its introduction.

CHAPTER XVII.

THE MOHAIR AND ANGORA GOAT INDUSTRIES OF THE CAPE COLONY 226

First export of mohair—Quantity and value of mohair export from 1857 to 1897—Fluctuations in quantity and price—Number and value of goat skins exported from 1885 to 1894—Numbers of Angoras and Boer goats in 1875 and 1891—Principal Angora goat districts—Mohair per goat—Principal Boer goat districts—1894 statistics.

CHAPTER XVIII.

THE ANGORA GOAT AND MOHAIR INDUSTRIES OF THE UNITED STATES OF AMERICA 235

The first importation—" Angoras or Cashmeres "—Colonel Richard Peters—First Angoras in California—" Billy Atlanta "—William M. Landrum—C. P. Bailey—Subsequent importations—W. W. Chenery—Diehl and Brown—John M. Harris—" Geredeh Angoras "—Cape Colony Angoras imported—U.S.A. Angoras exported to the Cape Colony—Numbers of Angoras in the different States—W. R. Payne—Imports of mohair—Dressed skins—William L. Black's pamphlet—Prospects of the industries.

CHAPTER XIX.

THE ANGORA GOAT AND MOHAIR INDUSTRIES OF AUSTRALIA . 248

Australia and the Cape Colony—First importation—Mr. Sechel—The Acclimatisation Society of Victoria—Cashmeres—Second importation of Angoras—Mr. McCullough—The Royal Park flock—Sale of the flock—Sir Samuel Wilson's flock—Mr. Price Maurice's importations—No government statistics with regard to Angora goats—The industry now practically non-existent—Imports and exports of mohair—Merino *versus* Angora.

	PAGE
PAPER ON THE OSTRICH 259	

How many species are there?—Colour of the plumage—Colour of the unfeathered parts—Colour of the tarsi and toes—The egg; and size of ostriches—Only one species—The egg and flesh of the ostrich—Its breast-bone and powers of kicking—Leaping and swimming—Waltzing and rolling—The cry of the ostrich—How it feeds, and what it will swallow—How the ostrich runs—Nidification, sexual relations and parental habits—The nest—Laying and sitting—Times of sitting well apportioned—Protective coloration—The little embankment around the nest—Guarding the nest—Eggs outside the nest—The hatching of the chicks—Newly-hatched chicks—Parents and chicks—Is the ostrich polygamous?—Why several hens often share one nest—Unattached hens—Large chicks mistaken for hens—Why no chicks result—Evidences for monogamy stronger than for polygamy—Curious and exceptional relations.

GLOSSARY.

Hamels.	Sheep wethers.
Kapaters.	Goat wethers.
Karoo.	A large, elevated, inland tract of country, hot, stony and dry, with small scattered shrubs and an absence of grass pasturage.
Kloof.	A wooded valley.
Kopje.	A small hillock, often standing alone.
Rand.	A long, low elevation or undulation.
Veld.	Open country, unused except for grazing stock.
Up-country.	The inland parts: generally far inland.
Kraal.	A fold for stock. Throughout almost the whole Karoo, and many other parts of South Africa, small stock are kraalled at night, to protect them partly from thieves, but mainly from wild carnivora, and to collect their droppings for purposes of fuel.
Mist.	The droppings of small stock trodden into a solid mass in the kraals. This is dug out in cakes, dried and used for fuel where wood is scarce or unobtainable.
Kuif.	A tuft on the forehead.
Boer.	Literally, a farmer. Used to denote the Dutch farmer.
Voer-bokken.	Fore-goats: goats which lead a flock, generally used of such as are trained to lead sheep.
Brandziekte.	Scab, generally of sheep or goats. Very prevalent in South Africa.
Izak Bok-Boer.	Isaac goat-farmer.

ERRATA.

Glossary. *For* "mist" *read* "mest".
" *For* "voer-bokken" *read* "voor-bokken".
Page 9, line 7 from bottom. *For* "Arauca" *read* "Arauco".
" 10, line 7 from top of footnote. "Kaross," a skin rug with the hair on.
" 11, note to illustration. *For* "mist cakes" *read* "mest cakes". (Since writing this note an Afrikander sheep has been killed at Graaff Reinet, whose tail weighed 28 lb.)
" 32, line 7 from bottom. *For* "pastural" *read* "pastoral".
" 33, line 11 from bottom. *For* "pastural" *read* "pastoral".
" 36, line 13 from bottom. "Undergrowth." The word "undergrowth" is used here as it is used on pages 97 and 167, and as the word "bottom" is used on page 101, to signify the soft, longish undergrowth corresponding to the "poshm" of the Cashmere goat. It is not used by me in the sense in which Mr. Hoerle has used it on page 96, to signify the short, smooth coat (like that of a smooth-haired fox-terrier) which is seen on the Angora goat when it has shed its normal fleece. The two meanings of the word should be noted on pages 96 and 97. On page 96 Mr. Hoerle uses it to signify the short coat of the nature of kemp; on page 97 I use it (as I have used it throughout the book) to signify the fine lougish undergrowth of the nature of mohair. Attention is called to this point because some American critics have apparently confused the two meanings of the word.
" 44, line 4 from top. *For* "£277,619" *read* "£527,619".
" 50, top line. *For* "mist" *read* "mest".
" 79, line 2 from bottom. *For* "$\frac{1}{1540575}$" *read* "$\frac{1}{1540575}$".
" 90, line 10 from top. *For* "had" *read* "has".
" 117, about middle of page. *For* "slippy" *read* "slipy".
" 125, lines 21 to 25 from top. The reference is of course to unwashed hair.
" 134, line 7 from top. *For* "to" *read* "by".
" 173, footnote. A reliable farmer tells me he has seen a Boer goat kapater which, killed and cleaned, weighed over 100 lb. Farmers in the district of Hanover, Cape Colony, consider the average weight of Boer goat kapaters, killed and cleaned, should be about 70 lb.

Page 173, last word on page. *For* "voer-" *read* "voor-".
" 181, last line. The firm was at that time a Cape Town house, and the 1856 goats were landed at Cape Town. For many years past, however, the firm has been at Port Elizabeth, at which port all its subsequent importations have been landed.
" 231. *For* "2,161,925" *read* "2,161,937".
" 231. *For* "395,502" *read* "397,502".
" 231. *For* "3,695,202" *read* "3,065,202".
" 232. *For* "2,073,601" *read* "2,873,601".
" 244, line 12 from bottom. *For* "Menard, Co. Texas" *read* "Menard Co., Texas".
" 249, footnote. *For* "See Chapter XI." *read* "See Chapter XII.".
" 264, line 2 from top. *For* "cocks" *read* "hens," and *for* "hens" *read* "cocks".
" 265, note to illustration. The three photographs on pages 265, 271 and 273 are all of the same ostrich, and were taken on the same day.
" 269, line 4 from bottom. *For* "steeplechaser" *read* "hurdleracer".

S. C. C. S.

Hanover, Cape Colony,
February, 1902.

THE ANGORA GOAT.

CHAPTER I.

THE DESCENT OF THE ANGORA FROM THE WILD GOAT.

WILD goats are divided into two sub-genera, ibexes and goats proper, and are restricted to the Old World.[1] Geologically, according to Lydekker,[2] they appear to be somewhat older than the sheep, remains of certain species having been obtained from the pliocene rocks of the Siwalik Hills of Northern India. In the superficial deposits of the plains of Central Europe, the remains of a species of ibex have been found. This, as the same authority points out, is a matter of some interest as showing how species of goats came to be differentiated. In a remote geological epoch, when Central Europe was much colder than at present, and the mountain ranges inaccessible, being covered with perpetual ice and snow, goats lived on the plains, and were probably homogeneous, or almost so. With an increase of temperature, they migrated to the various mountain chains, and, different herds becoming isolated, gradually de-

---

[1] The Rocky Mountain *goat* of North America is erroneously so called.

[2] *The Royal Natural History* (Lydekker), 1894.

veloped, in the course of long ages, into distinct species.

In some such manner, it seems probable, the various species of goats were evolved from a common very remote ancestral stock.

There are about ten species of true wild goats, now mainly confined to Europe, and to Asia north of the southern peaks of the Himalayas. They are, as already remarked, divided into two groups, the classification being mainly based on the shape of the horns.

Group 1, the Ibexes, have horns "flat in front, with a horizontal triangular section, furnished with large transversal knots".[1]

Group 2, the Goats proper, " may be distinguished from the ibex and the sheep by the peculiar formation of the horns, which are compressed and rounded behind and furnished with a well-developed keel in front".[2] The essential distinction is concisely expressed by another authority: " The horns of the former sub-genus are destitute of the keel in front so characteristic of the latter".[3]

Group 2, which comprises the Goats proper, is divided into two sub-species:—

(*a*) CAPRA FALCONERI, known also as the Markhor, or Wild Goat of Thibet.

---

[1] *The Angora Goat: Its Origin, Culture and Products*, 1882, by John L. Hayes, LL.D.

[2] *Natural History*, 1865, by J. G. Wood. Dr. Hayes describes Group 2 as having horns "compressed and carinated in front".

[3] *The Riverside Natural History*, edited by J. S. Kingsley; article on "Goats" by R. Ramsay Wright, Ph.D.

(*b*) CAPRA AEGAGRUS, known also as the Paseng (the "rock-footed"), the Bezoar Goat, or Wild Goat of Persia.

CAPRA FALCONERI has a beard which extends from the chin to the shoulders and chest, and long

Photo. Naudin]   [Kensington, W.

Capra Falconeri. Photograph, by kind permission of the authorities of the British Museum, of a specimen in the South Kensington Natural History Museum, August, 1897.

spirally-twisted horns, the twist being outwards from the base. The males, when old, become whitish all over. The ewes have a beard confined to the chin, and small horns with a slight spiral twist.[1] It is a native of the Western Himalayas, Northern Afghanistan, and possibly of Persia; it is also found generally in Cashmere and on the Thibetan side of the Himalayas.[2] Fossil remains show that it is one of the oldest types of goat.[1]

CAPRA AEGAGRUS is chiefly remarkable for its enormous horns, which are larger proportionately than in any other ruminant animal;[3] they are obscurely triangular in form, transversely ridged, and are bent backwards as in the domestic varieties, being scimitar-like in shape of curve, and having no spiral twist. Large horns of *Capra Aegagrus* measure 40 in. along the curve, but a length of upwards of $52\frac{1}{2}$ in., with a basal girth of 7 in., has been recorded.[1] According to Darwin,[4] when this goat happens to fall accidentally from a height, it is said to use its enormous horns to save itself, bending forward its head and alighting on them, thus breaking the shock. It stands somewhat higher than any of the domesticated varieties of the goat (an adult male stood 37 in. at the withers[1]), from which it further differs in its short and powerful neck, its stouter limbs and slender body.[3] In the female the horns are exceedingly diminutive, or are altogether wanting. The fur, which over the greater part of the body is short, is of a greyish-brown colour, with a black line running along the entire length of the back, while the under surface of the neck and the beard, which is present in both sexes, are of a brown colour.[3] In the winter coat

---

[1] *The Royal Natural History* (Lydekker), 1894.
[2] Brehm, *Tierleben*.
[3] *Encyclopædia Britannica*.
[4] *Descent of Man*.

the hair on the neck and shoulders is rather longer than elsewhere, and in the same season, in the colder part of the animal's habitat, a coat of woolly fur is developed beneath the hair.[1] The

Photo. Naudin]   [Kensington, W.

Capra Aegagrus. Photograph, by kind permission of the authorities of the British Museum, of a specimen in the South Kensington Natural History Museum, August, 1897.

young are dropped in May, to the number of one or two. It lives in herds, though the males sometimes keep apart from the females, and are

[1] *The Royal Natural History* (Lydekker), 1894.

occasionally solitary.[1] It is exceedingly wary and agile; and shy, except during the rutting season, when the herds are led by the oldest male if danger is suspected.[2] Like some antelopes, its horns appear to be the seat of the larvæ of a species of bot-fly (*oestrus*) which makes its way inwards through the frontal sinuses.[2] It is known as the Bezoar Goat, from the concretions or bezoar stones (formed of various lime salts round some indigestible substance as a nucleus) believed to have been originally obtained from its intestines or stomach, and formerly much used in medicine and as antidotes to poison.[2,3] Its range is extensive, and was formerly even more so than at the present day. There is evidence that, in classic times, this goat was widely distributed over the Grecian Archipelago; although in Europe it is now found only in Crete, the island of Antimelo, in the Cyclades, and perhaps also in Giura to the northeast of Eubœa. Eastward it is found in the hills and mountains of Asia Minor, being especially common in the Taurus range, and it extends thence through Persia into Baluchistan, Sind, and Afghanistan. In India its range does not extend beyond the western side of Sind. It is found in Sind and Baluchistan in hills a little above the sea level; in the mountains of Persia it ascends to an elevation of 11,000 ft. or 12,000 ft.[4]

[1] The habits of *Capra Falconeri* are, in these respects, similar.

[2] *The Riverside Natural History*, edited by J. S. Kingsley; article on "Goats" by R. Ramsay Wright, Ph.D.

[3] *Encyclopædia Britannica*.

[4] *The Royal Natural History* (Lydekker), 1894.

All varieties of the domestic goat (*Capra Hircus*) are, of course, descended originally from wild species. There was, at one time, much diversity of opinion as to whether there still existed representatives of the wild parent stock, and, if they did exist, whether the domesticated varieties were all descended from one species exclusively, or from one main stock crossed to a greater or less extent with other species. But now it seems to be fairly well established that *Capra Aegagrus* is the wild parent stock from which all domesticated varieties of goats are descended. The subjoined opinions indicate the conclusions arrived at by those most competent to decide the point:—

J. F. BRANDT, formerly director of the Museum at St. Petersburg, asserts that *Capra Aegagrus* "is incontestably and exclusively the source of the domestic goat of Europe"; but he further intimates that the domestication of other wild species than *Capra Aegagrus*, and perhaps *Capra Falconeri*, had produced the Angora goat.[1]

Dr. HAYES[2] says that, although there does not appear to be a development of fleece in *Capra Falconeri* corresponding to that of the Angora goat, yet Sacc, professor in the faculty of sciences at Neuchatel, does not hesitate to declare that "all the characters of this species (*Capra Falconeri*)

---

[1] *Considérations sur la C. Aegagrus de Pallas, souche de la Chèvre Domestique,* par J. F. Brandt. Quoted by Dr. Hayes. *Capra Aegagrus* was first defined by Pallas from a cranium alone from the mountains of the north of Persia.

[2] *The Angora Goat*, 1882, by Dr. Hayes. *Capra Falconeri* appears at that time to have been but recently known to the scientific world.

seem to indicate that it is the source of the beautiful and precious Angora goat, whose horns are spirally twisted like those of Falconer's goat"; and he mentions that Geoffrey St. Hilaire, the highest authority at that time upon the origin of domestic animals, refers to the opinions of Brandt and Sacc without dissent, thus : " He (Brandt) is led especially to see in the Angora goat, produced according to Pallas by the cross of the sheep with the goat, an issue of *Capra Falconeri*. This opinion is also admitted by our learned *confrère* M. Sacc." [1]

[1] *Sur les Origines des Animaux Domestiques*, by Geoffrey St. Hilaire. Quoted by Dr. Hayes. It might, with equal force, have been argued that Geoffrey St. Hilaire refers, without dissent, to Pallas' opinion that the Angora was produced by a cross of the goat with the sheep; but it is clear that St. Hilaire does not, in this passage, give the weight of his authority to either opinion.

The idea, however, of there being at least a close resemblance between the Angora goat and the sheep has been very widespread. Pegler remarks that the Angora approaches more in its appearance and character to the genus *ovis* (sheep) than to the genus *capra* (goat) and adds : " Even the bleat of this goat resembles more that of the sheep than the goat, the cry being softer and more approaching the 'baa' of the lamb. It is doubtless owing to these facts that Pallas regards the breed as a cross between the goat and the sheep," a conclusion which Pegler does not seem quite sure is erroneous. Dr. Hayes says : "The cry is wholly different from that of the common goat, and resembles that of the sheep". Even the *Encyclopædia Britannica* falls into the same error. It says : " The face has a sheepish expression. . . . This variety of goat approaches nearest in its nature, form, and habits to the sheep, even the voice having a strong resemblance." Other authorities might be adduced expressing similar opinions. I have only to say that, having farmed with Angoras for many years, having seen nearly all the best animals in South Africa (many of them

Dr. JOHN BACHMAN,[1] a prominent naturalist of America, was instructed by the U.S.A. Congress to bring up a report on Asiatic goats in 1857.

being of unmixed descent from imported stock) and all those recently imported, and knowing most of the leading breeders intimately, I have never noticed any resemblance whatever, in cry, habits, or appearance, to the sheep; nor have I ever heard of any one else in South Africa having observed it, though, since 1856, over 3000 Angoras have been imported into the Colony from Asia Minor. The fact is, no such resemblance exists: the Angora is a perfect goat in cry, habits, and appearance, only it is the most refined, highly-bred, and blood-like of all the various varieties of domesticated goats.

The *Encyclopædia Britannica* remarks that "Hybrids between the goat (it does not specify the Angora particularly) and sheep are known to have occurred, but are rare". Pliny mentions that in his time the Corsican goat interbred with the sheep, and other instances of this strange union are on record. Thomas Southey (*On Colonial Wools*, 1848) shows that not only are hybrids between the goat and sheep common in Chili and Peru, but that in those countries goats and sheep are mated intentionally to produce them. He also quotes Dr. Adam Smith (*Peru As It Is*, 1839) to the effect that "in Chili it has been frequently found that, by crossing the goat with the sheep, the fleece has resulted of a long, lank, lustrous, and consistent quality, and when woven has greatly imitated the finest camlets. The intention of this was originally to avoid the tedious process of plaiting the sheep's fleece on the skin to make it suitable for 'pellones,' or saddle covers, and the experiment succeeded beyond expectation." The largest and best "pellones" come from Arauca, where the Indians, chiefly leading a pastoral life, take great care in selecting the best breeds for mixture, and in preparing them (by a peculiar method) for their own use, and for purposes of trade. The skins are large, light when dry, and the wool is allowed to grow to a great length (10 or 12 in. at times) before the animals are killed. The colour is generally bluish. They

---

[1] *Patent Office Report, U.S.A.*, 1857.

He says that the varieties of the goat are equally numerous and equally varied in different countries, but are all of one species, the varieties mixing and multiplying with each other *ad infinitum.* "All claim as their origin the common goat (*Capra Hircus*), which, it is admitted by nearly all reliable

are used as covers for the deep saddles of those countries, sometimes three or four skins being thrown over one saddle; and, in the sudden and violent rains, which are common there, these pellones are found useful as a shelter for rider and horse. They make a comfortable soft bed, and in that part of the world are as indispensable to the traveller as the kaross is at the Cape. These hybrids are always perfectly barren.

Crossing between the goat and the sheep is not unknown in the Cape Colony. I have seen four animals represented as being the hybrid progeny of such a cross, three exhibited at Port Elizabeth Shows, and one at a Queenstown Show—all, I think, purporting to be crosses between the Angora goat and the Cape (Afrikander) sheep. That exhibited at Queenstown was said to be such a cross. I examined it closely, and am quite satisfied it was a hybrid between an Angora and a sheep, probably an Afrikander sheep. It was a well-grown animal, about six or eight months old, not having yet cut its teeth; and was fat and healthy. Looked at not too critically from a few yards' distance, it would be mistaken for a sheep, owing mainly to the shape of the horns, which were curled close to the skull, imparting to the head a sheep-like appearance, and to the fleece, which had an even "top" and showed no ringlets. When examined closely, however, the face, although covered with soft down and quiet in expression, more resembled a goat's, and the compact fleece, when opened, was found to be of mohair, peculiar-looking and crimped somewhat like wool, but undoubtedly mohair, about two inches in length, the inch-length nearest the skin being bright lustrous yellow—the colour due, no doubt, to the exudation of some natural secretion of the skin. The animal's legs were not woolled. It was such a perfect blend that, the more critically one examined it, the more one realised the impossibility of deciding whether to class it as a sheep or a goat: it was, in fact, a creature *sui generis*.

DESCENT OF THE ANGORA FROM THE WILD GOAT.

naturalists, derives its parentage from the wild goat (*Capra Aegagrus*)." The goat has, he continues, in several of its varieties, become a wool-bearing animal; various breeds have been formed and have become permanent, but they are all of one species descended from a common wild ancestor.

Photo. W. Roe] [Graaff Reinet.

Afrikander Sheep Rams. These sheep are notable for the enormous size of their tails, of pure fat, which weigh, in some cases, as much as 20 lb. The kraal wall behind them is built of "mist" cakes.

CUVIER[1] says: "*Capra Aegagrus* appears to be the stock of all the varieties of the domestic goat". He adds, as mentioned by Dr. Hayes, that the domesticated goats vary infinitely in size and colour, in the length and fineness of the hair, in

[1] *The Animal Kingdom*, by Cuvier. Cappadocia was a province of Asia Minor, adjoining, on the south-east, the province of Galatia, in which Ancyra was.

the size of the horns and even in the number, the Angora goats of Cappadocia having the longest and most silky hair.

Israel S. Diehl,[1] in an article on the goat in the Report of the Department of Agriculture, U.S.A., in 1863, says that although a great variety of goats now exists throughout the world, nearly all reliable naturalists maintain that they derive their parentage from the wild goat (*Capra Aegagrus*).

Brehm,[2] the great German authority, says that the origin of the domestic goat is quite unknown, and of the wild species so little is known, that it is even impossible to say how many species there are; but that the Bezoar Goat (or Boz-Paseng, *Capra Aegagrus*) is usually credited with being the ancestor of the domestic goat. He adds that the Angora goat is believed by some to be descended from *Capra Falconeri*.

Dr. Hayes[3] holds that *Capra Aegagrus* is the parent stock of all domesticated breeds except the Angora, which he maintains is a distinct species descended from *Capra Falconeri*.

Pegler,[4] an English writer, says: "There is but little doubt that the numerous varieties of the domestic goat are all descended from *Capra Aegagrus*, but it is not improbable that *Capra*

---

[1] The Hon. Israel Diehl, formerly U.S.A. Consul at Batavia, was sent by the U.S.A. Government to Asia Minor in 1862 to report on Angora goats. His report was presented to Congress in 1863.

[2] *Tierleben*, by Brehm.

[3] *The Royal Natural History* (Lydekker), 1894.

[4] *The Book of the Goat*, 1885, by Pegler.

Aegagrus occasionally crossed with some allied species, as with *Capra Falconeri*"; but he continues: "The Angora, known also as the Mohair goat, cannot be regarded otherwise than as a distinct species. ... It is the general opinion of naturalists at the present day that it is descended from the *Capra Falconeri*, while other varieties have their origin in the *Aegagrus*."

The "ENCYCLOPÆDIA BRITANNICA" says that "considerable diversity of opinion has been expressed by naturalists as to the original stock of the domestic goat, which is met with in nearly every quarter of the globe—the now prevalent and most probable opinion being that the various domestic breeds are descended from wild stock now extinct".

Dr. WRIGHT[1] in a very able article says: "Many naturalists agree in considering *Capra Aegagrus* to be the original stock of the tame breeds of goats. Sundervall, however, thought that *Capra Falconeri*, from Thibet and Cashmere, comes nearer to the domestic goat. Danford is of opinion that the *Aegagrus* is the principal stock of the Western breeds, but that the presence of a beard in the tame females, as well as a tendency to a flattened and spiral form of the horns of both sexes, indicate some admixture with the European ibexes."

"THE ROYAL NATURAL HISTORY,"[2] contains the most recent and probably the most correct statement on the subject, the best *résumé*, I believe,

[1] *The Riverside Natural History*, edited by Kingsley; article on "Goats" by R. Ramsay Wright, Ph.D.

[2] *The Royal Natural History*, 1894, edited by Lydekker.

yet published. It says: "The Persian wild goat (*Capra Aegagrus*) is a species of special interest, as being the chief ancestral stock from which the various breeds of domestic goats are derived". Further: "It has already been mentioned that the various breeds of domesticated goats have been mainly, if not exclusively, derived from the Persian wild goat. In saying that domestic goats are mainly derived from that species, it should, however, be mentioned that it is probable that many races have been crossed with other wild kinds. . . . The Angora has been regarded by some as a direct descendant of the Markhor (*Capra Falconeri*). . . . It is not improbable that some races of the domestic goat may have a larger or smaller proportion of Markhor blood."

It is at once apparent, on considering these authorities, that there is a general consensus of opinion that *Capra Aegagrus* is the wild parent stock from which the domesticated goat is descended. But another fact, equally apparent from its peculiarity, is that several of them hold, more or less firmly, that the Angora goat is a separate species, descended from *Capra Falconeri*, and distinct from all other domesticated varieties. It will be noticed, however, that though the most reliable authorities, such as Brehm, Wright, and Lydekker, mention that this idea obtains, not one of them identifies himself with it. If the idea is correct, it means that *Capra Aegagrus* is the parent stock of all domesticated breeds (from the Cashmere and the Maltese down to the dwarf goat of Guinea and the Boerbok of the Cape) except the

Angora, which is alone and exclusively descended from *Capra Falconeri*, and is therefore a distinct and peculiar species. This contention has found an earnest exponent in Dr. Hayes; and as he more than any one else has identified himself with it, and most ably stated it, and as he is the author of the most careful and exhaustive book[1] on the Angora goat which has yet appeared, it is instructive to discuss his arguments.

After deciding that *Capra Aegagrus* is the parent stock of all domesticated breeds, except the Angora, he discusses the origin of the Angora at considerable length, showing great familiarity with what was known of the subject at that date; and he comes to the conclusion (a conclusion, in my opinion, in no way warranted by the evidence he adduces) that the Angora is descended from *Capra Falconeri*, and is a distinct species of itself. He quotes only one authority, Sacc, who definitely holds this opinion, though Brandt, whom he also mentions, evidently considered the Angora was not quite satisfactorily accounted for by tracing its descent solely to *Capra Aegagrus*. Sacc's words are: "All the characters of this species (*Capra Falconeri*) seem to indicate that it is the source of the beautiful and precious Angora goat, whose

[1] *The Angora Goat: Its Origin, Culture, and Products.* The foundation essay of this valuable book first appeared in 1868. In 1882 it was issued in book form, with many additional notes and other supplementary matter. It is the most valuable book on the subject which has yet appeared; but, in many respects, when compared with more recent, full, and accurate knowledge, it is now somewhat out of date; though it still contains much valuable information, especially such as relates to the early days of the Angora industry in the States.

horns are spirally twisted like those of Falconer's goat ".

Dr. Hayes' theory is that *Capra Falconeri* was ages ago domesticated in Central Asia, the ultimate result being a fleece-bearing goat, of which the Angora is the modified form; and that these goats were taken into Asia Minor in comparatively recent times, when that country was invaded and occupied by one of the barbarous and pastoral tribes of Central Asia, probably the Turks. In support of this, he urges that the Angora goat is diffused around the mountains of Thibet, where *Capra Falconeri* abounds (and, indeed, though perhaps sparingly, over the whole of Asia); that two branches of the Turkish race successively installed themselves in Asia Minor in the eleventh and thirteenth centuries, taking possession of the precise region in which Angora is included; and that the Angora goat was not known to the writers of classic antiquity (nor earlier).

It may be allowed here, for the sake of argument, that the Angora goat is diffused around the mountains of Thibet, and sparingly throughout Asia, as Dr. Hayes claims; it may also be allowed that certain barbarous tribes did invade and instal themselves in Asia Minor six and eight hundred years ago. But this will not greatly affect the argument, unless it be clearly shown that the Angora has been but recently introduced into Asia Minor, and that it was unknown there prior to the advent of these invaders from Central Asia. This point is discussed at some length in Chapter ii.; it is sufficient to say here that his contention is by no means proved; that, in fact, evidence seems clearly to show that some thousands of years ago a valuable fleece-bearing goat was farmed in those regions of Asia Minor where the Angora now abounds.

Dr. Hayes concludes by formulating certain alleged material points of difference between the Angora and other domesticated varieties to prove that they are two distinct species, only one of which, in the light of more recent and exact knowledge, is of sufficient importance to be noticed, namely, the difference in the shape of the horns. The importance of any radical difference here can hardly be overrated, as this point is the chief basis of classification for the goat family.

The horns of *Capra Falconeri* have a spiral twist; so have those of the Angora.[1] The horns of *Capra Aegagrus* have no twist; neither have those of the "common" breeds. It seems to be on this, to them, most striking and unique similarity between the Angora (and no other breed) and *Capra Falconeri*, that M. Sacc and Dr. Hayes found their hypothesis. In fact, one is tempted to think that this apparent similarity may have suggested the hypothesis. For the similarity has been proved to be only apparent: they had not observed the essential dissimilarity, namely, that the spiral twist of the horns of *Capra Falconeri* is invariably *outwards*, while in the case of the Angora it is invariably *inwards*. This dissimilarity is so essential that it at once invalidates their whole argument.

There is, however, another objection to Dr. Hayes' contention, which he does not surmount,

---

[1] According to Dr. Hayes, the Angora alone of all domesticated breeds has spirally twisted horns.

namely, that the progeny got by crossing the Angora with any domesticated breed of goats are perfectly fertile. The force of this fact he somewhat evades, dismissing it with the remark that "the theory of the difference of species of these two races (the Angora and the non-Angora races) is not invalidated by the fertility of the products of their crosses; such fertility having been observed in the mixed offspring of the more widely separated species, the horse and the ass". That this analogy tells against his theory is evident; it is not established that *Capra Falconeri* and *Capra Aegagrus* are less widely separated than the horse and the ass, and it is exceedingly rare for a mule to be fertile. If the Angora and the "common" races were to-day two distinct species, the product of a cross between them would be infertile. But the progeny of a cross between the Angora and any "common" breed are as invariably and as perfectly fertile to any number of generations, both with either parent and *inter se*, as are the progeny of any one variety bred pure; which clearly shows a common ancestry, and finally destroys the theory, of which Dr. Hayes is so earnest and able a champion.

However, having, as he considers, clearly proved that the Angora is a distinct breed, he follows the argument to its legitimate conclusion. "The practical deduction," he says, "to be drawn from this separation of the two species is thus clearly stated by M. Sacc: 'There is then no utility in creating flocks of the Angora by crossing with the ordinary goat. We must limit ourselves to preserving the species in entire purity, and devote ourselves to improving the race by itself, as has been done with the justly celebrated merinos of Rambouillet.' A leading object of this paper is to enforce the opinion of this sagacious and practical naturalist."

He then proceeds at considerable length to enforce this teaching, that there should be no grading-up from common (non-Angora) goats, as no good could possibly result; and that the Angora should be kept pure and in-bred, and thus, and thus only, increased.

This was his opinion in 1868; but when his book was published in 1882, guided by the inexorable logic of facts, he had modified his views greatly; and although he does not specifically abandon his contention that the Angora is a distinct species (completely as his theory had failed on the essential point of the doctrine he was inculcating), he candidly acknowledges that he went too far in saying that there could be "no utility in creating flocks of the Angora by crossing with the ordinary goat," and that efforts should be strictly limited to preserving the species in entire purity, and to increasing the breed solely by in-breeding; that he was mistaken in saying, for instance, that there should be no grading-up by putting thoroughbred Angora rams to common ewes and their progeny, as it had been clearly proved that this had been accomplished with such pronounced success as to surprise even the most sanguine advocates of this method; in proof of which, among other examples, he instances the Angora industry of the Cape Colony, the remarkable success and rapid growth of which are due mainly to grading-up from common ewes.

The contention that the Angora goat is a distinct species thus appears to break down at every point. All domesticated varieties are of one and the same species, descended from one common ancestral stock. The wild stock from which they are descended, mainly if not exclusively, is *Capra Aegagrus*. Similar circumstances to those which have produced the different varieties of sheep have given rise to the various breeds of domesticated goats. But it is also probable that many domesticated varieties have at times crossed with wild kinds other than *Capra Aegagrus*, and that some may have a larger or smaller proportion of *Capra Falconeri* blood.[1] Both these wild species interbreed with the common goat; and the ibex is said to do the same. Even at the present day it not infrequently happens that rams of the wild species obtain access to the ewes of domesticated varieties as they wander, often in a semi-feral condition, on the mountains where the wild species live. The progeny of such crosses are not always fertile; but the fact that some are shows how other blood has been introduced into the main strain, and how the *Capra Aegagrus* stock may have become modified to a slight extent. This may, perhaps, help to account for certain subtle modifications in some domestic breeds which might seem anomalous on the theory of perfectly pure descent from *Capra Aegagrus*.

[1] The fact, however, that the outward twist of the horns, so pronounced in *Capra Falconeri*, is unknown in the Angora (whose horns have the twist inwards), or any other domestic variety, appears to indicate that the cross with *Capra Falconeri*, if there was such a cross, is very remote, and that this strain of blood is almost, if not quite, eliminated.

CHAPTER II.

EARLY RECORDS.

There is no record of the first domestication [1] of the goat; as with the sheep, it was domesticated by man long before he was advanced enough to leave any record of his doings. In the earliest times it was worshipped. The veneration in which the goat was held in ancient times, says Southey, may be imagined from the fact that Pan (in the heathen mythology represented as the supreme power over nature) was portrayed with the insignia of this animal, and the Libyan Jupiter with the horns of the ram; while the Grecian Jupiter and Minerva claimed the ægis, or goat-skin, for a breast-plate.

The goat was, however, domesticated in the time of the prehistoric inhabitants of the Swiss lake cities, and was well known to the ancient

[1] Dr. Louis Robinson, in an article on the goat, in *Blackwood's Magazine* for March, 1897, has the following: "Probably in nearly all cases where savages have habitually tamed wild animals, the custom has arisen in the following way. The hunter, having killed the dam and captured the little ones, carried the latter home, very likely as playthings for his children. If the little orphans were pretty and playful, they would be cherished by the 'squaws' and 'papooses,' and would become, as it were, members of the family circle. Now, young kids have very engaging manners, and are to this day universal favourites with children; hence they would be very likely to be kept and brought up in some such manner."

Egyptians, and worshipped by them from so remote a period as 2700 B.C. The Romans used either to shear[1] or pluck the hair from the goats; a fact which Ælianus, 250 A.D., mentions with regard to the goats of Lycia, a province in the south-west of Asia Minor. Dr. Hayes mentions that Appianus, about 100 A.D., refers to stuffs made under the name of *kilikia*, from Cilicia (the ancient name of the country in which Angora is situated), as a means of protection against projectiles; that Virgil refers to goat's hair as used in camps, and as a covering for poor sailors; also that Columella,[2] the great writer on Roman agriculture, quoting Virgil, says the goat should be black.

Some very curious ideas, says Pegler, existed among the ancients with regard to the goat. For instance, Pliny says, on the authority of Archelaus, that goats breathe through the ears and not through the nose. An equally absurd idea held by some of them was that the animal breathed through the horns. It does not become us, however, to assume too superior an air over the "ancients," for the belief yet so prevalent among up-country South African farmers that because locusts (unless there is no wind) fly sideways they have their eyes behind their legs, is not one whit less absurd.

Mr. Julius Mosenthal writes to the *Cape Monthly Magazine*, in 1857, as follows: "The

---

[1] From Lucian, 165 A.D., it appears that the same custom prevailed among the Greeks.—Pegler. The Latin *vellus*, a fleece, is from *vello*, I pluck.

[2] Columella, about 50 B.C., wrote *De Re Rustica*. He was contemporary with Seneca.

softness, durability and flexibility of Angora wool, the brightness of the colour when dyed, its long staple and fibre are well-known facts traceable to remote antiquity. When the children of Israel left the slavery of Egypt and took with them their cattle, the goats they had must have been wool goats, for Moses commanded them to bring white silk and goat's wool [1] to weave the altar covers and the curtains for the Tabernacle (Exod. xxxv. 23). Much goat wool must have been at hand, and of excellent quality, for we read further (Exod. xxxvi. 14), 'and the wise workmen wove eleven curtains of goat wool, thirty ells [2] long, four ells broad, all of the same size'. For slaughter purposes we find (Ezek. xxvii. 21) that these goats were exported from Tyre to Arabia."

Dr. John Bachman also says there are satisfactory evidences that from the time of Moses, who in several places refers to the fine linen and goat's hair spun by the women, the manufacture of fine fabrics from the hair of the goat has been uninterruptedly kept up.

In the same magazine Mr. Mosenthal publishes an extract from a letter to him from Mr. Adler, his brother-in-law: "The Phrygians [3] were long celebrated for paying great attention to the keeping of live stock, especially sheep (Xenophon, *Anab.*,

---

[1] In the revised version "wool" becomes "hair". From the purpose for which it was required, and the fact of its association with "white silk," it may perhaps be inferred that this hair was white.

[2] The English ell is forty-five inches.

[3] Ancyra, modern Angora, was at one time in the province of Phrygia.

Op., p. 527, *et alibi: et* Herodotus).[1] The sheep reared in the vicinity of Celænæ,[2] one of their cities, were celebrated for the fineness of their fleeces, in which respect they rivalled those of Miletus[3] (Strabo, p. 867). The goats of the country were not less distinguished for this quality than the sheep, for in ancient Phrygia the Angora is found. The hair of this goat was woven into cloth in the time of the Persians. 'Ciliciæ capræ tondentur ut alibi oves' (Aristotle's *Hist. Anim.*, viii., *Op.*, p. 791).[4] These goats were shorn like sheep themselves, and garments woven of their wool (*Geographical Survey of the Persians*, c. i., 113). These garments were dyed in brilliant colours indigenous to the country, such as the red of cochineal, and robes of such extreme beauty and splendour made from them that they were worn by the kings of Persia (Ctesias Indica,[5] cap. 21; Ælian, *Hist. Anim.*, iv., 46; Arrian, iii., 28)."

It seems clear that the ancient Egyptians owned fleece-bearing goats whose hair was of a quality sufficiently beautiful to be used with white silk in the manufacture of the altar covers and curtains of the Tabernacle in the time of Moses; and that fleece-bearing goats were farmed in Asia

---

[1] Xenophon lived from 450 to 360 B.C.; Herodotus, about 484 B.C.

[2] In Phrygia.

[3] A city on the west coast of Asia Minor. Strabo, about 54 B.C.

[4] "The goats in Cilicia are shorn as sheep are elsewhere." Aristotle lived from 384 to 322 B.C.

[5] Ctesias Indica, 400 B.C.; Ælian, 250 A.D., wrote *De Animalium Natura*; Arrian, 134 A.D.

EARLY RECORDS. 25

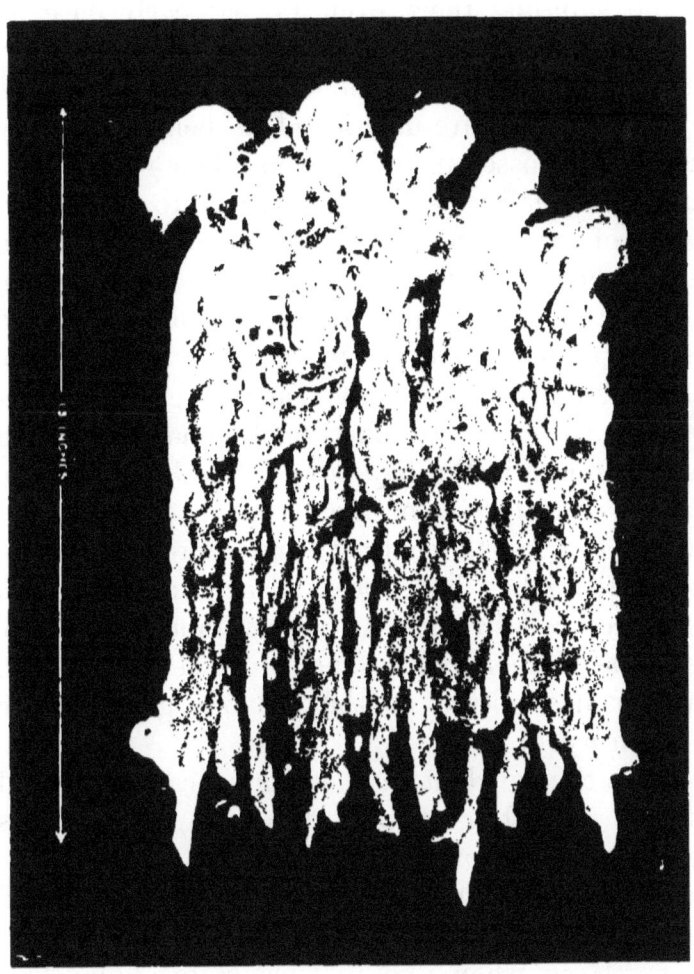

Photo, W. Roe. [Graaff Reinet.

Sample of selected locks of Mohair, eleven months' growth, thirteen inches long, cut from an ewe bred and owned by C. G. Lee, Klipplaat. This is a very choice specimen of the best style of mohair; the locks are solid curled ringlets, running thick to the points, of great length, beautiful quality, and with only that small modicum of oil (scarcely appreciable) necessary to the growth of hair of the highest excellence.

Minor in the fifth century B.C., the industry being of old standing there even at that early date, as Phrygia and Cilicia (comprising Central Asia Minor, the home of the modern mohair goat, where Angora is now situated) are mentioned as being especially famous for possessing goats whose hair was of such superfine quality as to be woven into regal garments of great beauty and splendour, dyed in the most brilliant colours.[1] After this, as has been shown, they are frequently mentioned as being in their present habitat up to the third century A.D. Later, as Mr. Mosenthal remarks, gleanings respecting the early manufacture of mohair in Angora may be found in the *Expositio Totius Mundi* (in the *Geographica Antiqua* of Jac. Gronovius), a composition of the fourth century; and there can be no doubt that they have been farmed in the region now occupied by them in Asia Minor ever since. In 1555 Father Belon, and in 1654 Tournefort, gave a description of the Angora goat to the modern world.

It is thus evident that, as far as can be traced back, a valued and famous fleece-bearing goat has continuously belonged to Asia Minor, and more especially to that part of the country which is still considered, *par excellence*, the home of the Angora goat. How, when, and in what state of development the fleece-bearing goat first appeared there, it is impossible to say; but it seems to have been there, in a fairly high state of development, as far back as historical records carry us.

Thus the arguments against the recent intro-

---

[1] The suitability of the hair for thus being dyed would seem to indicate that it was white.

duction of the Angora goat into Asia Minor seem overwhelming. But it is nevertheless worth while to examine Dr. Hayes' arguments, or rather the arguments of Tchikatcheff, the Russian traveller, which Dr. Hayes adopts and amplifies.

He contends that there is nothing in the references in the Bible which justifies the supposition that the Israelites were possessed of a race of goats with fine and white fleeces; that the classic writers do not specifically refer to goats so clothed, but rather indicate that the hair was coarse; and that the most careful research among the Byzantine writers, after the Roman possessions became the patrimony of a barbarous people, has not afforded any indication of fine and white-fleeced goats.

The evidence just adduced seems to cover and dispose of these contentions.

Dr. Hayes then proceeds, on the same authority, to show that two branches of the Turkish family, the Suldjeks and Oghus, successively installed themselves in Asia Minor in the eleventh and thirteenth centuries, taking possession of the precise region in which Angora is included, and which their descendants still occupy; and that these Turks came originally from Central Asia, bringing the Angora goat with them.

Beyond maintaining that the Angora goat is at the present day diffused around the mountains of Thibet, and sparingly over the whole of Asia, he does not bring any evidence to show that these Suldjeks and Oghus had mohair goats, or that such goats accompanied them, or that the Angora appeared in Asia Minor simultaneously with their arrival, or even about that time. Whereas, it has just been conclusively shown that 1300 or 1400 years before this invasion Phrygia and Cilicia in Asia Minor were noted for goats with fleeces of superfine quality. In fact, it would seem as though, having become thoroughly convinced of the idea that the Angora goat was a distinct species descended directly from *Capra Falconeri*, the wild goat of Thibet, Dr. Hayes felt it was necessary to establish the introduction of a goat, domesticated and evolved in that country, into Asia Minor, to account for its presence there. Against this we have the facts that the Angora goat is not descended from *Capra Falconeri* but from *Capra Aegagrus*, the parent stock of all domesticated varieties, and that the mohair goat has been known in its present habitat for at least 2400 years.

Dr. Hayes is, however, not alone in this idea of the comparatively recent introduction of the Angora into Asia Minor. Sacc quotes De la Tour d'Aigues, President of the Royal Agricultural Society of France, that "there is a constant tradition that the goats of Angora did not originate in that country, but were derived from Central Asia". This statement does not carry much weight, for, as Dr. Hayes remarks, the president probably derived this opinion from the Turkish shepherds who accompanied the flock introduced by him into Europe in 1787. But Pegler (who, like Sacc and Dr. Hayes, holds that the Angora is a distinct species) supports this opinion. He says: "Although Asia Minor is at the present time the home of the Angora, it has been established beyond doubt that the introduction of the breed into that country is of comparatively recent date, having been imported originally from the mountains of Thibet". But he gives no proof of this at all, and quotes no authorities, except "A Writer to the *Field*," as follows : " Busbek, the Dutch ambassador at Constantinople in 1641 (? 1554), explains that he was informed that they (Angora goats) had been recently introduced into Asia Minor from Armenia. All later inquiries support this theory, for, in districts where they have succeeded best, the graziers assert that they came from the eastward. . . . At the present time it (the Angora goat) is extinct in the regions where it derived its origin." Pegler does not give the writer's name, or indicate the scope or trustworthiness of these "later inquiries"; but it may be remarked that the concluding sentence of this extract is quite erroneous, for the Angora is not extinct in Armenia: the goats there are undoubtedly Angoras, though of very inferior quality.

Wishing to know whether a tradition of the Angoras having come from the eastward still existed in the mohair area of Asia Minor, I wrote to Mr. Henry O. Binns, a gentleman who knows the Turks intimately, and speaks their language, having lived many years among them, engaged in the Angora goat industry and the mohair trade. His reply is to the following effect :—

The Kurds, a nomadic tribe, live in Van (Armenia), and every year take their hamels (sheep wethers) overland to Constantinople, passing the city of Angora on the way. In consequence of this, some people have thought the Kurds first brought the Angoras from Van. This supposition is incorrect; for, in the first place, the Kurds farm with sheep mainly, and take hamels, not kapaters, to Constantinople; in the next place, it is far more probable that, when flush of money on their return journey, the Kurds would have purchased some of the beautiful Angoras to take back with them; and lastly, the Van goat is exactly the inferior creature one would expect the Angora to become when taken from its home to a part of the country quite unsuited to it, and when constantly crossed with the coarse straight-haired Kurd goat. It is pointed out, says Mr. Binns, by those who hold that the Angora goat came from Van, that the Persian cat is common in the city of Angora. This, however, he adds, is an argument of no weight, as the Kurds might easily have brought them for the merchants in the way of business as household pets, having described them as they passed through with their sheep.

The tradition of the Angora goat having come from the eastward crops up in the explanation the peasant Turks give as to how it originated. According to this legend, there was, in the Angora district, some 400 or 500 years ago, a white common goat which had been bred to produce a thick crop of fine undergrowth hair (called "derhem"). To this district at that date there came from Van, fleeing probably from a drought, some refugee Kurds, bringing with them flocks of white mohair goats. The two breeds crossed, the result being the famous Angora goat.

It seems probable that these traditions (of whose incorrectness there can be but little doubt) may have arisen from the fact of the Kurds making frequent journeys to Constantinople through Angora, accompanied by stock.

At any rate, I take it to be thoroughly established that the Angora has not been introduced into Asia Minor in comparatively recent years; while it is perfectly clear that a valuable fleece-bearing goat has existed where the Angora is now found from remote antiquity.

CHAPTER III.

THE EVOLUTION OF THE ANGORA.

It seems likely that the evolution of the Angora proceeded somewhat as follows:—

It will be remembered that *Capra Aegagrus*, the parent wild stock, has hair longer on some parts of its body than on others, and that in winter the hair on the neck and shoulders grows longer than elsewhere; also that, in the same season, in the colder parts of its habitat, an undercoat of woolly fur is developed. When domesticated, the tendency to vary, present in all living things, would have much freer scope, unrestrained by the conditions which tend almost irresistibly to make wild animals conform to one type; and variations would tend to perpetuate themselves under the new conditions, which, being greatly artificial, would not act towards the elimination of departures from the normal type. There would thus gradually be formed various types adapted to various local climatic and pastural conditions, aided by the conscious or unconscious controlling influence of the different owners, chiefly through the selection of sires. The natural tendency would be to bring each type to that condition most suitable to the particular locality in which it was bred, and the owners would strive, unconsciously at first, and then with increasing deliberate intention, to preserve any variation which they noticed and valued. Varying rapidly and more rapidly as the original type became unfixed, as the goats would do under domesticated conditions, some of them would have more hair and tend to develop a better fleece than others. This being a valuable property, rams possessing the desired characteristic, other things being equal, would be used as sires; and the idea once being possessed by the owners, it would be a matter of comparatively easy achievement, gradually, and no doubt intermittingly, and through the course of many years, to develop a fleece on an animal which at certain times of the year had a natural tendency to produce it spontaneously. That this fleece-yielding property was favoured by natural conditions, and valued and early developed by the owners of the goats, is shown by the fact that all the varieties of domesticated goats found about the widely-extended natural habitat of *Capra Aegagrus* are fleece-bearing to a greater or less extent; and that these fleeces were gradually developed under different owners, under different climatic and pastural conditions, and not in contact with one another, is shown in the numerous distinct varieties of fleece-bearing goats, and in the widely diverse character of their fleeces. If the conditions of any particular locality tended to produce, for instance, fineness of fleece, and if this quality was valued, it would be bred for; and if any district produced this quality in a surpassing degree (as the country about Angora undoubtedly does), goats of this description would gradually become localised there; other desirable qualities would be gradually bred on; and that district would eventually be considered the habitat of that peculiar type or breed of goat.

This seems to have happened in the case of the Angora goat. Before there was any export of mohair, except as yarn, from Asiatic Turkey, this goat, as will presently be shown, was confined in the most remarkable manner to a comparatively small extent of mountainous country around (principally north-west of) the town of Angora. Of this there can be no reasonable doubt whatever. Of course a hard and fast line could not have been drawn absolutely confining the pure Angora to a certain defined piece of country, and excluding it from the immediate neighbourhood. There was (and is) a certain limited portion in which the Angora reached its greatest perfection; and as this region was departed from the Angoras gradually deteriorated, crossed with, and merged into the common Kurd goat, indigenous to the whole of Asia Minor. But, practically, there is no doubt that the pure Angora was found only within a limited region, of which the town of Angora may be taken as the chief point, on the inland elevations of Asia Minor. This region has long been noted as tending to produce, in a conspicuous degree, the qualities which have made the Angora goat famous and valuable. Apropos of this, the *Encyclopædia Britannica* says: "The fineness of the hair (of the Angora goat) may perhaps be ascribed to some peculiarity of the atmosphere, for it is remarkable that cats, dogs, and other animals of the country are to a certain extent affected in the same way as the goats, and that they lose much of their distinctive beauty when taken from their natural districts". Dr. John Bachman (*U.S.A. Patent Office Report*, 1857) says: "The Angora goat derives its name from the country where this peculiar variety has originated. It is remarkable that nearly all the domesticated animals carried to Angora have, in the course of time, produced varieties, the whole pellage of which is formed of white hair of uncommon length and fineness. Not only the goat has thus been changed, but also the sheep, cats, rabbits, etc." And Captain Conolly, quoted by Southey (*On Colonial Wools*, 1848), says: "It is remarkable that wherever these goats exist, the cats and greyhounds have long silky hair also, the cats all over their bodies, the greyhounds chiefly on their ears and tails. . . . Possibly hares and other furry animals in this region have their coats altered also, more or less." There has been much speculation as to why this region should possess this peculiar quality; it is probable that the atmosphere is the chief factor. At any rate, there seems to be no doubt that a limited and comparatively well-defined region around the town of Angora possesses in a degree unapproached elsewhere in Asia Minor, and probably in the world, those conditions favourable to the development of the soft, silky, lustrous, white mohair goat. This being so, it is but natural that such a goat should have been evolved there and localised there.

It is indeed most probable that the fleece-bearing goats of the time of the Egyptians, and even in the time of the Greeks and Romans, did not closely resemble the modern thoroughbred Angora any more than they resembled those of a much earlier period. There has doubtless been a continual progression towards evolving the beautiful goat of to-day. But it seems quite clear that from remote times the mohair goat developed in the region of Central Asia Minor, and gradually became localised there, the territory which it occupied eventually being restricted to that portion which pre-eminently suited it, the region around Angora, until at last the pure-bred animal was found only there. A continuous course of in-breeding, through a long period of time, fixed it true to type, and made it essentially a thoroughbred; but this also made it small and delicate.

Thus was evolved the modern pure-bred Angora goat, as it was known forty or fifty years ago before the increased demand for mohair induced the breeders to cross it extensively with the common goat of the country; since when its characteristics have greatly altered.

As to the actual mohair of the Angora goat, I am tempted to hazard the speculation that it is the elongated soft undergrowth (which is found shorter and finer beneath the outer hairy covering of the Cashmere, and also on the *Capra Aegagrus* in winter), while kemp is the remnant of the common hair of the original outer coat.

By some writers (not of any great authority on this point) the Angora is thought to be a "sport" from the common Kurd goat—a goat which has a fleece, generally dark or black, of coarse, long, straight hair. They think it may be an albino. Tournefort says: "The delicacy and lymphatic temperament of the white Angoras, which seems to be inherent in this race, appears to be closely related to their colour; some physiologists see in the colour and delicacy of this animal the evidence of an imperfect albinism". It is merely a suggestion, and, as far as I know, is unsupported by any other considerations than those contained in the above quotation. There is nothing inherently impossible in the "sport" theory; the "otter" sheep was a sport, and a breed was founded on it; the nectarine is a sport from the peach, and now throws true; but there is no necessity whatever to adopt such a theory to account for the Angora. The sheep is descended probably from a dark, hairy ancestor; and there seems no more reason to suppose that the white mohair goat is a sport than that the white woolled sheep is. The evolution of both is due to domestication through many ages, aided by climatic and pastoral conditions and man's controlling influence.

CHAPTER IV.

THE PROVINCE OF ANGORA.

It is interesting to learn what we can about the province of Angora, a portion of which (to be more particularly described later) was the cradle of the Angora goat industry, and is the home from which the beautiful and precious white mohair goat has been exported to other countries to enrich them with a new industry, and to which, more than any other country in the world, the Cape Colony is deeply indebted.

The *Encyclopædia Britannica* gives the following historical particulars: "Angora or Enguri, the ancient Ancyra, a city of Turkey in Asia, capital of the vilayet of the same name, is situated upon a steep hill near a small stream, which flows into the Angora, a tributary of the Sukaria or Sangarino, about 220 miles E.S.E. of Constantinople. . . . Ancyra belonged originally to Phrygia, and afterwards became the chief town of the Tectosages, one of the three Gallic tribes that settled in Galatia about 277 B.C. In 189 B.C. Galatia was subdued by Manlius, and in 25 B.C. it was formally made a Roman province, of which Ancyra was the capital. Ancyra was the seat of one of the earliest Churches, founded probably by the Apostle Paul, and councils were held in the town in 314 and 358 A.D. In 1402, a great battle was fought in the vicinity of Ancyra, in which the Turkish sultan, Bajazet, was defeated, and made prisoner by Tamerlaine, the Tartar conqueror. In 1415 it was recovered by the Turks under Mahomet I., and since that period has belonged to the Ottoman Empire."

Photo. W. Roe] [Graaff Reinet.

Angora Goat Ewes, bred and owned by C. G. Lee, Klipplaat.

Mr. H. A. Cumberbatch, British Consul at Angora, in his report to the Marquis of Salisbury, dated 15th July, 1895, says: "The vilayet, or province of Angora,[1] is essentially an agricultural one; the rural population gives itself up entirely to the

[1] In 1893 a railway was completed, connecting the town of Angora with Constantinople.

cultivation of the soil and the rearing of cattle, while the inhabitants of the towns, themselves to a great extent owners of farms and vineyards, trade on the result of the cultivators' labours. . . . The entire province is more or less mountainous, and furrowed by deep valleys. Its mean altitude is estimated at 2900 ft., the town itself being 2854 ft.[1] above the sea level.

"The elevated masses are here and there shaded with forests, but the plateaux, which form the most extensive portion of the country, are very little wooded, and consequently the absence of trees and shrubs gives them a dreary aspect.

"The scarcity of trees permits the summer heat to dry up the little humidity acquired by the soil in winter, and droughts of any length bring about partial or complete failure of crops.

"Wherever the mountain soil is carried down by the spring floods to the valleys and plateaux it makes them very fertile and suitable for the cultivation of all kinds of cereals and vegetables. Wherever artificial irrigation is practicable the fertility is greatly augmented.

"In this province there are to be found light and friable soils, both suitable for wheat and barley culture, and, although rarely manured, good crops are raised, thus proving their great fertility.

"In many parts, however, and in the Cesarea district especially, the soil is very poor, with no consistency, being nothing but dust and stones.

"The climate is extreme. In the months of January and February the thermometer will mark

[1] The same altitude as the town of Cradock, which is 2865 feet.

a minimum of 10° Fahr. for several days at a time, reaching as far as 0° Fahr., whilst in June and July the maximum readings of 85° Fahr. are maintained day after day, with little or no rain.

"The country is covered with snow in the winter, rain and snow falling frequently. In 1894, the total rainfall at Angora was 8·12 inches, but that was an exceptionally dry season. For the first six months of 1895 the rainfall was 10·10 inches, which is somewhat above the average, the heaviest rainfall in twenty-four hours having been 1·20 inches."

It will be seen from this description that the province of Angora, as to geographical configuration, pasture and climate, bears a remarkably close resemblance to those up-country Karoo districts of the Cape Colony where the Angora goat thrives best; for instance, the five leading districts of Willowmore, Aberdeen, Somerset East, Cradock, and Graaff Reinet. The height above the sea is almost the same; the kloofs and the mountains of Cradock and Somerset East are in some parts densely wooded with forests; and the sides of the kopjes and rands are covered with scrub. The description of the elevated plateaux, covered with stunted vegetation, and parched in summer, might serve equally well if applied to the Karoo. Here, too, are valleys in an arid country rich with an alluvial deposit from the hills; here is veld in abundance to which the description "dust and stones" is peculiarly applicable; and, in the summer, the vast treeless flats are exhausted of all humidity by a scorching sun. The temperature of the province of Angora is, on the whole, colder than that of the chief goat districts of the Cape; 20° Fahr. here is very cold, and is rarely attained except on still frosty nights, whereas 100° Fahr. in the shade is a common occurrence in summer during several months. The Cape winter is warmer and much shorter and drier. The rainfall is almost the same. The average annual rainfall for the five districts named, for eight years (from 1884 to 1891), was about 17 inches, which seems to correspond almost exactly with that of Angora. Here, however, the rain falls in greater quantities at a time. The heaviest rainfall in Angora for twenty-four hours, during the first six months of 1894, was 1·20 inches; here it is no uncommon occurrence for that amount to fall in an hour or even half an hour.[1]

It is thus evident that the Cape up-country districts are, on the whole, considerably hotter than the province of Angora. They are also probably much drier, for they are further inland, the rain falls mostly within a few months of the year in heavy thunderstorms, and the water runs rapidly off. Our up-country air is seldom moist, even during a rainy season. Now dryness is one great essential to the growth of good mohair, and in this the Cape excels. Although, perhaps, our climate is too warm, yet it may be that its excessive dryness counterbalances this; for it cannot be doubted for a moment that tens of thousands of square

---

[1] At Aberdeen Road in March, 1896, an inch and a half of rain fell in fifteen minutes; and between Richmond and Middelburg in January, 1897, two and a half inches fell in twenty-five minutes. Such downpours are not uncommon in the summer up country.

miles of the up-country districts are peculiarly adapted to the Angora goat, probably more so than any other country in the world, except that portion of Central Asia Minor which is its natural habitat.

The reasons for the rapid growth of the Angora industry in the Colony, and for the superb excellence of the hair grown by the foremost Cape breeders, are abundantly apparent when it is seen that our veld and climate are almost identical with those of the province of Angora.

According to Mr. Cumberbatch, the population of the province of Angora is under 1,000,000 souls in an area of 29,000 square miles, the average number of inhabitants per square mile being about 34½. In some parts it is as low as 15 per square mile. There is an export trade in wheat and barley; it is excellently adapted for fruit, and the grape industry promises to be large and remunerative.

There were 1,230,000 Angora goats in the province in 1893, and 310,356 common goats. The average annual mohair clip of the province reaches 30,000 cwt. (3,360,000 lb.), valued at £200,000; the annual clip of the common goats' hair is about 710 cwt. (79,520 lb.), nearly all of which is used locally in the manufacture of sacks, tents, etc.[1]

Comparing these figures with those of the Cape, according to the census of 1891, the white population of the Colony is about 377,000 (or 1·70 to the square mile), and about 1,527,000 of all nationalities (or 6·90 to the square mile). The area of the Colony is 221,311 square miles. In 1893, the Cape had

---

[1] It must be remembered that the province of Angora does not include the whole of the mohair area of Turkey in Asia.

2,811,206 Angora goats[1] and 2,819,749 common goats. In the same year there were exported from Cape ports 9,457,278 lb. of mohair, valued at £277,619. The following table shows an instructive comparison between the province of Angora and the Cape Colony.

(The figures represent the annual average. To obtain that of the Colony, I have taken the four years 1891 to 1894 inclusive.)

	Angora.	Cape.
Mohair goats	1,230,000	2,891,233
Mohair	3,360,000	9,982,709 lb.
Per goat	$2\frac{3}{4}$	$3\frac{1}{2}$ lb. (nearly)
Total value of mohair	£200,000	£419,501
Per lb.	1s. $2\frac{1}{4}d.$	$10\frac{1}{4}d.$ (nearly)
Money yield of mohair per goat	3s. $3\frac{1}{4}d.$	2s. $11\frac{1}{2}d.$

The superiority of the Turkish hair is at once apparent, there being a difference in its favour in the above figures of nearly 4d. per lb.; and also a difference in its favour in the net return per goat of nearly 4d., although the Turkish goats shear ¾ lb. of mohair less per goat than the Cape goats. It must be remembered, moreover, that the mohair exported from Cape ports is not all grown in the Cape. Transvaal and Free State hair (an unknown quantity) is included in the figures given above, but the goats of those states are not. This would, perhaps, not make a very great difference, for practically the Transvaal has no goats, and the Free

---

[1] It is worth remarking that in December, 1895, the then five leading mohair goat districts of the Colony (Willowmore, Somerset East, Jansenville, Aberdeen and Cradock) had about 100,000 Angora goats more than the province of Angora, being together about half as large in superficial area.

State not a very large number. But the superiority of Turkish hair becomes accentuated. Against this, a large quantity of the best hair of Asia Minor comes from the province of Angora. The great superiority of the mohair goats of Angora, as a whole, over those of the Cape is, nevertheless, thoroughly established. Cape farmers have been breeding for quantity—oily hair; the Turks more for quality—non-oily, silky hair; and the consequence is that Turkish goats surpass those of the Cape. Cape farmers are, however, rapidly breeding out the excess of oil, and producing a longer, silkier mohair, which in the best clips is already rivalling super Turkish.

The system of farming in vogue in the vilayet of Angora is of a most primitive character. Mr. Cumberbatch says that farms, in the proper acceptation of the term, cannot be said to exist. Except in the immediate vicinity of towns, the land is owned and cultivated by peasants belonging to the neighbouring villages. (Dry, unirrigated land is worth 5s. 9d. to 11s. per acre, irrigated land 28s. to 80s. per acre; but, in the vicinity of towns, irrigated land, where it is adaptable for garden purposes, is worth from £15 to £45 per acre. The price of ordinary grazing land is not given, but it is, presumably, very cheap.) The plots owned, or rather, cultivated, by the peasant farmer vary from 10 to 100 acres.[1] Apart from irrigated land, which is generally reserved for barley, and is always sought after, the peasant does not care much

---

[1] There are 2,500,000 acres of cultivated land, 125,000 of vegetable gardens and orchards, and 75,000 acres of vineyards.

whether he owns land or not. Arable land is more than plentiful, close at hand. Any one is free to cultivate Crown land, and becomes the legal owner thereof after ten successive years of cultivation, the calculation being that in ten years the cultivator pays the full value in tithes. (The tithe, *ashar*, is the only direct duty levied on farm produce, and amounts to 11¾ per cent. of the yield.) On the other hand, land left uncultivated, or unused for pasturing or other purposes, for ten years, reverts to the Crown. The peasant farmer and his family depend entirely on the yield of their plot, supplemented by the produce of one or more cows [1] and of the sheep and goats which are either his own or are supplied by his "partner". A system of partnership is commonly resorted to, especially if it offers the peasant a chance of securing a little hard cash. He never resists the temptation of a loan, no matter what interest is demanded. Hence he is never out of debt; and, considering his destitute condition, his natural laziness, the extortions of the tax collectors, and the terms of his usurious partner, his chronic state of misery is not to be wondered at. The "outside" partner is generally a wide-awake Greek or Armenian of the nearest town. The system pursued in this partnership is broadly that the "outside" partner supplies the seed and sells the oxen to the

---

[1] There are about 570,000 cattle, of small size and weight; and 1,600,000 sheep, clipping 4,144,000 lb. wool annually. These sheep are of the Koramanian breed, and are distinguished for their long tails, but both the mutton and wool are inferior. Half of the wool is exported, and half made up locally into carpets and wearing apparel.

peasant on credit, the peasant supplying land, labour and implements. The produce is halved. The ploughs, worked generally by one pair of oxen, which are calculated to plough ten acres per annum, are of the most primitive kind, being made entirely of wood, except the share and coulter. Often nothing more than the curved branch of a tree, with a piece of iron as the share, is met with. Other agricultural implements and methods are equally primitive. This system of partnership is very general; in a bad year nearly every peasant farmer is forced to resort to it. All the members of the family assist, while several farm hands, who receive about £4 10s. per annum and their food, are employed. Day labourers receive 6d. to 10d. per day without food, and reapers, during harvest time, 1s. 4d. to 1s. 8d. per day and their food.[1] Sheep and common goats are taxed at the rate of 7d. per head per annum; Angora goats at the rate of 6d. per head. Large sheep and goat owners possess more or less extensive tracts of land with a few cottages on them, but beyond the pasturing of the animals no serious agricultural or dairy operations are indulged in by them. The great majority of the stock, goats, sheep and cattle, are owned by the peasant farmer in very small lots, for, as has been remarked, farms, in the proper acceptation of the word, cannot be said to exist.

With regard to the Turkish farmer himself,

---

[1] The yield of wheat is fivefold, and the average annual crop is 8,000,000 bushels, which, at the rate of 58 lb. to the bushel, gives 2,320,000 bags of 200 lb. each. The yield of barley is tenfold, the average annual crop being 3,000,000 bushels, or 1,160,000 bags of 200 lb. each.

and his manner of life, a vivid description is furnished in an extract from a letter written by one who had lived among the peasant farmers for many years, published in Consul Cumberbatch's report of 1895.

"Inured, as he has been, to a struggling existence, it has had the effect of making him gloomy and taciturn. In place of a neat homestead, we find a hovel constructed of sun-dried mud bricks. This one-roomed hovel, without any windows (the only light and air admitted come down through the chimney), serves him and his family as their residence. Adjoining this we find a cellar-like building which serves to house his live stock. All the surroundings are dirt and untidiness. In the place of a garden, we see heaps of manure. The walls round the premises are studded over with lumps of cow-dung undergoing the process of drying for fuel. On the whole, a Turkish farm hovel has a desolate and cheerless look about it, and it is no wonder, with all these miserable surroundings, that the owner should partake of their nature. Frugality is a great characteristic of the Turkish farmer, and it is owing to this that he has been able to eke out a miserable existence. His tastes are simple and his requirements few. He produces everything for his sustenance at little cost; his food consists for the greater part of bread, for which he grows the wheat. This is sometimes varied by a soup made of sour milk and crushed wheat boiled; this is a most nourishing and satisfying dish. He also cooks another dish, equally good, of crushed wheat boiled and flavoured with fresh butter. Sometimes he indulges in a dish of fried eggs. Coffee he drinks occasionally. This completes his dietary, and, simple as it is, he is strong and healthy, and generally of fine physique. He thinks nothing of a twenty or thirty-mile walk, or of doing a day's work of sixteen hours. He would fare badly under the eight hours' system. His clothing costs him even less than his food. He cultivates the cotton from which the women spin the yarn and weave the calico for his clothes. He also allows himself a jacket made of bright-coloured Manchester print. The sheep finds him material for a warm covering; he knits his own stockings. Boots are unknown to him; he manufactures out of a piece of untanned cow-hide a pair of sandals. His cattle find him in fuel; he collects all their manure and dries it in the sun. This warms his house, it makes a good bright fire, and also serves to light his room. Lamps and candles are too great a luxury. Tobacco he seldom indulges in. In spite of all his frugality, he remains poor. The low price of cereals in the past and occasionally bad seasons have been against him."

The Turkish methods of Angora goat farming will be dealt with in Chapter x. But the foregoing details about the peasant farmer have been given because they have a direct bearing on the goat industry, helping us to understand the class of men by whom the Angora is farmed in Asia Minor. One is immediately impressed with the close resemblance of many of the circumstances of his life to those of a portion of the farmers of the Cape Colony, especially the poorer classes in outlying up-country districts. The desolate mud-floored houses, the absence of gardens, the heaps of kraal manure, the "mist" packed on the kraal walls to dry for fuel, and other minor points of resemblance, constitute a parallel with the Turkish farmer's life, as close as unexpected; so close, probably, only because the conditions of the two countries are so similar. This is the type of Turkish farmer who has bred the mohair goat for centuries, possessing it exclusively till near the middle of the present century. It is more than probable that such a farmer would not have produced such a goat as the Angora, even through centuries of breeding, unless he had been greatly aided by the peculiar climatic and pastoral conditions of his country. The men who are building up the Angora industry of the Cape are, however, of a very different type; compared with them, the Turk is antiquated and ignorant. It seems inevitable that, even though in climate and pasture Angora may be superior to the Cape for the production of the best mohair, yet, in the future, Cape mohair will equal, if not surpass, Turkish; for the cultured intellect and more modern and scientific methods of the Cape breeders will probably more than counterbalance the natural advantages which Angora seems to possess.[1]

[1] I desire to thank Mr. C. J. Rhodes for very kindly and promptly supplying me with a copy of Mr. Cumberbatch's report on the province of Angora.

CHAPTER V.

THE ORIGINAL PURE ANGORA GOAT.

THE mohair goat, spread over a large extent of Turkey to-day, is a product of, at most, the last eighty or ninety years, mainly of the last fifty or sixty, and differs materially from the original Angora, which was confined in a remarkable way to a small tract of country peculiarly adapted to it. During the present century, the original type has been largely modified by widespread crossing with the common Kurd goat. This general crossing was resorted to to supply the European demand for unmanufactured mohair, which arose rapidly and assumed large proportions within a very few years, and which could not be met by the normal increase of the pure Angora.

This chapter and the next describe the original Angora goat and its peculiar localisation; Chapters vii. and viii. detail when and how the breed became modified and with what results.

The first detailed account of the Angora seems to have been given in 1654 by the celebrated academician, Tournefort, chief botanist to the French king. In his *Levant Voyage* he observes: "They rear the finest goats in the world in the Champaign of Angora. They dazzle by their whiteness, and their hair, which is as fine as silk, curling naturally in tresses eight or nine inches long, is the material of many beautiful stuffs." But the ancient geographer, Strabo, mentions that the goats of Phrygia were as celebrated for the fineness of their fleeces as its renowned sheep were, and says that the first quality of mohair is "fine, white and bright".

Captain Arthur Conolly, in a paper read before the Asiatic Society in 1840, writes thus: "The long-famed goat peculiar to the province of Angora and certain adjoining districts is invariably white, and its coat is of one sort, namely, a silky white which hangs in long curly locks". Further: "After the goats have completed their first year they are clipped annually in April and May, and yield progressively until they attain full growth, from 150 Turkish dirhems ($1\frac{1}{32}$ lb.) to $1\frac{1}{2}$ okes ($4\frac{1}{8}$ lb.)".[1]

M. Boulier, the French *savant*, says: "The length of the locks of the white Angora reaches 0·25 m. (nearly 10 in.), and the weight of the best fleeces 2 okes (2 kil. 500, *i.e.*, $5\frac{1}{4}$ lb.)".

M. Brandt, director of the museum of St. Petersburg in 1855, described a specimen of the Angora goat brought by the Russian traveller, Tchikatcheff, as being of inconsiderable size, with thick fleece of long, soft, fine, silky hair of pure white, here and there slightly inclining to yellow (stained, no doubt), silky and greasy to the touch, showing distinctly the brilliancy of silk. The horns, he says, are of a greyish-white tint, and longer than the head, being 14 in. in direct diameter. The body was 2 ft. 2 in. in height, covered with long

---

[1] The oke is 400 Turkish dirhems (drachms), and is equal to about $2\frac{3}{4}$ lb.

hairs twisted in spirals, having the appearance of loosened ringlets.

Dr. John Bachman says that the Angora goat, as described by Hassilquist, Buffon, Pennant, and others, is in general a beautiful milk-white colour, the hair on the whole body being dispersed in

Photo. R. Nicholson] [Cradock.

Angora Goat Ram, bred and owned by Robt. Featherstone, Groenfontein, Cradock. Age, 4½ years, with ten months' fleece weighing 9¾ lb.

long pendent spiral ringlets. He also mentions that Dr. G. C. Schaeffer, after having examined, microscopically, the mohair of some pure Angoras belonging to Colonel Peters, Atlanta, Ga., U.S.A., says: "The degree of fineness is about that of the finest Saxony wool".[1]

The Hon. Israel Diehl, in his report to the

[1] *Patent Office Report, U.S.A.*, 1857.

U.S.A. Congress in 1863, says that "the wool (mohair) is described by Buffon and others as a 'very beautiful curled or wavy hair, of silvery whiteness, with a fine downy wool at its base'".

Dr. John L. Hayes says: "An infallible proof of the fineness, not mentioned by M. Boulier, is insisted upon by other writers, viz., the curling of the wool, which is observed upon the young individuals only when they are of pure blood; so that all the young bucks are rejected from the flocks with the utmost care, as not being of the pure race, whose wool is not curled".

Some goats were imported to the Cape by the late Mr. W. R. Thompson, of Grahamstown, in 1858, before the original pure Angora was so greatly modified by crossing. The pure-bred progeny of these goats some years later, when the property of Mr. D. Watson, Llangollen, Alice, were "non-oily, and clipped from 4 lb. to 5 lb.; their hair was very fine and had no kemp". It is likely that these goats grew more robust out here in consequence of the change, and thus that their fleeces were somewhat heavier than those of their imported, perhaps pure-bred, ancestors.

Mr. T. B. Bayly, writing to the *Cape Monthly Magazine*, for 1857, says of the Angora: "Its drooping curls of pure glossy white, together with the high symmetry and gallant bearing of the animal, mark its high caste".

Mr. Julius Mosenthal, whose brother had been to Angora and brought out thirty "pure-bred" animals in 1856, writing to the same magazine, says: "A grown-up (Angora) goat will carry from 3 to 4 lb. of wool of twelve months' growth".

The *Encyclopaedia Britannica* says: "The average amount of wool yielded by each animal (the pure-bred mohair goat of Angora) is about 2½ lb. The kids are born very small, but grow fast, and arrive early at maturity," and it describes the hair as "soft, silky, and about eight inches long".

Chambers' Encyclopaedia says each goat clips from 3 to 4 lb.

Mr. D. Hutcheon, C.V.S., in his article on "The Angora Goat" in the *Official Handbook of the Cape and South Africa*, 1893, speaks of the (original) "pure-bred, silky-fleeced goat of Angora and surrounding districts," and describes it as "the fine, lustrous, silky-fleeced goat, producing the most valuable hair, but an animal of comparatively small size, with only a moderate weight of fleece as a rule".

Mr. Henry O. Binns, in correspondence with me, frequently refers to the original pure Angora which had almost been bred out as early as 1863. As a man who spent twenty years in the mohair-goat districts of Asia Minor, between 1864 and 1886, a breeder and large purchaser of goats and mohair, who not only was thoroughly conversant with all the various types and grades, but who also saw specimens of the original pure Angora, and who knew and watched the causes and manner of its gradual elimination, his testimony is particularly valuable. He describes the pure Angora ram in his prime as about the size of a five months old Cape kid, with small thin horns, woolled all over the body, the hair almost covering the eyes; exceedingly delicate, and so subject to disease that no one cared to keep him. "What is to-day called the pure-bred Angora is," he says, "like the English thoroughbred horse, the result of crossing and re-crossing, until body, class, points, etc., have attained to what is generally considered that the thoroughbred Angora ought to be." He adds that "this pretty little animal did well to give $2\frac{1}{2}$ lb. of hair," and that a really fine silky fleece cannot be heavy. Further, this goat had not a dry fleece, but only a slight modicum of oil, which, however, in so small a goat would make but a trifling difference in the weight of the fleece.

In 1848, the Sultan selected nine pure-bred Angoras from the best flocks in Angora, and sent them as a present to Dr. J. B. Davis, who had been sent to Turkey on some mission by the U.S.A. Government. These goats were the first Angoras ever imported into the United States, and were, I think, among the best bred goats that have ever left Turkey. They and their pure-bred progeny afterwards passed into the possession of Colonel Richard Peters, from whom Mr. Joseph P. Devine, San Antonio, Texas, obtained some. Colonel Peters says a flock of Angora wethers, "if kept fat the year round, could be made to produce wonderful fleeces, say 6 or 8 lb., while breeding ewes would not average over 4 lb., or less". Mr. Devine says: "The heaviest clip I ever took from a pure-blood billy was $6\frac{1}{2}$ lb. from a three-year-old Peters' goat, and I have had several to shear 5 lb." (at twelve months). He says Colonel Peters was surprised at his obtaining such heavy clips, for in Georgia such weights were not obtained. The heaviest fleece he "ever took from a pure nanny was $3\frac{1}{2}$ lb., also from Colonel

Peters' stock," whose pure-bloods, he thinks, cannot be rivalled.

As regards the constitution of this goat, Dr. Hayes, from whose book the particulars given in the preceding paragraph have been obtained, says: "All authors agree that these animals (the original pure Angoras), though able to resist both heat and cold, except immediately after shearing, when they are liable to be destroyed by moderate depression of temperature, cannot withstand much humidity either in their pastures or folds. In a moist atmosphere they are specially subject to maladies of the respiratory organs.[1] In severe winters, while the common goat of the country is unaffected, the mortality among goats of the pure race is frightful. This is due largely to their confinement, where the temperature is 15 Cent. (60° Fahr.), in very bad stables, completely closed and unventilated, and to their nourishment on fodder imperfectly dried, a very little barley being given only when the snow falls."

Tournefort says: "The delicacy and lymphatic temperament of the white Angoras, which seems to be inherent in this race, appears to be closely related to their colour. Some physiologists see in the colour and delicacy of this animal the evidence of an imperfect albinism."

Dr. Hayes also mentions the statement of Tchikatcheff, that when the losses among the pure Angoras are very considerable (from the causes detailed above), the people of the country repair them by crossing the Angoras with the common

---

[1] See Chapter xv.

goats, and then grading up the progeny until purity is regained.

Mr. Binns says the Angora was a delicate goat, in fact so delicate and liable to disease that, when there was a large European demand for mohair, no one cared to have it in its original pure-bred form, but desired a hardier goat, clipping a heavier fleece. He also says that this Angora goat required better feeding than the common goat, and was extremely liable to pneumonia,[1] from which the common goat is exempt, and that the purer it was the more liable it was to pneumonia.

South African experience also shows that the progeny of such imported goats as most closely approximate to the original pure Angora are more delicate than those not so closely related.

I think it is certain that the original pure-bred white mohair goat was a small, very refined, delicate animal of great beauty, clipping at twelve months' growth of fleece about from 2 to 4 lb. (according to sex and age: kids considerably less) of dazzling white, fine, soft, silky, very lustrous mohair, *curling in ringlets* from 8 to 10 inches long, with merely the minimum of oil in its fleece requisite to the growth of hair of the highest excellence, so small in amount as to be inappreciable to the unskilled observer. It was perfectly clothed in every part; it had short, silky, curly hair about the face, and down the lower parts of the legs to the hoofs; a soft, silky, curly "knif" (tuft on the forehead), and small, thin, light-coloured horns. The ewe was, of course, smaller and finer than the ram, and had

---

[1] See Chapter xv.

only one kid at a birth (of this there is abundant evidence). Its delicacy was no doubt mainly due to a long course of inbreeding;[1] perhaps also partly to the desire that it should yield hair of exquisite fineness. In a goat, refinement and delicacy of body and fleece to some extent go together. I do not think it possible for a large, powerful, big-boned goat to produce such a fleece as it seems evident the original pure Angora carried. This long course of inbreeding, however, while it rendered the goat delicate, at the same time also made it a thoroughbred in the truest sense of the term. There seems to be no doubt that, speaking generally, it had been bred true to type for many centuries, and thus had acquired, to an almost unique extent, that one distinguishing quality of the thoroughbred —great antiquity of fixed characteristics. This gave it prepotency of unusual strength, as was shown by the certainty and rapidity with which the rams impressed their peculiar characteristics upon their progeny got by common ewes, a fact fully established and remarked upon with wonder by all who used them to grade up from common ewes before the breed had lost its pristine purity.

[1] I would not be understood to condemn inbreeding; there is probably no thoroughbred stock in the world which has not been produced and which is not maintained, to a large extent, by inbreeding; there seems to be no other way of securing fixity of characteristics. But it requires an accurate knowledge of the science of breeding and a rare skill in mating, amounting to genius, to secure fixity of certain desired qualities without sacrificing others, especially without impairing the constitution. These requisites the Turkish farmer did not, and does not, possess.

CHAPTER VI.

THE LOCALISATION OF THE ORIGINAL PURE-BRED ANGORA.

I HAVE remarked that the original pure-bred Angora was practically confined to a certain portion of Central Asia Minor peculiarly adapted to it.

Of this localisation there can be no reasonable doubt. It appears to date back at least several centuries before the Christian era, for, as has been shown, the goats of Phrygia (comprising that portion of the country in which Ancyra, the modern Angora, was situated) and Celaenae were celebrated for their beautiful fleeces. It seems clear that if the Angora was not then as definitely localised in as small an extent of country as it came to be later, yet the best goats were found in that region which was probably the centre of the industry, namely, in the neighbourhood of the town of Angora.

Mosenthal, writing to the *Cape Monthly Magazine* in 1857, says: " In Porter, vol. ii., p. 720, you will find that Angora is the Ancyra of the ancients, situated in the N.E. part of Phrygia, afterwards called Galatia—' the hills about Ancyra are covered with thousands of these goats '".

Tournefort in his *Voyage to the Levant*, 1654, says: " It would appear that Strabo speaks of those beautiful goats—'in the neighbourhood of the river Halys (Kizil-Irmak), a river running N.E. from Angora, they cultivate sheep whose wool is very thick and very soft; and, moreover, they have goats there which are not found elsewhere'. Be that as it may, these beautiful goats are not to be seen at present more than four or five days' journey (thirty miles) from Angora and Beibazar; their progeny degenerate if carried to a greater distance."[1]

Captain Arthur Conolly[2] wrote thus in his paper read before the Asiatic Society in 1840: "The country within which it ('the long-famed goat, peculiar to the province of Angora and certain adjoining districts') is found was thus described to us—'Take Angora as a centre: then the Kizil-Irmak (or Halys River), Changeré, and from eight to ten hours' march (say thirty miles) beyond; Beybazaar, and the same distance beyond, to near Nalahan; Sivree Hissar; Yoorook, Tosiah, Costamboul; Geredeh, and Cherkesh'—from the whole of which tract the common bristly goat is excluded. Kinnier did not see a long-haired goat east of the Halys; we marked the disappearance of this animal to the westward, a little before Nalahan. Our informants agreed that the boundary is decided on all sides, and remarked that, if taken out of their natural districts, these goats deteriorate,

[1] Quoted by T. B. Bayly, *C. M. Magazine*, 1857.

[2] Southey, *On Colonial Wools*, speaks of Captain Conolly as "the highest authority on this particular subject which can be quoted". Conolly's paper was written in 1839, but read in 1840.

in point of coat especially, till scarcely recognisable; adding that it is difficult even to keep them alive elsewhere, particularly if they are taken to a low or damp soil after the high and dry land to which they are accustomed."[1]

The extreme boundaries here mentioned, as far as I can ascertain, seem distant from Angora about as follows: East, 80 miles; west, 80 miles; south, 100 miles; north, 150 miles; but the area indicated is, I think, perhaps not more than 25,000 square miles, if so much.

Dr. Hayes quotes from Tchikatcheff,[2] who devoted five years to the study of natural history in Asia Minor. The region marked out by this distinguished Russian as the peculiar domain of the Angora goat is situated between 39 deg. 20 min. and 41 deg. 30 min. north latitude, and between 33 deg. 20 min. and 35 deg. longitude east of Paris, and is in extent about 2350 metric square leagues (*i.e.*, 14,514 English square miles), equivalent to about one forty-fourth part of the peninsula of Asia Minor, and about the same fraction of the area of France.

Dr. Hayes himself observes that "the localisation of this species (the pure Angora) in certain districts within the general domain assigned to it is quite remarkable, and appears to be mainly determined by the altitude of the country; the flocks of the pure race being rarely distributed upon the

---

[1] Quoted by Southey.

[2] *Considérations sur la Chèvre d'Angora.* The whole area comprised within the limits mentioned is 21,016 English square miles; but over a portion of this, about 6500 square miles, the Angora was not found. Paris is about 2 deg. west of Greenwich.

most elevated districts, in the deep valleys, or the neighbourhood of the forests. This localisation is doubtless encouraged by the native proprietors, who unanimously assert that this goat cannot be transported from the place where it is born to a neighbouring village without suffering a deterioration of fleece. Even the intelligent travellers (Tchikatcheff and Boulier) above referred to seem to partake of this opinion."

Boulier,[1] he says, shows that the common goat, spread everywhere in Asia Minor, upon all soils, and at all elevations, is the black or Kurd race. The variety confined to the narrow limit is the white race.

Sir Samuel Wilson, a great sheep breeder of Australia, in his pamphlet, *The Angora Goat*, published in 1873, says that the valuable mohair goat of commerce exists only in a tract of country extending for about thirty miles around the town of Angora.

Gavin Gatheral, H.B.M.'s Vice-Consul at Angora, in a paper read before the Royal Colonial Institute in 1878, says that the Angora goat "has for many centuries been a native of the central plateaux and mountains of Asiatic Turkey," and specially singles out the goats of the three districts in the immediate neighbourhood of the town of Angora as being "undoubtedly thoroughbred," and smaller in size than other varieties. The last part of this statement may not be exactly correct, but it seems to indicate that the original region still retained its superiority in 1878. And further

---

[1] *Sur la Chèvre d'Angora*, par M. Boulier, Pharmacien Aide Major.

evidence in support of the localisation of the mohair goat in the region already indicated may perhaps be drawn from another statement of his, that it had been introduced into certain adjoining districts in comparatively recent times.

George Gatheral says: "It is true that for a long time the district of Angora alone produced mohair. The traditional home of the Angora goat was the mountainous region to the north of Angora."

The latest utterance on this subject shows that even to-day the old tendency to localisation still persists. Consul Cumberbatch, in his report of July, 1895, says: "The hilly north-west districts of this province (Angora) and those of the conterminous province of Kastamouni form the natural zone within which the greatest number (of Angora goats) producing the best fleeces are found. As this centre is departed from, the numbers decrease and the fleece depreciates in quality. It is also to be noted that where the Angora goat predominates the common goat hardly exists at all."

Mr. Binns frequently refers to the spread of the Angora goat into districts beyond that region to which it was originally confined; to which may be added that, from the earliest days, the town of Angora has been the centre of the industry, and has given its name to the mohair goat.

I think it is established that the original purebred Angora goat was, for many centuries at least, confined to a comparatively well-defined area in the neighbourhood (chiefly north-west) of the town of Angora, and that it was not found elsewhere; also, that region being peculiarly suited to it, it could not be removed from it without deteriorating, and perhaps in some cases without risk to its life; also that, even at the present day, when the original pure breed has been succeeded by a robuster (and,

Photo. H. Würdemann] [Cradock.

Angora Goat Ram, "Sam," bred and owned by R. Cawood, Ganna Hoek, Mortimer. Born August, 1888. Heaviest fleece, as a six-tooth, 15 lb. 2 oz. (at twelve months' growth). Exhibited, for many years, at all the chief Agricultural Shows, and never beaten except on one occasion, in 1894, by R. Featherstone's "Turk" (a judgment reversed at subsequent shows in the same year). "Sam" is the most famous goat in South Africa; with splendid weight of fleece, he combines a fineness of fibre rarely seen in an old ram; and he has scarcely any "oil". The photograph, taken in February, 1897, shows him carrying, when nine and a half years old, a fleece of nine months' growth, weighing 9 lb.

probably, more remunerative) animal, it is still in this region that the greatest number of Angoras, producing the best fleeces, are found; and that, as this centre is departed from, the hair deteriorates.

Of this region Tournefort wrote: "All this country is dry and bare, except the orchards. The goats eat nothing except the young shoots of herbs, and perhaps it is this which, as Brusbequis observes, contributes to the consummation of the beauty of their fleece, which is lost when they change their climate and pasture."

Dr. Hayes summarises Tchikatcheff as follows: "This country is more or less mountainous and furrowed by deep valleys, its mean altitude being estimated at 1200 metres; while the more elevated masses are generally shaded with pine forests, the plateaux, which form a large part of the country, are very little wooded. The absence of trees, bushes and arborescent plants gives the country the aspect of immense steppes. This nudity permits the first heats of the spring to dry up the little humidity which the earth has acquired in winter. The climate is excessive, the winters being very cold and the summers exceedingly hot. The country is covered with snow in winter, the rain and snow being very frequent, the thermometer in the neighbourhood of Angora frequently descending to 12°, 15°, and 18° of the Centigrade thermometer, corresponding to 10·6°, 5°, and zero Fahrenheit. The cold season continues, however, only three or four months. During the rest of the year, the temperature is very hot, particularly in the valleys, while the fine days continue almost without interruption. Abundant pasturage is found for the white goats only after the frosts and snows, when the first rains revive the vegetation. This time is of short duration, and the stimulus given by a copious and succulent nourishment is exerted wholly in developing the fleeces in length. The shearing, which takes place in April, is hardly concluded when the vegetation called forth by the warm spring is arrested, and receives no moisture from the dews; persons lying at night in the open air finding in the morning no humidity upon their garments. This dryness, however, gives to the vegetation which flourishes (the only food for flocks during summer) an aromatic character, which makes it peculiarly digestible and stimulating."

Captain Conolly has also described this region: "The greater part of the area described above consists of dry chalky hills, on which there are bushes rather than trees, and these chiefly of the dwarf oak, or else of valleys lying 1500 to 2500 feet above the level of the sea, which are quite bare of trees and but scantily covered with grass. In this expanse of country there are spots which produce finer fleeces than others, *e.g.*, Ayash, Beybazaar, and Yoorook. These are districts where the goats are mostly kept on hills, and the natives attribute a general superiority to mountain flocks, which have, first, a rarer atmosphere; secondly, more leaves and a greater choice of herbs, for which, nevertheless, they are obliged to range widely, and so are kept in health, on which the quality of their coat mainly depends. The finest fleeces in the aforesaid country are said to come from the Yoorooks, roving tribes who keep their flocks out day and night throughout the year, except when an unusual quantity of snow falls, so that, not being enclosed and crowded together, they do not soil their coats by the heat and dirt of each other's bodies. The latter flocks, too, are more or less kept upon fresh food in winter, as they are then led down from the mountain heights to the tops of the lower hills, from which a little herbage can be gleaned, as the strong winds that prevail at this season drive the snow off them, while the plain flocks must be folded and fed on hay and branches."[1]

It will be noticed that, in a general way, these descriptions of the region to which the pure Angora goat was originally restricted correspond with that of the province of Angora, given by Consul Cumberbatch; but the more minute details given afford information of additional value. Mountain veld with an average elevation of several thousand feet above the sea level, a rare and extremely dry atmosphere, and sparse vegetation, with a great variety of shrubs of an aromatic character, seem to be its distinguishing characteristics. But it is to be remarked that the manner of farming greatly influences the character of the hair. If the goats are to produce the best fleeces they are capable of, they must have mountain veld, and be maintained in uninterrupted good condition; they must have a great variety of food, principally shrubs and aromatic plants, and lead an active life; they must, if possible, have running water to drink, and be kept free of dust; they must not be kraalled (or shedded) except when absolutely necessary; they must have clean sleeping places, and must not be crowded together. These are all vital truths which the best Cape farmers are rapidly recognising.

[1] From Southey's *On Colonial Wools*.

CHAPTER VII.

THE CROSSING OF THE PURE ANGORA WITH THE COMMON OR KURD GOAT.

"According to tradition, Angoras were first kept as household pets, and they still retain to a high degree the gentleness and tameness derived from this early method of domestication. The beauty and silkiness of their fleece attracted the admiration of the female members of the household, who quickly appreciated its value as a fibre for the private manufacture of articles of adornment in female attire, each family at that period keeping from five to ten goats for their special use. All the extra fleeces, not required for the purpose mentioned, were sold for stuffing beds, etc. In this way this delicate and valuable animal was preserved before mohair came to have a commercial value."[1]

It is probable that the information contained in this letter is correct, at least to this extent, that the goats were kept in very small lots by the different families; for, when there were no manufactures, no markets, and no demand for mohair, there would be no inducement to produce it in large quantities. Individual families would grow what

[1] Quoted from a letter to *The Field* by Pegler in *The Book of the Goat.*

was needed for their own use, and perhaps a little more as a medium for barter. It may be surmised that, as the utility of this hair was more widely recognised, more goats were kept and the hair more variously and extensively utilised, until it came into use beyond the confines of the region to which the goat was originally restricted, eventually becoming an article of commerce in Europe.

Long before this, however, the primitive method of keeping these goats solely as household pets (if ever this did generally obtain) had been superseded by more modern methods; and they were farmed in flocks of inconsiderable size. Gradually the manufacturing trade of Angora grew, and the export trade in yarn and manufactured goods increased; but the mohair goats were kept pure. In 1820 the first unmanufactured mohair, a few bales, was exported from Constantinople. In 1839 spun yarn ceased to be exported, being entirely superseded by raw hair; and soon Turkey was taxed to its utmost to meet the European demand. The phenomenally rapid growth of the demand for this product necessarily required a correspondingly rapid increase in the number of mohair goats; but so rapidly grew the demand that the pure Angoras could not increase fast enough to supply it. The Turkish farmers, in consequence, as a means of quickly increasing the number of mohair-yielding goats, resorted to grading up the common or Kurd flocks by introducing into them pure Angora rams in the place of Kurd rams.

It seems certain that, well into the present century, the original Angora goat was kept pure; though it is more than probable that the growth of the mohair trade had, in some localities, induced this crossing of the Angora with the common goat to a slight extent. There is no doubt, however, that after 1836 such crossing was resorted to with increasing frequency, until in the sixties and seventies it became very general; but since 1880, in consequence of the great decline in the demand for and the price of mohair, it has ceased to be common. It seems still to be persisted in, to a slight extent, in outlying border districts; but 1880 may be taken as the date when the general, systematic crossing-out process practically ceased. Since then the breeders have been content with the normal increase of the mohair goats, recognising that the supply of mohair was, for the time being, adequate to the demand; and consequently there appears to have been an improvement in the goats in recent years, as compared with those of twenty years ago, and some tendency towards uniformity again. But the original pure Angora has been eliminated, and the uniformity is towards a new type. Since 1880, also, the area over which the mohair goats had spread does not appear to have materially increased.

It will be remembered that the original pure Angora was a small, delicate goat, clipping a comparatively light fleece of very white superfine hair. When the losses among these goats were heavy, in consequence of the flocks being decimated by severe winter rains and snows or by an epidemic of contagious pleuro-pneumonia, the people of the country used to repair them by putting pure rams to common ewes, and then grading up the progeny by in-breeding to the pure stock. That this was done, at any rate occasionally, is generally agreed by the various authorities. It is further stated by some writers that this expedient was resorted to, at times, for another purpose, namely, to impart physical stamina to the pure race, purity being regained as before. When stamina alone was the object sought, *white* common ewes seem to have been preferred, as might have been expected.

Thus the Turks were familiar with the method and effects of crossing, and knew how to grade up; and when the unprecedented demand for mohair arose, it was but natural that they should resort to the expedient of grading up. They did so, their object being threefold: first, rapidly to increase the number of mohair-yielding goats; second, to obtain a white mohair goat of sufficient physical robustness to live in regions where the pure-bred would have died; and third, to produce a goat which would yield a heavier fleece. The demand for mohair was so great in proportion to the supply that quantity was more desirable than quality; it paid better to have a goat clipping a fairly good heavy fleece than a light fleece of extrasuper quality, even within the original area itself.

These are three varieties of domesticated goats in Turkey:—

1. The white Angora.
2. A goat with a rough outer and extremely fine under coat.
3. The common or Kurd goat.

The white Angora in his original purity has been described—a small, delicate animal, found only within a certain limited region in the neighbourhood of Angora, with a fleece of dazzling white, exceedingly fine, soft, silky, non-oily hair, hanging in curled ringlets.

The second variety is thus described by Mr. Diehl in his report to the U.S.A. Government in 1863: "There is also a second or other variety of Angora or shawl-wool goat besides those generally described. This goat has an unchanging outer coat of long coarse hair, between the roots of which comes in winter an under coat of downy wool that is naturally thrown off in spring, or is carefully combed out for use. A remarkably fine species of this breed exists throughout the area to which the white-haired goat is limited." And Mr. Binns, in a letter to me, says: "There is, however, yet another class of common goat to be found in small numbers in the centre of Asia Minor, chiefly between the towns of Angora and Koniah, which, though it can scarcely be called a Cashmere, is yet undoubtedly a descendant of it. This goat is larger than the common goat, and has a long, very coarse fleece of hair, at the roots of which, instead of the coarse kemp, there grows a remarkably soft coat of extremely fine wool of an almost silken texture. In spring this hair, of which each goat yields from about 2 to 4 ounces, gradually works its way to the outer extremity of the coarse hair, and is then combed away and stored up, to be later on entirely separated from any odd coarse hairs which may have come away with it, after which it is woven into fine goods."

There can be but little doubt that this goat is closely related to the Cashmere; and it is highly probable that, though it may not have been generally crossed with the Angora, some of its blood, especially when crossing was so indiscriminately resorted to, has at times been introduced into the Angora breed and modified it, though perhaps almost imperceptibly.

The third variety is the common or Kurd goat, indigenous to and spread over the whole of Asia Minor, on all soils and at all elevations (except where it has been ousted by the more remunerative Angora). Boulier refers to it as the black or Kurd race, and describes it as larger than the Angora, with a slightly longer and much heavier fleece of black straight hair without undulation.[1] Gavin Gatheral describes it as somewhat larger than the Angora; and Pegler says it is "a black goat rather larger than the white or Angora proper, the hair of which, although long and of a fleecy nature, being at the same time coarse in quality". Mr. Binns says it is indigenous to the whole of Turkey. He describes it as a very hardy goat, larger, of stouter build, and healthier than the modern Angora, and very much more so than the original pure Angora. It is not subject, or but slightly subject, to pneumonia. It is a little smaller than the Boer goat of the Cape. Its fleece, which is kempy, is not denser than that of the pure Angora, but is very coarse and often very long. Its colour is not confined to black, but varies as much as does that of the Boer goat. It has thick horns, thicker than those of the original Angora, but not so thick as those of a large horned

---

[1] Length of hair of Kurd goat, 0·27 m., equal to nearly 11 in.; that of Angora, 0·25 m., equal to nearly 10 in. Weight of fleece of Kurd goat, from 3 to 4 okes (3 kil. 750 to 5 kil.), equal to from 8½ to 11 lb.; that of Angora, 2 okes (2 kil. 500), equal to 5½ lb. – Boulier.

ram of the modern Angora. Its hair is used for weaving into the Kurd cloths for tents, sacks for mohair, hand-bags for rubbing down horses, etc., etc. It is kept chiefly because it is very hardy, increases with wonderful rapidity, and gives much milk. Ewes seldom have less than two kids at the birth, and are so hardy that with her two or more kids a ewe will do better on less food than an Angora with one kid. Its large supply of milk is specially valued because milk cheeses, a highly-prized food, are made from it.

It was with this goat that the original pure Angora was crossed when the increased demand for mohair sprang up. It will be seen that both varieties were fleeced; but, while one was a small, delicate, refined, pure-bred animal, thin-horned, small-boned, with a white fleece of exquisite beauty and fineness, hanging in curled ringlets, the ewes having only one kid at a birth; the other was a large, hardy, thick-horned, big-boned mongrel, with a kempy, very coarse fleece without undulations or ringlets—blue, black, grey, red, or almost any other colour or combination of colours, the ewes seldom having less than two kids at a birth, and often three or four.

All writers with any knowledge of the subject are agreed that this crossing did take place. The first mention of it that I am aware of is made by M. Boulier.[1] "Seventy years ago," says Boulier,

---

[1] Boulier seems to have written about 1855. It is evident that he is not a reliable judge of Angora goats. A man needs to have farmed them for some years to be a competent judge. It is plain, also, that he knows but little of scientific breeding.

"at Zchiftela Gentchibe Yallaci, the natives possessed no goats. Since that period they have crossed the black female goats of the village with the buck of the white race, and at present there are not less than 8000 goats of the latter race upon the territory of that district. We have examined the flocks, and the fleeces are in no respect inferior to any of those which we have seen elsewhere. It is now established in respect to these new generations that, after three years of experience, the newly crossed race has not degenerated; it is distinctly established, since for a long time the regenerators are taken from the flocks themselves. At Sidi Ghazi the crossing by the same procedure has been commenced within only six years. The flocks are magnificent."

Thus early we have an indication as to the method pursued when it was desired to have white mohair goats in regions where they had not previously existed.

Boulier says that purity is regained after inbreeding to five generations, and thus describes the effects of the crossing and the gradual elimination of the inferior qualities of the Kurd goat in the successive generations:—

"1. The cross of a black female with a white buck will present a fleece marbled with a yellow colour upon an impure white foundation. The flanks, the shoulders, and the head will preserve more particularly the marks of the colour of the mother; the fineness of the fleece will be sensibly ameliorated.

"2. The cross of this first product with a white buck will cause all the dark tints to disappear.

The fleece will become white. The shoulders and flanks will be covered with wavy ringlets; but the whole line of the back and the forehead will remain furnished with coarse, straight hairs.

"3. On coupling this new cross always with a buck of the pure race we shall obtain a greater fineness in the long ringlets of the flanks and shoulders; the dorso-lumbar portion of the vertebral column will no longer retain coarse hairs, which will remain still on the upper part of the neck and forehead.

"4. A fourth cross, carried on with the same precautions as before, will fix a stamp of purity on the product; the coarse hairs will have disappeared on the forehead and neck.

"5. The consecutive crossings will render more stable the modifications already formed, and already, after the fifth generation, the individuals will be able to reproduce as if they were pure blood."

This information of Boulier's with regard to the effect of the cross on five in-bred generations is palpably incorrect almost throughout, but I give it as showing how primitive and unscientific are the Turkish ideas of breeding, for Boulier was but expressing what he had heard from the Turkish farmers.

The effects of thus grading up have been much more carefully and scientifically noted by the earliest American breeders of the Angora, and they are all agreed that, after the fifth in-bred generation, the goats give excellent hair; but the best breeders are unanimous in saying that the rams must on no account be used for breeding purposes, as their progeny varies greatly. Colonel Richard Peters, of Atlanta, Georgia, U.S.A., whom Dr. Hayes considers the highest practical authority in America on this subject, says that the hair of such goats "is not inferior to much of the mohair imported from Asia Minor"; but with regard to the use of scuh "full-blood" rams, as the Americans call them, for breeding purposes, he adds: "It is a fact that no breeder, however experienced in raising Angoras, can by his eye select a flock of so-called 'full' or 'pure' bloods from a flock of thoroughbreds; but the get of kids by 'full-blood' bucks will invariably enable any intelligent shepherd to detect the fraud upon the thoroughbreds". This is only what any scientific breeder would expect, but the Turk is not so careful; he sees that, after the fifth in-bred generation, goats are produced which yield excellent hair, and, judging each goat on its individual merits, caring nothing about its descent, he is satisfied that they are equal to the thoroughbreds for breeding purposes. In this he is undoubtedly incorrect, but it goes far to explain why, crossing having been commonly resorted to, the Turkish goats are now so mixed, and why so many Angoras, imported from Asia Minor as thoroughbreds, throw coloured progeny. The fact, of course, is that it needs most careful breeding over a long time to so fix desirable qualities in an animal that it may be depended upon to get progeny like itself, and thus merit the proud title of thoroughbred. Dr. Randall has well said: "Base blood runs out rapidly by arithmetical calculations, but, practically, *it stays in*, and is ever and anon cropping up by exhibiting the old base characteristics in a way that sets all calculations at defiance". How true this is is shown by Fleischmann in his work on the "German Fine Wool Husbandry" (*Patent Office Report, U.S.A.,* 1857). He shows that after crossing the merino with the common country sheep, and then breeding in with constant regenerators of the pure blood,

Photo. Arthur Green] [Port Elizabeth.

Six-tooth Angora Ram, bred and owned by R. C. Holmes, Karree Hoek, Pearston. Winner of numerous First and Second Prizes in 1895, 1896, and 1897. Weight of fleece, 12 lb. (at twelve months).

even in the twentieth generation coarse hair will be found, and that, while in the pure merino there are 48,000 wool hairs to the square inch, in the twentieth generation there are only 27,000. Such an animal of the twentieth generation will have only $\frac{6}{1048576}$th part of base blood; whereas one of the fifth generation will have $\frac{1}{32}$nd. If the twentieth generation cannot be trusted to breed true *inter se*, how much less can the fifth or sixth!

In fact it needs no argument to convince the scientific breeder that the fifth or sixth in-bred generation will not throw true. Yet the effect of in-breeding to thoroughbred stock is extraordinarily powerful and rapid, even when the first cross is between two pure and most distinct breeds. This is strikingly shown in the crossing of the pure bull-dog on to the pure greyhound, when the latter, through a long course of in-breeding, has become enervated, the object being, without impairing the qualities of the greyhound, to impart to it greater tenacity of purpose and to overcome the excessive timidity which it sometimes displays. It is instructive to note that, according to Stonehenge, the great authority on the dog, the fifth generation in-bred to the greyhound (after one cross with the bull-dog) has produced a greyhound, perfect as a show-dog, but not very fast: a defect overcome in subsequent generations.

Coming down to a later date, there is ample proof that this crossing was resorted to. Dr. Hayes refers to it, and Pegler refers to certain variations in the Angora goat in shape of ears, horns, etc., "due in a great measure to crosses more or less remote with a common kind, known as the Kurd race, which is distributed generally over Asia Minor". G. A. Hoerle, Corresponding Secretary to the American Mohair Growers' Association, about twenty years ago wrote as follows to the *Texas Live Stock Journal*: "All we know about practice in use with Angora goat breeders in Asia Minor is what we have learned from people who have visited that country, and looked into the Angora goat husbandry. They all, without exception, agree that the practice of grading up the scrub (Kurd) goat of the country is common, even very common, there in the Angora-raising districts." And he adds that "Angoras have been badly mongrelled up in Asia Minor".

In a paper read before the Royal Colonial Institute in 1878, Mr. Gavin Gatheral, H.B.M.'s Vice-Consul at Angora, discusses "the breeding of the mohair goat, and cross-breeding with a common species". There are two methods, he says, for beginning to form a flock of Angoras. One is to obtain "a few thoroughbred goats of both sexes, and trust entirely to their natural increase". The objection to this method is the initial outlay, and the long time that must elapse before a large number of goats is obtained. The second method is to introduce thoroughbred Angora rams into flocks of common (Kurd) ewes. By this method large flocks, clipping excellent hair, may be obtained within a very few years. "Theorists," he says, "object to this system, that perfect purity of blood cannot be reached; but, practically, every trace of under-breeding can be eliminated, and the standard of the pure goat reached." The most profitable manner of applying the second method is to keep a small flock of pure Angoras to breed rams for service to the flocks which are being graded up; and to use no crossbred rams. This does away with the necessity of constantly purchasing new rams, and enables the owner at the same time gradually to acquire a thoroughbred flock.

It is thus evident, on Mr. Gatheral's testimony, that crossing and grading up of Kurd goats was most common.

Mr. D. Hutcheon, C.V.S., in his article on the Angora goat in the *Official Handbook of the Cape*, 1893, after remarking upon the different types of the Angora to-day, says: "The manner in which these different types of Angoras were originally formed, is generally represented to have been by means of a cross between the black Kurd goat common to the whole of Asia Minor, and the pure-bred silky-fleeced goat of Angora and neighbouring districts".

Mr. George Gatheral, of Constantinople, in a letter to me in 1896, after remarking that for a long time the district of Angora alone produced mohair, mentions a tradition among the Turks as to how other parts of Asia Minor came to produce mohair. According to this tradition, at a time when Angora alone possessed the mohair goat, there was a great drought or some other calamity in that district, and, in consequence, the pure Angora goats were sent to other parts, and scattered over a wide extent of country in which the common goat alone existed. The two breeds mingled, the common goats were extensively graded up, and thus other centres came to produce mohair. And he further states: "It has been and still is the custom to cross the black or brown or white *straight-haired* goat with the mohair goat, and give the latter a stronger physique, the fifth cross being considered thoroughbred. It is said that, after thirty years, there is no chance of a cast back. If a goat has blue stains under the eyes, it may now and then have a black kid; but it is considered that a goat with these stains will produce stronger progeny when it produces a white one, that is, a blue face stained animal may have one kid in ten black, but its white ones will be more vigorous than those of an animal always producing white kids." And in a letter to the *Eastern Province Herald*, dated Constantinople, 4th November, 1895, he mentions as evidence of the excellence and purity of the goats of the district of Beibazar that they have been "most carefully bred, uncrossed with black or red goats, for thirty years or more". Now, the town of Beibazar is only about forty-eight miles from that of Angora, and is within that portion of the country to which the Angora goat was originally confined. Thus, according to Mr. Gatheral, even the goats of that famous district were, some thirty or more years ago, crossed directly with the common goat. It will be seen presently that this is corroborated by Mr. Binns, who, however, adds that they still are crossed even there, to some extent. If direct crossing was resorted to in Beibazar, it may be gathered how general it was in less central districts when it was desired rapidly to increase the number of white mohair goats; and the effect upon the original pure Angora and upon its descendants to-day may easily be inferred, when the Turkish farmers' unscientific methods of breeding are remembered, and the fact that the fifth in-bred generation was considered by them to have acquired *all* the properties of the thoroughbred.

Mr. Binns gives most valuable information. He writes to me that he cannot say when crossing began to be general; when he went to the Angora districts in 1864, it was in full swing, and must have been commonly practised for some years, as there were even then many more cross-bred goats than pure-bred. The fact that these cross-bred goats were in large numbers and yielded excellent hair, shows that crossing had been generally resorted to a good many years back. Even at that time the original pure Angora was becoming very rare. To-day he is probably extinct, or almost so. The districts outside the mohair-producing region were, he says, thronged with the Kurd goat. Angoras were introduced amongst the various flocks of these goats, which in due course were all graded up, and yielded white mohair. From inquiries made, he concludes that the Angoras were first generally crossed with the common goat when a large European demand for mohair sprang up, after unmanufactured mohair was allowed to be exported, and lustre goods became fashionable. The result is seen in the Angora of to-day, which is a product of the cross. The greatest endeavours[1] to increase the numbers of Angoras and to produce them in other parts of the country, by means of grading up the common goats, were made, he says, from about 1863 to 1876, when not only were other districts, where the Angora had never been before, induced to buy rams to cross with the common ewes, but, so eager were the farmers in Angora itself to increase the number of their mohair goats, that common ewes were actually imported into that

[1] Mr. Binns is, of course, speaking of what came under his own observation, but the statement is probably correct without reservation.

and neighbouring districts, and graded up there by means of pure rams. No wonder goats became mixed, and the pure goat eliminated, replaced by this heavier-fleeced, more prolific, more remunerative cross. These endeavours were due to the great demand for mohair during these years, for the price per pound was never lower than 2s. 9d., except for a short time in 1868, when it touched 2s. 3d., and was generally at from 3s. 3d. to 3s. 9d. Thus there was a large increase, not only in the numbers of white mohair goats, but also in the area over which they were distributed. The common goat was then first graded up in such districts as Eskischehr in Broussa, Soungourlou in Yozgat, Devriken and Tosia in Kastamouni, and sundry other districts. So general has been the crossing that not only is the original pure Angora extinct, or almost so, in Asia Minor, to-day, but even in Beibazar, one of the very purest districts, hardly a flock is to be found which does not contain one or more grey, black or white common ewes and their various crosses. Such common goats, and the various grades between them and the modern Angora, are much more common in less central, less pure districts. Throughout the whole of the mohair districts any ewe (or ram) which has originally come from a cross (and almost all have now) is liable to have coloured, kemped kids, red, blue, black, or other colours; and in almost every flock in Beibazar, as well as in other districts, coloured kids, the progeny of white sires and dams, are to be found.

The general and systematic crossing practically ceased in 1880, when there occurred the great decline in the demand for and price of mohair; but for four years before that date it had ceased to be so general. Since 1878 or 1880 there has been no material increase in the area over which the mohair goat is distributed. In 1896, however, mohair suddenly jumped from 1*s.* 2*d.* to 2*s.* 7*d.*, which was the first rebound since 1880. If high prices should continue, crossing may again be resorted to, to some extent, in outlying districts; but, if they should not continue, it is unlikely that further crossing will again be resorted to, except in isolated cases, or for the purpose of increasing the stamina of the thoroughbreds, according to the old custom. Nor is it likely that under present conditions the Angora goat will spread much beyond those portions of the country in which it is now found, for the Turk is most unenterprising, and values his common goats for their remarkable prolificness, their extreme hardiness (necessitating little attention), and their abundant milk from which he makes cheeses of which he is very fond.

Thus I take it that, well into the present century, the original Angora was generally kept pure, and was not found, except, perhaps, to a very limited extent, outside the region which had been his peculiar habitat for many centuries. The number of Angoras had, however, up to this time, been slowly increasing, and perhaps spreading by means of slightly modified crosses; for before unmanufactured mohair was permitted to be exported from Asia Minor, an export trade in spun mohair yarn had sprung up, the town of Angora being the chief manufacturing centre. In 1820 the first unmanufactured mohair was exported, and the trade grew gradually, the demand being small till after the Greek Revolution, when it soon assumed large proportions, and increased with extraordinary rapidity till about 1878 or 1880. The European demand for mohair became so great that it was impossible for Asia Minor (which practically had a monopoly of the trade till the early seventies) to meet it merely by the normal increase of the pure Angora goats. It was, therefore, necessary quickly to obtain a more rapid increase in the number of mohair goats than could be obtained through the normal increase of the pure Angoras; and, at the same time, a larger area of country was essential for the production of the amount of mohair required. To secure these ends the Turkish farmers resorted to grading up the common ewes by means of in-breeding to Angora rams. The mohair demand being so great in proportion to the supply, quality ceased to be the first essential; weight of fleece was required and a large number of goats. So, in crossing, the aim was not to breed right back to the original pure Angora, but to produce a goat which, under the then conditions, should be more remunerative: a large, hardy goat which would live almost anywhere, yielding a heavy fleece which would net more money in consequence of its weight though lacking to a considerable extent, as compared with that of the pure Angora, in other characteristics. And as one very efficacious way of packing mere weight on a goat is to cultivate the secretion of an abnormal amount of "grease" in the fleece, "oily" goats became fashionable.[1]

[1] The terms "oily" and "non-oily" (signifying a great excess of "grease," or a scarcely appreciable amount) are

With these ends in view, crossing became very general, and was so persisted in that in the early sixties the original pure Angora was becoming very scarce. A further and most marked impetus was given to the mohair trade in the sixties and seventies, when lustre goods became the fashionable craze, and mohair went up to, and maintained, an abnormally high price. This, of course, at once reacted on the Angora industry of Asia Minor. Crossing became more general than ever; by its means, entirely new districts were rapidly populated; indeed, such a hold had this method of increasing the numbers of the mohair goat obtained on the Turkish farmers, and so eager were they to avail themselves of it, that, not content with introducing Angora rams into flocks of Kurd ewes in outside districts, they actually imported the Kurd ewes into the very centre of the mohair region—the home of the pure Angora—and, putting them to Angora rams, graded them up there. When crossing became so general (especially when considered with what is known of the Turkish farmer and his unscientific methods of breeding), and districts far from the region where the pure goat was found became thus populated with mohair goats, it may be safely inferred that the grading up of the common ewes was not brought about solely by the use of pure rams, but that cross-bred rams were commonly used in many parts; indeed, the fifth and sixth in-bred generations, used by the

common in the vocabulary of the Angora farmer of the Cape Colony. The secretion so designated is, however, not an oil or a grease; it is more of a soapy nature, being largely composed of potash.

Turks as thoroughbreds, are really crossbreds. At this stage, principally in the sixties and seventies, mohair goats must have been badly mixed, almost, if not quite, throughout the whole of the then mohair-producing districts. Writing of this period, Mr. Binns says that the out-breeding of the pure goat not only caused the average quality of Turkish hair to become lower, but that the Turks went to the other extreme and completely neglected the quality of the hair as long as they got the quantity. " During the years 1863 to 1870, when lustre goods were in such demand that any and every class and quality were eagerly bought up to make quantity, this paid them well, but since the price of mohair has fallen so low,[1] the Turkish farmer has been forced to the conclusion that, unless he produced a mohair of a certain class and containing the right proportion of the finer qualities, his mohair was often utterly unsaleable even at a very low price, and he has consequently had to study how to get the heaviest weight compatible with the most saleable qualities."

When the price of mohair again declined, as it did from 1880 onwards till it became very cheap, crossing was no longer generally resorted to ; the Angora ceased to spread to new districts, and, quantity of mohair ceasing to be almost the sole desideratum, the farmers set about improving the quality and reducing the " oil ". For buyers became more discriminating ; they purchased good mohair readily, but inferior stuff with great caution, especially if greasy, in which case they discounted

[1] Written in 1893, letter to the *Midland News*, Cradock, by H. O. Binns.

the grease as well. But so general and thorough had been the mongrellism that, even to-day in the very best most central districts, even in the old original limited mohair region, there is hardly a flock which has not coloured members, and perhaps not a flock in which even some of the best white ewes may not throw "red-kemped," or some other coloured progeny. Every country into which Angoras have been imported, especially the Cape Colony and the United States, had borne witness to the fact that, judging by the goats imported since 1860, Turkish flocks are woefully mixed. Not only have many most inferior goats been imported, but even specially selected stud rams and ewes have frequently thrown off-coloured and quite black kids. That matters should have come to this pass in Asia Minor was inevitable, as is clear when the method resorted to, and the men who resorted to it, are remembered. That the Turk should have resorted to this method was natural; the same method obtained generally at the Cape and in the United States; but the Turk is not so intelligent a farmer as are those of the Cape and America, nor are his methods comparable to theirs; he knows nothing of the scientific principles of breeding; and, having thoroughly mixed his goats, he does not seem able to again breed them to the thoroughbred standard, at least not without being allowed very many years to do it in.

CHAPTER VIII.

EFFECTS OF THE CROSSING.

In tracing more particularly the effects of this crossing, perhaps the most important matter is that relative to the prevalence of kemp in the modern Angora. The data one has to go upon do not admit of an absolutely definite conclusion, but from what I have been able to gather from many sources, I believe that the best examples of the original pure-bred Angoras had no kemp; that kemp is a sign of common blood; and that its prevalence in the fleece of the modern Angora is due to crossing the pure Angora with the common or Kurd goats. I am of course aware that kemp in the modern Angora is so common that it can generally be detected without a very careful scrutiny in the best Cape stud flocks; but, on the other hand, it is undeniable that some of the foremost Cape breeders, starting, I believe almost invariably, with kempy stock, and often solely through grading up by careful in-breeding by selection, have already, in the short time that they have had, produced many goats, some perhaps quite devoid of kemp, others with so little that only the most careful examination can detect it.

The opinion that the original pure Angora was kempless is supported by most men who have given the subject the careful study that its intricacy demands.

It must be borne in mind that kemp and mohair are, in their nature, essentially different hairs; they do not grade into each other, and cannot, by a competent judge, ever be mistaken.

Photo. G. Watson] [Aberdeen Road.

Angora Goats owned by R. F. Hurndall, Somerville, Aberdeen Road, standing among mimosa trees.

From an examination of the specimen Angora goat brought to Russia by Tchikatcheff, Brandt says that those strands of mohair "corresponding most to external hair have only a third, or, at most, do not attain to half the thickness of the external hair of the common goat; and that the external hair of the wild and domestic goats is not only closer, stiffer and more massive, but has a more considerable torsion and a less even surface, that is to say, it is rougher and more scaly. He also remarked that 'the walls of the hair of the Angora goat being thinner than those of the hair of the common goat, the substance contained in the fatty cellules oozes out more rapidly, which renders the hair of the Angora goat softer and more flexible, and gives it the lustre of silk'."[1] Dr. Hayes says that mohair is extremely slippery, and has the aspect, feel and lustre of silk without its suppleness; that it lacks the felting property of wool; and that it is dyed with great facility, being the only textile fabric which takes equally the dyes destined for all tissues.

Mohair is undulated with a smooth surface, very fine, and of a lustrous appearance, and a living-white colour. Kemp is not undulated; I have never seen it as long as mohair; it is stiff, rough, very coarse, and of a pronounced lustreless appearance and a dead-white[2] colour; it will not work up with mohair, and will not take the dye as mohair does; it is never found in locks or ringlets as mohair is, but always as separate individual hairs.

The essentially distinct nature of mohair and kemp will be more clearly comprehended from the following observations, by Colonel R. W. Scott, of Kentucky, U.S.A., referred to by Dr. Hayes as " one of the most reliable and eminent breeders within my knowledge," and by Mr. G. A. Hoerle,

[1] *The Angora Goat*, by Dr. Hayes.
[2] Mohair and kemp are also found in other colours.

Corresponding Secretary of the American Mohair Growers' Association, whose letter to the *Texas Live Stock Journal* shows him to be thoughtful and well posted in the subject.

Colonel Scott says: "When the wool[1] of the Angora goat is being shed, the cups or bulbs in the skin which produced the fibres are also shed, as well as the cuticle or outer skin. This is a peculiarity of the Angora goat; but a still greater one and of far more practical importance, is the capacity of the bucks to transfer, or impart, this rare quality to other goats which do not possess it. . . . The kid of an Angora buck, out of a native ewe, invariably has in its skin those bulbs, or cups, which produce and secrete the fine *wool* of the Angora or wool-bearing goat, while it has the power to secrete the hair[2] also, as its ancestry, on the dam's side, always had. The wool of goats is finer, longer, or thicker, in different individuals of the same blood, just as is the case with sheep; and, like sheep also, the same animal produces finer wool when young than when advanced in life. But the *wool* of the half-blood kid or goat is of the standard and fineness of full-blood[3] or of pure Angora goats' wool, but it is short. The *wool* and the *hair* of the half-blood grow together, and seem to constitute one covering; but a closer inspection shows the different fibres issuing from the different bulbs in the same skin; and when the shedding season arrives, the fine *wool* may be combed out of

---

[1] We should say mohair now.   [2] Kemp.

[3] The term "full-blood" was used in America to indicate graded-up goats of the fifth or later generation, in-bred to pure Angoras.

the *hair* on the animal's back, and, on being separated from it, bears a close resemblance to the finest fur, or to Saxony wool, or to the Angora mohair. A friend who was travelling in Europe sent me a sample of mohair, which exactly resembles this fine *wool* of the first cross, having also some of the coarse *hair* and of the cuticle in it, showing that it had been shed and not shorn. The two products of the half and of the three-quarter blood being nearly of the same length, they cannot be separated by shearing, and to gather it by combing it out of the hair on the backs of the animals is too tedious. The specimen to which I have alluded is most probably the product of some other species of wool-bearing goat, and not of a half-blood cross of different species."[1] He goes on to say that, as grading up is persisted in, the *wool* gradually becomes much longer than the *hair*, and that eventually goats of the fifth inbred generation and later "bear wool which in every essential particular resembles closely that of the pure-bred or imported Angora".

The implication here is clear that the bulbs of the roots of mohair and kemp respectively are essentially different, and that, when kemp is shed, its bulbs remain in the skin; while, when mohair is shed, the bulbs are shed too, and must re-form to produce the next fleece. The assertion that whatever *mohair* may be found upon any cross will always be of the same nature, irrespective of the quantity, quite distinct from kemp, and practically of one uniform degree of fineness, is borne out by

[1] *The Angora Goat*, by Dr. Hayes.

a host of independent observers, and is supported by my own experience. Colonel Scott states (it is also implied in the above extract) that mohair and kemp are both naturally shed, but not exactly at the same time of the year. This, I believe, is also correct.

Mr. Hoerle says: "A really thoroughbred Angora should have no kemp". Further: "I have not the slightest doubt that any vestige of kemp in the fleece of an Angora goat is itself proof positive of an admixture of common blood of the coarse and long-haired goat type. . . . Here I may mention that, practically speaking, kemp is the degenerated coarse hair of a long-haired common goat.[1] It grows less and less and degenerates more the higher the animal is bred up. But it is quite distinct in character from the mohair. Its bulbs or roots have the same shape and character as those of the hair of the common goat, or the undergrowth of the hair of the Angora, and they remain in the skin after the hair is shed, whereas the bulbs of the mohair are shed with the hair, and new ones form in the skin shortly before the mohair begins to grow." He, however, holds that the progeny of a pure-bred kempless Angora ram by a common smooth short-haired ewe cannot possibly have kemp, as the ram cannot impart what he does not possess, and it cannot be supposed (he says) that the short hairs of the common ewe would elongate to form kemp, the short undergrowth of the ram (corresponding to her *hair*) being even shorter than her own. It will be seen that on this point Colonel

---

[1] The Kurd goat of Asia Minor.

Scott and Mr. Hoerle differ. I agree with Colonel Scott. I have said in Chapter iii. that I believe mohair is the elongated undergrowth. There can, I also think, be but little doubt that kemp is the hair of the coarse outer coat. It must be remembered that all domesticated goats have a common ancestry;[1] that thus even the purest bred kempless Angora potentially has kemp; and that, therefore, when crossed with another variety whose hairs, though quite short, are of the nature of kemp (or, in fact, when crossed with any other variety), the forces of atavism come into effect, and there is liability to reversion, to a greater or less extent, to a common ancestor which had kemp. As has been said, the original pure-bred Angora was probably kempless; it was not innately kempless, but through a very long course of in-breeding to produce the finest fleece possible, kemp had gradually been eliminated. Of course, all the Angoras of (say) 100 or more years ago were not kempless, because the Turkish farmers occasionally crossed the rams of the pure race with the common ewes to make up losses, and to impart hardihood to the breed; but I have very little doubt that there were many which were pure-bred and kempless. It is probable that *very* few kempless Angoras have ever been imported into the Cape Colony; therefore the prevalence of kemp in the Cape flocks may justly be imputed to the imported goats. But experience has also shown that when put to smooth

[1] Mr. Hoerle's theory is probably accounted for, in part, by the fact that he held the Angora to be a distinct species, descended from *Capra Falconeri*, though modified by late infusions of other blood.

short-haired Boer goats, these imported Angoras have produced progeny more kempy than themselves. If, therefore, Angoras, when crossed with short-haired goats, produce kempy progeny, it is much more probable that, when crossed with a long-fleeced goat whose hair is not mohair, the offspring will have kemp, and have it long and in great abundance. If the Angoras that have been imported to this country, chiefly within the last sixteen or seventeen years, and especially if those imported in 1895 and 1896 are to be taken as but fairly representative of the Angoras of Asia Minor, then there can be no doubt that kemp is extremely common there, for not one of these goats was free from kemp, and most had it in large quantities. Believing that the original pure Angora was kempless, it follows that, in my opinion, the great prevalence of kemp to-day in the goats of Asia Minor is due to the crossing of the Angora with the common Kurd goat of that country. Even those who may not believe that the pure Angora was kempless, still acknowledge that it was almost so. In such a case it follows with equal conclusiveness that the crossing produced the large amount of kemp so prevalent in the Angoras of to-day, which are the product of that cross. Even if it be maintained that the ordinary fleece of the Kurd goat is not identical with, or does not closely resemble, kemp (and I do not know that this can be reasonably maintained), yet, if it once be granted that kemp was, at least, very scarce in the pure Angora, there is but one way to account for the great prevalence of kemp to-day, namely, that it is due to the crossing; for the modern Angora is the product of that cross, and it is incontestable that kemp is very common in the goats of the Kurd race. It is further supported by the fact that the nearer the modern Angora of Asia Minor approximates to the Kurd goat, the more abundant is kemp.

Kemp is often found scattered over the whole body, always shorter than long mohair; but, generally, it is found along the back, and on the hinder part of the body, especially in the breeching, which, when much kemp is present, is usually short, wiry and matted. Kemp varies in length; it is sometimes found shed throughout some of the long locks of a good goat, and is then short and not so coarse; when long and very prevalent it is never found in a fleece which, as a whole, is long, fine, soft, silky and lustrous. Other things being equal, it is more prevalent in the flat locks, characteristic of what in the Colony is called the Geredeh, than in the round, curled ringlets of the goat with only a small modicum of oil in its fleece. The nearer a goat approximates to the original pure-bred Angora, the less prevalent is kemp, and already in many instances the modern Angora has been bred almost, if not quite, free of kemp. That kemp can, and will, be entirely eliminated from the best stud goats of our most intelligent breeders I have no doubt whatever.

There are other variations in the modern Angora, due, I believe, to the original Angora having been crossed with other breeds. For instance, Conolly says: "A curious statement made to us at Angora was, that only the white goats which have horns wear their fleece in the long, curly locks that are so much admired; those that are not horned having a comparatively close coat". I cannot add anything to this statement, not having had the point suggested when I was farming goats; but Mr. Binns says it is devoid of fact. It may, however, be remembered that the female of *Capra Aegagrus* is occasionally hornless, though I cannot see that this has any bearing on the statement made to Conolly. It will be interesting if observant men engaged in the industry will notice if hornless goats (which, by the way, are very rare in this Colony) have not, as a rule, the curled locks in so pronounced a degree as those that are horned. This peculiarity, if it does exist, may not, of course, be due to the influence of some cross; the variations may simply be collateral. Further, crossing has been so universal and has had such an overwhelming effect that a variation which might have been pronounced in 1840 (the date of Conolly's paper) might be almost obliterated now, especially in the Cape, where the Boer goat has exercised such a powerful and far-reaching influence. However, there can be but little doubt that, as a mohair merchant remarked to Conolly, "in Angora, as elsewhere, the finest fleece naturally is that which more readily curls".[1]

[1] The shape and style of the lock are points to which I think great importance should be attached. Since writing this chapter, I have met Mr. Amos Crabtree, one of the leading mohair merchants of Bradford. Mr. Crabtree insisted very strongly on the necessity of a fleece being in curled ringlets, as that style of fleece yields the best mohair; from the manufacturer's point of view it is superior, because it works up best and is preferable to all other types. My own experience as a farmer is that, speaking generally, fleeces

Some Angoras have a soft, downy undergrowth. Mr. C. Lee, senr., for instance, whose son, Mr. C. G. Lee, certainly possesses some of the purest, finest and most remunerative goats in South Africa, recently wrote to the *Eastern Province Herald*, remarking upon this undergrowth in his goats, adding that it is the finest and most valuable part of the fleece, being used by manufacturers in the place of silk. Mr. Binns speaks of this as "bottom," and says that the Turkish goats produce it as a protection against the intense cold of late winter, but that it is not produced in South Africa, at any rate not to the same extent, on account of our milder climate. It will be remembered, however, that round about Angora and Koniah there is a breed of goats whose fleece is characterised by a soft, fine undergrowth; in this respect resembling the Cashmere, to which, I doubt not, they are closely related. It seems, therefore, probable that such Angoras as have this undergrowth owe it to some remote cross with this Cashmere-like goat. Now, the horns of the Cashmere are not long, and are not spirally twisted. It would be interesting to observe whether, among such rams as have this fine silky undergrowth, there is a tendency to have lightish horns with no spiral twist, or with a spiral twist less pronounced than in the horns of rams which have no undergrowth at all. Mr. Hoerle, referring to such goats, says: "The downy Angoras are most likely animals of

of the curled ringlet type contain the finest and best quality and longest hair, and that such fleeces are freer from kemp than fleeces characterised by any other style of lock.

rather short breeding crossed up with any wild species, or perhaps with the Cashmere".

With regard to another point, Mr. Hoerle, commenting on the "mongrelling up" of goats in Asia Minor, observes: "We find, for instance, fine, well-covered, heavy-fleeced ewes with only a few remnants of a beard left, and also just as fine ewes entirely without beard . . . and I have seen many females of the fourth and fifth crosses (with the common scrub goat of America), as well as so-called "pure bloods," with absolutely no beard at all, whilst thoroughbred Angora ewes, with the very best points, have heavy flowing beards".

Mr. Hoerle's explanation of this seems to be incorrect. He holds that the Angora is a distinct species, descended from *Capra Falconeri*, of which both sexes are bearded; and that the Kurd goat is descended from *Capra Aegagrus*, the female of which, he says, is beardless; and upon this he founds his explanation. More recent observations have shown that the Angora is also a descendant of *Capra Aegagrus*, and merely one of the varieties of the domesticated goat (*Capra Hircus*), and that the female of *Capra Aegagrus* is bearded. This upsets Mr. Hoerle's explanation, but it does not necessarily touch his facts. I can only suppose that the absence of beard is a fortuitous variation which would have some tendency to be hereditary. No beardless goats have come under my own observation; in the Colony I have only heard once of a few beardless rams, and this statement requires confirmation. Mr. Binns, supporting Mr. Hoerle, says there certainly are some beardless *ewes*, but that he has never heard of beardless rams. However, of this there is no doubt, that the purer bred an Angora is, the smaller and softer should be the beard; in a very fine goat, perfectly covered up to and under the jaw, the beard is scarcely discernible, and is invisible to the casual glance. The "kuif" or tuft of hair on the forehead at the base of the horns should be very soft, silky, curly, and lustrous; absence of such a tuft, or coarse straight hair in its place, is an indication of common blood. The hair on the tip of the tail, though somewhat harsher and coarser than the beard, should also in a first-class goat be very fine and soft. The "kuif" should be mohair, but the beard and the tip of the tail never are.

There is, at times, some considerable variation in the shape of the horns of rams, due probably, to a great extent, to the crossing. Normally, the horns should have a spiral twist, branching backwards and outwards, and should not be very large; yet frequently rams are found with straight-up horns, with no twist, running close together almost, sometimes quite, to the points; or with short horns, diverging at the points, with just the slightest half twist; or with horns of immense size.

With regard to the ears, the pure race are lop-eared.[1] This is an indication of long domestication. Wild species have prick ears, but, in the long-domesticated and carefully-bred varieties, the ears are pendent, the muscles having become

---

[1] "The Scinde and Syrian goats, especially, are noted for the length of their ears, which are often 22 in. long, and touching and dragging on the ground."—Diehl.

Dr. Hayes says that some breeds have ears 19 in. in length and 4¾ in. in breadth.

atrophied through long disuse. In the modern Angora, though lop ears preponderate, there is much difference in their droop and in their size; "mouse ears" being by no means infrequent. There are other variations also. As Dr. Hayes says: "There is a kind of suture or keel-like seam which runs up the centre of the ears of many of them," and it is by no means uncommon to find the tips of ears in some goats turned back and lying as flat and close as though stuck fast.

These and many other variations, such as defects of covering, style of locks, etc., are evidently in the main due to the Angora having been crossed with the common goat, and to a less extent (at any rate in Asia Minor) with other varieties. The crossing, however, has not only tended to engraft on to the Angora some of the numerous variations of the unstable breed of common or Kurd goat, but it has brought into effect the powerful forces of atavism, and given free scope to fortuitous variation.

Another and different effect of the crossing may be mentioned as of great importance, which is that the modern Angora often has two kids at a birth.[1] This is characteristic of the Kurd goat, which seldom has less than two. It is clearly established that it is an extremely rare occurrence for a pure Angora ewe to have more than one kid at a birth, once a year. And it is to be remarked that as Angoras in the Colony are becoming purer and

[1] The tendency to produce more than one kid at a birth is further strengthened in such Cape Angoras as have been descended from a cross with the Boer goat, which generally has twins, often triplets, and sometimes four young at a birth.

more what they should be, the tendency of ewes to have more than one kid (even now not common in the best stud flocks) becomes less and less.

To sum up: The main results of crossing the

Photo. Arthur Green] [Port Elizabeth.

Six-tooth Angora Goat Ram, bred by R. Featherstone, Groenfontein, Cradock; owned and exhibited by R. C. Holmes, Karree Hoek, Pearston. Champion at Port Elizabeth Agricultural Show, 1895. Weight of fleece, 12 lb. (twelve months' growth).

original pure Angora with the common or Kurd goat, in Asia Minor, have been:—

1. To do away with the practically exclusive localisation of the Angora goat industry in its original limited area.

2. To eliminate the original pure Angora and substitute for it a made breed, the product of the

cross between the pure Angoras and the common or Kurd goats.

3. To impair the purity of the breed of Angoras throughout all the mohair districts.

4. To produce a white mohair-bearing breed of goats, the modern Angora, differing considerably from the original pure Angora.

(This breed, which is not yet quite fixed, but is gradually tending to become so, is a larger, somewhat coarser, hardier breed, with an oilier and much heavier fleece, which, though not attaining to the high level of that of the original pure Angora, is, nevertheless, in the best specimens, of great beauty and excellence, and equal to the most exacting demands of the present mohair manufacturing trade.[1] As the fleeces combine with increased weight a sufficiently high standard of excellence, and as the goat is hardier and healthier, it is the more remunerative breed; and, when stable at the high standard it has attained to in the hands of the most intelligent breeders, it is superior and preferable to the original pure breed.)

5. To spread this made breed over other districts of Asia Minor, where the original pure Angora could not live, or so deteriorated as, to a

---

[1] It seems likely that, as this type is improved and fixed by careful selection and judicious in-breeding, the oil will cease to be even as pronounced as it often is at present, and will eventually be reduced to just that small, almost inappreciable modicum necessary to hair of the highest excellence. The modern type, having somewhat more oil than the original breed, has, to a great extent, lost that glittering white appearance so often commented upon. The ideal goat in Turkey to-day has a leady-white tint of fleece (unwashed), while, in the Cape, the tendency is towards straw-colour.

large extent, to lose the valuable properties of its fleece.

6. To do away with a close uniformity among Angoras, and to produce different types; for the made breed, not yet fixed, was rapidly spread over a large extent of country, with widely diverse climatic and pastoral conditions. The style of fleece being largely determined by local conditions, different types of goats have been produced in different parts of the country.

7. To reduce the number of common goats, which, as with the Boer goats of the Cape, have been, to a great extent, ousted in the mohair districts by the more remunerative animal.

CHAPTER IX.

THE MOHAIR AREA OF TURKEY.[1]

TURKEY in Asia is divided into Provinces, or Vilayets, or Sandjaks ("flags"). The provinces are subdivided into kazas and nahies, which are again sometimes divided into divans.

The area over which the Angora goat is farmed embraces the provinces of Angora and Kastamouni, and portions of the provinces of Broussa, Yozgat, Koniah and Sivas. Its extreme boundaries may be said to be as follows : *North*, Kureh, in the province of Kastamouni, about 186 miles north of the town of Angora, and about 18 miles from Ineboli, a port on the Black Sea ; *south*, Koniah, about 138

---

[1] This chapter has been written mainly from information supplied to me by Mr. Henry O. Binns, to whom I wish to express my indebtedness. Several other authorities have been consulted, but the real value of the chapter is due to Mr. Binns, who has given it his own careful revision. The information is of much importance to Cape Angora farmers, and may be taken, I believe, as reliable, for Mr. Binns was born in Turkey, and learnt the language of the country from childhood. He travelled and lived among the up-country mohair farmers for twenty years, buying and getting up mohair, farming Angoras on a large scale on his own account, and buying goats for exportation to the Cape, Australia, and America. Altogether he lived in Turkey for thirty-eight years, and, in addition, he had the advantage of his father's experience, who had been there for thirty years previously.

miles south of Angora; *east*, Sivas, about 260 miles east of Angora; *west*, Boulou, in the province of Kastamouni, about 108 miles north-west of the town of Angora, and about 40 miles from the Black Sea; *south-east*, Yozgat, about 97 miles south-east of Angora; *south-west*, Eskischehr, in the province of Broussa, about 120 miles west-south-west of Angora. Thus, the mohair area is, roughly, in its extreme limits, about 324 miles from north to south, and about 380 miles from east to west. But although the whole of the mohair area is comprised within these limits, all the territory included within them is not stocked with the Angora goat. Much of the country east and north-east of Angora is not devoted to this industry to any extent. It is probable that not more than 60,000 to 80,000 square miles really constitute the mohair area; and, practically speaking, it is comprised in the two provinces of Angora and Kastamouni.

It must, however, be mentioned that about 900 miles east of the town of Angora is the kaza of Van, with the town of the same name, in the province of Erzeroum in Armenia, where a considerable quantity of very inferior mohair is produced.

The mohair area consists mainly of mountain ranges and elevated plateaux, averaging on the whole about 2500 feet above the sea level. Some of these mountain ranges are covered with an abundant growth of scrub oak. On the higher mountains are pine forests. In addition to this the plateaux grow only a scant supply of short tufted grass common to most high levels. In parts, however, there is an abundance of aromatic plants, principally thyme. A characteristic of the area is an extreme dryness, and a very cold winter, when, at times, for two or three months, the earth is covered with snow. Even in the town of Angora, the thermometer sometimes descends to zero Fahr.; and in the higher mountains it falls much lower. During the intense heat and dryness of summer, even the short grass is burnt up, and the whole country has a parched, arid appearance. Towards the middle of the area is the great central plateau of Hymané, covered with the scantiest vegetation. Being a mountainous country there is a great diversity of climate, and consequently a great variety of vegetation. One writer says that, at the end of December, he saw the orange and the lime growing at Tarsus, the birthplace of St. Paul, and thirty miles away (one day's journey on horseback) he was almost in perpetual snow, on the lofty Taurus mountains.

With such a wide diversity of climate, it cannot be expected that the mohair from the whole area will be of one uniform kind. In fact, about thirty different kinds are produced from as many different localities. These localities I shall call *goat districts*. The following table gives a list of these different goat districts. Each name is that of a locality which produces its own peculiar kind of mohair. It may be taken as a practically complete list of the principal goat districts. After each name there is indicated, in brackets, whether it is a kaza, which gives its name to the goat district, or a town, a village, or merely a place where a weekly bazaar is held. The distances between many of the localities are given, as well as the distance of each from the town of Angora. These distances are

THE MOHAIR AREA OF TURKEY.

Name of Locality.	Number of Miles and Direction from	Number of Miles and Direction from Town of Angora.	In which Province.
Angora (town and itch nahie or "inner circle")	Kastamboul, 130, S.		Angora.
Ayash (town and kaza)		27 miles W.	,,
Beibazar do. do.	Ayash, 21, W.	48 ,, W.	,,
Tschihirkhan (village)	Beibazar, 18, W.	66 ,, W.	,,
Nallikhan (town and kaza)	Tschihirkhan, 15, W.	81 ,, W.	,,
Mouhalitsch (village, weekly bazaar and nahie)	Beibazar, 24, S.	72 ,, W.S.W.	,,
Sivrihissar (town and kaza)	Mouhalitsch, 36, S.	84 ,, S.W.	,,
Soungourlou do. do.		42 ,, N.W.	,,
Chorba do. do.		27 ,, N.W.	,,
Yabanova do. do.	Chorba, 18, N.W.	45 ,, N.W.	,,
Tschiboukova (village and kaza)		30 ,, N.	Kastamouni.
Kastamboul (town and itch nahie)	Port of Ineboli, 54, S.	150 ,, N.	,,
Devriken (kaza and bazaar)	Kastamboul, 18, N.	168 ,, N.	,,
Kureh (town and kaza)	Devriken, 18, N.	186 ,, N.N.W.	,,
Araj do. do.	Kastamboul, 24, W.	174 ,, N.N.W.	,,
Tosia do. do.	Do. 42, E.	192 ,, N.N.E.	,,
Merguzeh (nahie and weekly bazaar)	Do. 15, S.	133 ,, N.	,,
Bostankeui (village)	Merguzeh, 15, S.	118 ,, N.	,,
Kotch-hissar (town and kaza)	Bostankeui, 12, S.	106 ,, N.	,,
Changura do. do.	Kotch-hissar, 30, S.	78 ,, N.	,,
Cherkesh do. do.	Changura, 36, W.	92 ,, N.W.	,,
Geredeh do. do.	Cherkesh, 40, W.	90 ,, N.W.	,,
Boulou do. do.	Kastamboul, 120, S.W.	108 ,, N.W.	,,
Mondournou do. do.	Geredeh, 18, W.	138 ,, W.N.W.	,,
Yozgat (capital town)	Boulou, 22, S.W.	97 ,, S.E.	Yozgat.
Koniah do.	Soungourlou, 26, S.E.	138 ,, S.	Koniah.
Broussa do.		210 ,, W.	Broussa.
Eskischehr (town and kaza)	Sea of Marmora, 18, E.	210 ,, W.S.W.	,,
Sivas do. do.	Sivrihissar, 42, W.	268 ,, E.	Sivas.

only approximate, but are accurate enough for the purpose to which they are applied. Turkish roads are reckoned by hours, as at the Cape, and the Turkish "hour" is supposed to be three miles (at the Cape it is six). This has been taken as the basis of computation in reckoning the various distances.

It is at once apparent from this list that, as has already been said, the mohair area is practically comprised in the two provinces of Angora and Kastamouni; and one is immediately struck by the fact, how short are the distances that separate many of the different goat districts from one another.

In some of these goat districts there are district markets, where each of the leading mohair merchants has his agent: these are Eskischehr, Sivrihissar, Beibazar, Ayash, Nallikhan, Geredeh, Cherkesh, Changura, Koniah, Sivas (and Van); Angora and Kastamboul being, of course, the two great markets. But every goat district mentioned in the above list is characterised by its own particular variety of mohair; the hair grown in each has some special characteristic which enables an expert at once to distinguish it from all the others.

This seems strange, considering the short distances that the various centres are from one another; but there can be no doubt of its correctness, for all authorities are agreed upon it. For instance, Mr. Gavin Gatheral, in his paper read before the Royal Colonial Institute in 1878, says that the mohair area (he makes it somewhat smaller than Mr. Binns) produces more than twenty varieties of hair, each of which is easily recognised by experts. Mr. Binns is very clear upon the point. He says that each district impresses some local peculiarity upon the hair grown in it. He adds: "Goats in Turkey are constantly being sold round in small lots, so that an intermixture continually goes on. Nevertheless, though out of each of many parcels of mohair from every district in Turkey, I could pick out many places which would so much resemble each other as to defy the best expert to tell which was which; yet, were lots of a few bales of the average mohair of each district placed in a row and cut open at the side, any one of our Constantinople merchants could tell which was which. . . . And we, who have lived some years in the town of Angora, could tell whether a small lot came from Hymané, Elma-Dagh, Stamos, etc., though in some cases but a mile or two might separate the villages. But this, of course, the Constantinople merchants could not do."[1] Again, regarding varieties of mohair (and necessarily of goats) he says: "One cannot say they are exactly *so* many types, definitely fixing the number, for there are endless subdivisions; but a connoisseur in mohair can tell you, from the bulk of the bales when opened, from which particular district it has come, provided it has been sent separately from the purchasing centre town of the same name. Each district displays a general type of its own, yet in each or most of them there are again other subdivisions, from the class or type of which a local agent can always tell in a moment where the mohair originally came from."

[1] Letter to *Midland News*, 1893.

Again, "each district has its own peculiarities in class of mohair, sufficient to enable a mohair expert to tell at a glance from which district or village a parcel had come". But there is sometimes a difficulty on the Constantinople market in identifying a lot of hair with any particular district, for the hair obtains its name from the town from which it was sent to Constantinople, irrespective of where it was grown or purchased. Thus the clips get mixed, many different kinds being ranked under one name, for the travelling agents go from village to village making their purchases, and then lump the different clips together, and take the hair to the best market, under whose name all that lot of hair is henceforth known. Thus, if the Angora local market be higher than the Kastamboul market, the hair grown in the kazas in the Ulgaz-Dagh mountains goes there, and *vice versâ;* and thus a part of the same clip might one year be known as Kastamboul hair, and the next as Angora hair. It seems, therefore, clear that the only reliable testimony as to where the hair really is grown, and comes from in the first instance, is that of the local merchants and buyers in the towns of Angora and Kastamboul.

It has been shown, in a previous chapter, that the original pure-bred Angora goat was practically of one uniform type, and confined to a limited, well-defined region; and that, when the European demand for unmanufactured mohair assumed large proportions in a short time, the pure Angora rams were put to Kurd ewes over a much larger extent of country, until that now indicated as the present mohair area was occupied. It was not difficult to maintain purity and uniformity among the Angora goats, when they were confined to a limited area and under conditions which tended to produce uniformity, and when only hair of super excellence was sought after. But when the original pure breed was broken up, when the product of the cross between the pure breed and the Kurd, as yet in an unfixed condition, was scattered over districts of the most diverse climatic and pastoral conditions, under owners unaccustomed to breed the Angora goat and unacquainted with what constituted the special characteristics of the breed, under such ignorant and careless breeders as the Turks, and when every kind of hair was saleable, the demand being so great—under these conditions uniformity was impossible. The breed, in a plastic state, was introduced into localities differing widely from one another; and these conditions, aided by the idiosyncrasies of the various breeders, rapidly stamped themselves upon the goats, until each district acquired a type of goat differing in some special characteristic from the others, characteristics marked enough to enable an expert to distinguish between them.

This is not only thoroughly well established, but it is exactly what might have been expected. Here, at the Cape, where the industry is so young, the same process is in operation. The difference, for instance, between grass veld and Karoo veld mohair is most marked, so much so that in the prize list of the Port Elizabeth Agricultural Society, separate prizes are offered for the two classes. Even on the same farm, grass-fed goats and Karoo-fed goats of the same flocks differ so pronouncedly, that even a comparatively untrained eye can detect the dissimilarity. Again, though there is a tendency for Karoo goats to conform to one type, yet trifling differences of veld and predilections of breeders suffice to mark distinct types.

It is quite incorrect to say that in Turkey there is more than one breed of Angora goats; they are all of the same breed; but there may be said to be different varieties, in this sense, that the character of the fleece is readily affected by local conditions; so that, for instance, the progeny of a goat in Sivrihissar with a comparatively light dry fleece would, if removed to Dortdivan, in Geredeh, and bred there for several generations, produce a heavy fleece with a great excess of oil. These different varieties are produced by different climatic and pastoral conditions, and are mainly due, as all authorities agree, to difference of food. Mr. Binns says: "Breed has nothing to do with it; it is entirely due to the accident of food, water, and climate". He insists particularly on the effect of food, and says that the goats characteristic of one district would soon acquire the distinguishing qualities of another if they were removed to it, bred there, and kept there. "For example," he says, "if a first-class ram from the celebrated ram-breeding village of Bostankeui were taken to Dortdivan, he would, in say two years, from being a radically different type of goat, possess most, if not all the characteristics of the Dortdivan or Geredeh with great excess of oil, it being only a question of time." Again, he says: "None of these peculiar characteristics are due to any breeding, but solely to climate and food". Experience at the Cape bears out this argument, for the rapidity with which the fleeces of Angora goats are affected by local conditions is remarkable.

In considering the special characteristics of the principal goat districts, and the manner in which the goats are affected, it must be remembered that often the differences between the various types of goats are not capable of being made clear through a written description; to be thoroughly comprehended, the goats themselves need to be seen. However, this is not the case with all the districts, and much may be learned that is useful to the Angora goat farmer by carefully considering such information as is obtainable.

Taking, first, the province of Kastamouni; the goat of Kastamboul, the best known goat district in the province of Kastamouni, has three special characteristics: its fleece is slippy (that is, it has no "bottom"), very fine, and exceedingly lustrous. Its locks are wavy, and not curled.[1] A good deal of misapprehension exists regarding this goat, owing to the loose use of the term Kastamboul. The town of Kastamboul is the chief market for all the goat districts in the province of Kastamouni. In this market, buyers discriminate between the hair of the various districts; but, in Constantinople, it is all known as Kastamboul hair. The Kastamboul goat's reputation suffers in consequence, for the hair forwarded from the Kastamboul market to Constantinople contains much inferior stuff, and is, on the whole, not good; for instance, the goats

[1] Mr. Amos Crabtree tells me that the hair of the Kastamboul goat does not work up well, and is not in good repute among manufacturers.

of Devriken, Tosia, and Kureh have been but recently graded up, and yield a large quantity of inferior and coloured hair. This is incorrectly called Kastamboul hair on the Constantinople market, though none of it comes from the Kastamboul goat. It is important to remember this. Mr. Binns says that to condemn the Kastamboul goat because a large proportion of the hair from the Kastamboul market is not of superior quality, is as incorrect as to condemn an English South African because the bulk of the people of South Africa are black.

Merguzeh, Araj, and the Ulgaz-Dagh mountains (a range running east and west, between Bostankeui and Kotch-hissar) are well-wooded and supply the goats in winter and spring with food and shelter in plenty. Thus the goats escape the weakness common to the flocks of the poorer peasants in the lower lands, who have to hand-feed during the winter, and the shelter of the forests enables the farmers to clip earlier. (These remarks also apply to Chorba and Yabanova in the province of Angora.) Bostankeui is a famous ram-breeding village. Some of the very best goats in the whole of the mohair area are found in Merguzeh, Araj, and the Ulgaz-Dagh mountains, for there men are found who make a speciality of breeding rams for sale. In fact, so excellent is the hair of the goats of the Ulgaz-Dagh mountains, that the Kastamboul buyers pay a higher price for it than for other kinds in the province of Kastamouni, to help them to sell the inferior classes of Tosia, Kureh, and Devriken. Changura produces goats whose fleeces generally have a reddish tinge, partially due to the colour of the soil, though in some instances the hair itself has this colour (due to the cross with the Kurd).

Geredeh is a mountainous district, about 4000 feet above the sea level, the chief town of which is about forty miles from the Black Sea. It is covered in many parts with pine and fir forests, which supply, almost exclusively, the winter food

Photo. W. Roe] [Graaff Reinet.

Angora Goat Ram, "Prince"; with a thirteen months' fleece weighing 16 lb. Bred and owned by C. G. Lee, Klipplaat.

for the goats; and it is extremely cold, the snow in winter lying thick on the ground for months together. Angora goats have been introduced into this district in comparatively recent years, and have developed into a very distinct type, the chief peculiarity of which is a fleece saturated with a great excess of grease, said to be due to pine feeding. Living in a well-wooded part, which affords abundance of food and shelter in the trying time of winter, the Geredeh goat has a large body, and is strong and healthy; having been but recently graded up from the Kurd goat, it is coarse, a characteristic accentuated, both as regards its body and fleece, by the quality of its food. Its fleece is coarse, and deteriorates rapidly with age, becoming short and wiry, especially if the goat is removed to other districts whose conditions are markedly different from those of Geredeh; and it has a tendency to be imperfectly clothed about the under surface of the neck and on the belly. The more its food is confined to pine and fir, the coarser and more oily is the fleece, and when the sub-district of Dortdivan is reached, all those traits which characterise the Geredeh goat are found in an exaggerated degree. The excess of grease is particularly noticeable, Gavin Gatheral describing the fleece as being "so surcharged with grease as to seem almost black" (the colour no doubt being due to the black soil which the grease takes up). This excessively greasy goat is to be found sparsely distributed among the flocks in some of the other subdistricts of Geredeh, but an enormous excess of grease is a peculiarity of the generality of goats in Dortdivan only. Though an excess of grease is the special characteristic of the Geredeh, yet every grade between the non-oily goat (whose fleece has the small modicum of grease natural to the mohair goat when it has a sufficiency and variety of food) and the Dortdivan goat is found in the district, which undoubtedly contains some most excellent animals. The Geredeh mohair known to the trade in Constantinople is that which is obtained from the whole of the district, and, as in other districts, quantities of the best hair are produced; but Geredeh hair is not in high repute in Bradford, its reputation apparently suffering on account of the proportion of coarse and excessively greasy hair which it contains. This inferior hair is grown principally in Dortdivan, which produces about one-seventh of the entire clip of the district of Geredeh. The average proportion of what are now called thoroughbred goats is much less in Geredeh than in any of the other good districts; and the Geredeh goats as a whole, and particularly the Dortdivan goats, are not held in high repute in Turkey; not to mention some of the goat districts of the province of Angora, they are greatly surpassed by the goats of Araj, Merguzeh, Bostankeui, and the Ulgaz-Dagh mountains.

Coming now to the province of Angora; the two goat districts whose names are most familiar to Cape breeders are Angora and Beibazar, the chief towns of which are about forty-eight miles apart, the town and kaza of Ayash lying between them. The soil of these districts is chalky, which gives a clean whitish colour to the fleeces. There is a considerable difference between the goats of Angora and Beibazar, those of Beibazar being much heavier and more curly. But the difference is not so much due to climatic and pastoral conditions as to enterprise. Mr. Binns says: "The Beibazar merchants were smart in the early days of mohair going up in price, and made money, which enabled them to pay greater attention to the improvement of their goats. Their influence extended to Chorba and Yabanova. Being wealthy men, they feed and look better after their goats, and this accounts principally for the immense improvement which has taken place in the Beibazar and Ayash goats in the last twenty-five years. The climatic and pastoral conditions of Angora and Beibazar do not much differ. I think it is likely that, since the wealth of Beibazar began to be spread around that district, the goats thereabouts have so much improved that there is not the slightest doubt but that the best breeding goats are to be found there, *not in* Beibazar, but from thence, mainly in the Chorba direction."

Ayash is one of the very best districts. Mr. Binns says that in 1877 a brother of his had sixty-three ewes, originally from Ayash, which in twelve months clipped 529 lb., or an average of $8\frac{1}{2}$ lb. each. Chorba is also one of the best goat districts of the province of Angora. Here, says Mr. Binns, "almost every variety of food loved by the goats is found in abundance, good grass, wild thyme, scrub-oak, pine and fir. The two last give an increase of yolk or oil to the hair, but as the variety of food is so great, the goats eat so little of the pine and fir that the yolk is generally only sufficient to preserve the hair in the best condition. Over the next rise is Yabanova, where pine and fir are more plentiful, and the goats' fleeces greasier and coarser." Ayash, Chorba and Cherkesh produce the largest proportion of good goats; they and Mouhalitsch, which is rapidly coming into the front rank, are noted ram-breeding centres. Gavin Gatheral had a particularly high opinion of the goats of Yabanova, Chorba, and Tschiboukova. And

George Gatheral says the best mohair comes from the valleys of the Ala-Dagh mountains to the north of the town of Angora, and instances Chorba, Yabanova, Murtad and Assa-Kassaba as producing particularly excellent hair. In Eskischehr, and more especially in Sivrihissar, in the plains, much of the mohair is harsh and dry, for the Angora is a mountain animal and degenerates everywhere in the plains. The white mohair goats of Koniah have no special characteristic, except that they do not throw very true to colour; for as Koniah lies on the outskirts of the mohair area, the colours of the Kurd goats have not yet been eliminated from the flocks, and coloured goats are common. But there seems to be a variety peculiar to Koniah; according to Mr. Binns this is a kind of fancy breed, mainly red or black, or red and black, producing, in some instances, exceedingly fine hair. Of this variety Mr. George Gatheral, writing in 1896, says: "In the Koniah district of Asia Minor, twenty years ago, there was another breed of mohair goat, whose fleece was altogether brown. It contained 90 per cent. of brown and 10 per cent. of black. It was called in the trade *Gingelline*, and was sold for special uses. But it went out of fashion; rams were brought from Angora, and the produce of Koniah is now all, or very nearly all, white mohair; it is, however, fine."

Lastly, there is the town and kaza of Van, in the province of Erzeroum, 900 miles east of Angora. "On the frontier of Armenia and Mesopotamia," says Gavin Gatheral, "is a province called Van, which has hitherto supplied a great weight of inferior mohair, more resembling sheep's wool than goats' hair." Mr. Binns describes the

Van mohair goats as of very inferior quality, not far removed from the common goats — hardy, shaggy animals of various and variegated colours, of little value as mohair goats; but he adds that the black and red goats, which, as in Koniah, seem to be a distinct variety in some respects, must not be included in the general run of the Van goats, as they are, as a rule, considerably superior. "In the province of Van in Kurdistan," says George Gatheral, " a goat existed, and still exists (though much reduced in number), of whose fleece 60 per cent. was white and 40 per cent. brown, black, and mixed colours. The market town where this mohair was sold is Gesireh, but it was known in the trade as Van mohair. This mohair was kempy, exceeding strong, coarse and long, and it was used for quite other purposes than the Angora mohair. It has gone out of fashion in a great measure, and the farmers now breed sheep instead of goats. In later years, the Kurds brought rams from the Angora district so as to improve the breed; but as prices fell, and the article went out of fashion, the breed was allowed to become extinct."

I gather from the information submitted in this chapter, that the mohair area of Asia Minor is an inland elevated region, practically comprised in the provinces of Angora and Kastamouni, characterised by a scanty vegetation, excessive dryness, and a very cold winter, short in the lower lands but long in the mountain parts. The herbage consists mainly of dwarf-oak and scrub-bush, a variety of aromatic plants, and a hardy grass, in the valleys and on the plateau; while on the higher mountain ranges, pine forests predominate. All the mohair goats are of one breed, of various types and various degrees of excellence. Each locality which has any marked peculiarity of food and climate, quickly impresses it upon its goats, which soon come to yield a variety of hair sufficiently individualised as to be at once recognisable by an expert. Where there is a suitable variety of food and a comparatively equable climate, the best hair is produced; mountain veld, with a mixture of grass and oak, is especially suitable for the production of the best hair. Pine feeding produces an excess of grease and coarser hair. Hair grown on mountain veld is superior to that grown on the plains. The local peculiarities of a district are not impressed solely upon the hair; they also react, more of less, upon the general structure of the animals. The colour of the soil imparts local colour to unwashed hair; thus, Beibazar hair is clean and whitish in appearance, the soil being chalky; Geredeh hair is blackish, as the grease takes up the black soil; that of Changura has a reddish tint; and so on. The same peculiarity is noticeable in the Colony; for instance, goats from pure grass veld are generally beautifully clean and white, while Karoo goats as a rule tend to have a yellowish, straw-coloured tint. Though each district tends to impress local characteristics upon its goats, and though the goats (I refer now to their fleeces) of each district can, as a whole, be readily recognised by one thoroughly acquainted with the various districts, yet in each district goats with qualities characteristic of most other districts may be found; so much so, that an expert could not say where they came from. Indeed it is evident that goats which are not reared and maintained under quite diverse climatic and pastoral conditions, which are not bred scientifically, and are constantly being mixed, cannot possibly acquire characteristics so striking and definite as to preclude their resembling, in many instances, the goats of neighbouring and somewhat similar districts. A certain uniformity runs through all the flocks of any one of the districts; yet no one district possesses any one type absolutely peculiar to itself. In most of the other districts, perhaps in all, or nearly all, there will be found a number of goats, more or less numerous, of a practically identical type. But to say that, because a goat comes from a certain district, therefore it is of a certain type; or that, because it came from that district, therefore it is *ipso facto* better than a goat from another district, is quite incorrect. It is true that some districts have a larger proportion of the best goats than others; thus there may be a probability that a goat from one district will be superior to one from another; but, practically, *the best goats are all of one type*, in whichever districts they may be. There is no difference worth mentioning in the type of the best goats, whether in the provinces of Angora, Kastamouni, or Broussa; and no district can claim that its best goats are different from, or individually superior to, the best goats of other districts. *Throughout the goats of any one district there is, as a whole, a certain uniformity to type; but the best goats, no matter from which districts they come, are all of one and the same type.* This will be seen more clearly when the manner of breeding and farming the Angora in Turkey is explained, to the consideration of which the next chapter is devoted.

CHAPTER X.

THE FARMING OF THE ANGORA GOAT IN TURKEY.

THE number of Angora goats in a flock in Turkey is, on the average, about 300; the reason being that it would not pay to have flocks much smaller, for a man and a boy generally herd each flock; and it would not be safe to have them much larger, for the country is bushy and broken, and wolves are numerous. It is calculated that about 300 goats cover the expense of herding, and are as many as a man, or a man and a boy, can be expected to herd safely, even though assisted, as is generally the case, by several large wolf-dogs, which are trained to guard and protect the goats. The great majority of the goats, as has been pointed out, are owned in small lots by the poor peasant farmers. For the sake of economy, several of these peasant farmers run their goats together, until a flock of about the size mentioned is obtained, the expenses of herding being shared by all the owners as a joint cost; or the goats of an entire village will be herded in one flock, each villager owning from about two to twenty head, the flock altogether amounting to 200, 300 or 400. On the other hand, the man who owns (say) 1000 goats (a very wealthy owner may have as many as 4000) will probably divide them into three flocks, so that no herdsman may have under his care more than he can safely herd. Thus it comes, that flocks of Angoras in Turkey number, on the average, about 300 each. There are, however, portions of the country where larger flocks can be run with safety. In the Steppe of Hymané, for instance, where the country is so level that the eye can stretch in most cases for many miles, flocks numbering as many as 2000 may be found. But this is exceptional.

The goats, being owned in such small numbers and receiving a great deal of attention, become very tame and attached to their owners or herdsmen. The consequence is that towards nightfall they generally, even if not herded, return to the homestead to sleep — a habit which perhaps an experience of the dangers incurred by sleeping out has partly tended to form. This peculiarity is frequently remarked upon by the owners of the first Angoras in America, who kept them in small lots. The rams, and especially very choice animals, are much valued. They become household pets and the playmates of the children, and have pet names given to them. Sometimes amulets are fastened on them, or little bags are tied around their necks, containing pieces of parchment on which are inscribed verses from the Koran to protect them from the "Evil Eye".[1]

---

[1] If a jealous or covetous or "evil" eye is cast upon a goat on account of its superiority over other goats, it is supposed that the whole flock will be blighted; therefore the Turk makes away with exceptionally superior rams (unless he can with safety use them secretly), and protects the others, both from the "evil eye" and other dangers, with charms in the shape of verses from the Koran tied on them.

The herdsmen have a custom of attaching bells to the necks of the finest kapaters, and sometimes to fat ewes that are not bearing. The bells are of different sizes and tones, and often in great numbers, and as the goats move about, a monotonous musical jingle is produced. The herdsmen are very fond of this "music," and take a great pride in their bells, in whose chime they detect a certain musical harmony. If the chime is not quite to the herdsman's fancy, he will sometimes pay a considerable sum to procure a bell which strikes the desired note. Mr. Binns gives an interesting illustration of this custom. He hired a man to herd one of his flocks, numbering about 330. This man at once asked for leave to go and get his bells. On obtaining permission he asked to be allowed to take a donkey, explaining that he required the donkey to carry the bells. He set out and duly returned with 240 bells; and later he paid £2 for one particular bell, which he said he required to make the chime complete!

The goats are not kraalled. In summer they sleep near the homestead, unconfined; in winter, when necessary (as is often the case), they are provided with shelter. Such peasants as are very poor and have only a few goats, say eight or ten, house them in very severe weather in a room in their own dwelling; otherwise an outhouse or rough shed is provided. These outhouses, Mr. Binns says, are always built on a slope, so that, though they may become hot and close, they never become very moist or foul; he also says that it is an extremely rare occurrence for the goats to be neglected, and that he has never seen them standing almost up to their

knees in liquid filth, as is often the case in the Cape
Colony. Still it seems that a very severe winter
has an injurious effect upon the hair. This fact is,
by another authority, attributed mainly to the bad
housing of the goats, which, he says, are crowded
into foul, unventilated and undrained sheds, where
the fleeces become damaged and soiled with the
liquid filth in which they stand. At any rate, a
severe winter does injuriously affect both the goats
and their fleeces. If pleuro-pneumonia is prevalent, the conditions under which the goats are
kept during winter afford it every means of
spreading, and the consequent losses are sometimes enormous. Gavin Gatheral says that in
the Liberian winter of 1879 not less than 468,889
mohair goats, or 35 per cent. of the whole, died.
The hardships the goats have to endure in winter
are augmented by the neglect to which they are
subjected in the matter of feeding. Grazing is
sometimes impossible, because deep snow covers
the ground. At such times they are fed on hay
or straw, or oak or pine branches which have been
cut when green and stocked for winter fodder.
Sometimes a little dry barley is given. The hand
feeding in winter is, however, in a measure supplementary; for grazing, to a small extent, is generally
obtainable, as the bushes are not often entirely
covered under the snow, and sometimes the strong
winds expose the tops of the hills, and the afternoon sun melts the snow on the south side of the
mountains, and the herbage is exposed for the
goats to nibble at. But what with insufficient
feeding and indifferent shelter, Turkish goats fare
badly during the winter. Another reason for the

small flocks is now apparent; large flocks could not, under present conditions, be fed or housed in winter. Contrary to what might have been expected, goats on the high mountains fare best during winter (if their constitutions are robust

Photo. G. Watson] [Aberdeen Road.

Angora Goat Ram, bred and owned by R. F. Hurndall, Somerville, Aberdeen Road.

enough to endure the great cold), for there pine forests abound, providing excellent food and shelter. Pine feeding, too, is said to develop a great amount of grease in the fleece, which affords an additional protection in snow and rain.[1]

Among the Turks there is no attempt at

---

[1] Mr. George Gatheral says that feeding on vetches also produces grease in the fleece. It may be added as of interest that scab exists in the flocks of Turkey, and that, at times, the whole country is subject to the ravages of locusts.

scientific breeding; there are no stud flocks; goats are constantly being sold round in small lots, and a continual intermixture goes on. In some of the best and wealthiest districts there are men who make a speciality of ram breeding. It must not, however, be supposed that even these ram breeders are such in the scientific sense of the term; for, in addition to there being no stud stock, and no pedigreed animals, rams are simply selected from the general flock, each being chosen merely on his own individual merit without reference to the qualities of his ancestors; and, as regards ewes, no selection seems to be exercised at all.

Mr. Binns says that the idea of a really first-class thoroughbred Angora ram of to-day is not different in Turkey and the Cape, except as regards the horns. The Cape farmer likes a thin horn; whereas the thicker and larger the horn is, the better the Turk is pleased. This is an essential point. I incline to the Cape view. Mr. Binns says that, having tested the Turk's view thoroughly, he is convinced that it is the right one, "that the strength of the ram for breeding purposes is increased by the size of his horn; the thicker the horn and the larger the growth per year, the more ewes he can serve. Light thin horns are essentially characteristic of the original pure Angora; but though thick horns are characteristic more of the Kurd goat than the original pure Angora, yet the horns of even the Kurd are very much thinner than those of to-day's so-called pure-bred Angoras. I am therefore inclined to the opinion that the thick horn is a characteristic of genital strength more than an indication of reversion." Now, I think it may be granted Mr. Binns is correct in maintaining that a large and thick horn often accompanies great sexual vigour; but, though a sire of strongly marked masculine type is always desirable, it by no means follows that excessive sexual vigour is the chief requisite; and a thin, light-coloured horn by no means connotes any deficiency of sexual vigour. Excessive size of horns almost invariably connotes common blood and coarseness in body, head and fleece—a general inferiority; smallish, fine, light-coloured horns generally connote refinement (not necessarily delicacy) of body, head and fleece—a general superiority; and my own experience is that, as regards sexual vigour, the thick-horned animal has no material advantage (if any at all) over the thin-horned.

Gavin Gatheral says that many splendid rams have a parting down the middle of the mohair on the belly.[1] I have seen a typical example of this in a ram bred from imported stock on both sides by the late Frank Holland, which, however, was far from being a splendid animal. Mr. Binns says he has never seen such a ram in Turkey which could be correctly described as "splendid". Cape breeders, at any rate, will rightly have no such rams.

As regards the weight of fleece of goats in

---

[1] This must not be confused with a bare or imperfectly covered belly. There is simply a perfectly defined parting down the middle of the hair on the belly, like a well-marked parting on the human head. When the goat is thrown on its back, the hair opens in a straight line down the middle, and falls, evenly divided, to opposite sides.

Turkey, rams clipping over 14 lb., and ewes over 8½ lb., at twelve months, when full grown, are considered exceptionally good; yet these weights are often obtained. It seems strange that 14 lb. should be often reached and but seldom exceeded; yet this is the case; and it is satisfactorily accounted for to the peculiar ways of the Turk. Many of the wealthier breeders produce rams clipping this amount, and when they do, they boast of it; yet a ram is not used for more than two years in one flock, from fear lest he should serve some of his own progeny, the Koran strictly prohibiting incest. These circumstances are against the full benefits being derived from such exceptional rams. On the other hand, it happens at times that a ram is produced yielding more than 14 lb.; but here again the evil influence of the Koran, from the stock-farmer's point of view, is felt. The Turk would not feel uneasy if other farmers had rams equally good, but fears to have one greatly superior to theirs; and this is why one seldom hears of 14 lb. being much exceeded. He believes that if he has a ram superior to those of his neighbours, and this is known, it will bring the "Evil Eye" on his whole flock. So, if his flock produces such a ram, he will try to prevent its being known among his neighbours; if successful, he will generally use it as a sire for two seasons, secretly, and then castrate it. If, however, there is a danger of its being known that he has such a very superior animal, he will castrate it as soon as he is himself aware of the fact, from fear of the "Evil Eye". Any scientific breeder will at once see how powerfully these two facts (the prohibition against close in-breeding, and the fear of the "Evil Eye") must militate against the best results in breeding, and how heavily they must handicap continuous advancement towards the production of better goats.

Mr. Binns gives an interesting account of one of these secretly-used rams. It happened that a Turk who felt himself under an obligation to him wished to please him, and, knowing his fondness for a good goat, told him he knew of a ram in the Geredeh district which clipped 16 lb. 13 oz. of clean hair. This man had been sent by the owner of the ram into a cellar to get some wood. Curiosity prompted him to go further afield, and he saw the ram, which the owner was using secretly for fear of the "Evil Eye". Mr. Binns rode some 200 miles to see this animal, knowing that, if the tale were true, it must be a very rare and valuable specimen. The owner at first denied that he possessed such a ram, but, finding Mr. Binns persistent, he feared his neighbours would get to hear of it and bring the "Evil Eye" on his flock; so offered to show it to him. Mr. Binns went down to see it, and "found the *brute* chained to a manger, in a cellar where he was stall fed—an ungainly, vulgar-looking beast, with hair like wire". The owner jokingly asked if he would give £30 for the ram, and was much disgusted when Mr. Binns replied that he would not give 30 paras (1½d.).

It would seem that 14 lb. for rams and 8½ lb. for ewes are about the maximum weights of really first-class fleeces; and that if these weights are much exceeded, the quality of the hair is inferior, and a good deal of the weight is due to oil and dirt. "In Turkey," says Mr. Binns, "14 lb. of first-class clean hair from a ram in any district, for instance in Beibazar, Ayash, Chorba, or elsewhere, has been proved over and over again to return more money to the farmer than the same weight of even washed hair from rams of the Dort-divan type, the goat with fleece so surcharged with grease as to seem almost black." It must not, however, be imagined that these weights are common; they represent the clippings of the very best animals. If an adult ram of first-class quality clips from 11 lb. to 13 lb. at twelve months, he is considered very superior.

It thus appears that the Turks farm their goats, from the breeder's standpoint, in the most slip-shod and unscientific manner. When one considers that the great majority of the goats are owned in very small numbers; that frequently the goats of different owners are herded in one flock; that goats are constantly being sold round in small lots, and that thus an incessant intermixture is taking place; that there are no pedigreed stock and no stud flocks; that in-breeding is prohibited; that an exceptionally superior ram is held to bring the "Evil Eye," and is therefore quickly castrated—when one considers all these facts, it is clear that, the goats having become mixed, purity, in the scientific sense of the term, is unknown; it seems hopeless to expect that fixity of type which only in-breeding can produce, or that continual improvement among the goats of Turkey, which might with every reason be expected, if the goats were under more competent management. From the scientific breeder's standpoint, there is thus but little uniformity, and throughout the whole area, generally speaking, the goats are almost inextricably mixed.

Shearing takes place in April or May, and the hair is not sorted; the farmer merely removes and puts up separately the soiled ends and breechings. If the goats are not shorn, they shed their hair as the summer heat comes on. The kapaters are seldom kept after they are six years old, but are sold or slaughtered. Conolly says (1840) that "surplus he-goats and barren females are killed in the beginning of winter, when their flesh is parfried and potted by the smaller classes as a store for the cold season".

Prices paid for Angoras by Turk to Turk average about £3 to £4 for a good ram, and up to £5 for a really first-class one, while a fancy animal will generally realise a fancy price. Ordinary selected rams are worth about £2. Ewes range from 18s. to 35s. With regard to the amounts paid for rams for exportation, Mr. Binns's information is peculiarly interesting, as much misconception prevails in the Colony on the point. It is clear that an experienced buyer in Turkey should be able to procure the goats at a not much higher price than that ruling in the country. Most of the goats imported to the Cape would probably be classed as "ordinary selected" (as above), and be worth about £2 each for rams and 20s. each for ewes; though, undoubtedly, many have been good and some first-class. In confirmation of this, it may be stated that Mr. Binns, who bought a great many of the goats which were imported to the Cape, was limited to £2 a head, taking the average all round, free on board at Constantinople. To this sum, in some cases, would be added the Constantinople merchant's charges. Still it is clear that a very exaggerated idea of the actual prices paid for Angoras by the exporters in Turkey exists in the Colony. Mr. Binns says: "Let alone £25 a head, not even as much as £5 a head has ever been paid in Turkey for a lot of rams *all round*, though £25 has been paid in individual cases. There is little doubt, however, that sham sales have been affected and the invoices shown to gull the importer." Yet, he says, it must be thoroughly understood that a foreigner would not obtain goats at the price at which Turk sells to Turk if he went about it in his own way. It is necessary to understand the Turk if you are to buy from him without suffering. Mr. Binns gives an account of his own method of purchasing, which, as illustrating the character of the Turkish farmer, is interesting. "Whenever I went to buy goats," he says, "I used always to enlist privately the head men of the district, and then profess to be going to see some goats further on, when any one who had goats would suggest that he had as good goats himself. I would ridicule this till he would fetch them out to show me, and then, while talking of one thing and another, I would gain a lot of information as to who, in the district or out of it, was reported to have the best goats. As the Turks themselves say: 'When you go to purchase anything, talk of everything else than what you want to buy, and let trade come of itself; it is only the fool who cannot get to the point when the time comes'. The Turk is not only very superstitious, but greedy and exacting in his bargains, and the idea of a foreigner coming to his feet to ask him to sell his goats, is so strange to him that it causes his goats to have a fictitious value in his eyes. Those of the Turks who go out of the way to purchase rams for themselves (and they are such strong fatalists that this is rather rare) usually go to the districts around Ayash to obtain them." Further, he says: "The most potent influence in securing good animals is business pressure. The more influence you have, and the less anxious you appear to buy, the sooner and better does the business get done. As an example, in the summer of 1867, the Hon. Israel Diehl[1] was sent by the U.S.A. Government to look over the land of Angoras, and we travelled twenty-eight days, during which he had, against my protest, tried the American way of making buyer and seller meet, and only succeeded in buying ten goats, which we only obtained through my happening to hit on a man I knew, who bought mohair for me in that particular district. At last, Mr. Diehl, getting disgusted with our want of success, placed himself in my hands. It took us only a few hours to ride to the nearest town (Beibazar), where I was well known, and in another hour I had all the wealthier men collected; and I simply stated that I had a traveller who was anxious to get home to his family, but could not until he had 140 more goats. Within a few hours all their best flocks were collected within a space of four or five miles, and we were invited to take our pick, which we did, and Mr. Diehl went away happy. The curious part of it was that where I

---

[1] Mr. Diehl made two trips, in 1862 and 1867.

expected them to ask, and Mr. Diehl fully expected to have to pay, at least £5 a head (as we had picked), when we went to fix the price the Turks all said: 'It is not a question of price, but of your helping a friend to get his traveller home; let some one else fix the price'. A third party was called, and on the matter being put to him, he said: 'That being the case, Mr. Binns, pay them 30s. each, and some day, when any of them happens to be in a corner, you can help him'. The Turks simply said: 'The Lord be praised: He put us in the world to help one another; you have spoken; so let it be'—to the intense relief of Mr. Diehl. The Turks are a curious people, and need a lot of management in the case of a buyer coming to buy their goats. While out *seeking* goats, we were asked £35 for cross-bred goats on many occasions."

CHAPTER XI.

THE TURKISH MOHAIR TRADE.

THE manufacture of mohair into articles of apparel prevailed in Angora from very early times. When the industry was conducted on only a small scale, the women of each family spun the mohair into garments for themselves. Later, there were people who made it their business to spin yarn and weave textures, and gradually a local manufacturing industry sprang up in the town of Angora. Later again, an export trade in spun mohair yarn followed. This yarn became known and used, first in Western Europe, and gradually through the rest of the Continent, until, at latest by the middle of the seventeenth century, it was known in England. In 1554, the first European record of the Angora goat appears. In that year, Busbek, the Dutch ambassador of the Emperor Charles V. at Constantinople, procured a pair of Angoras, and sent them as a present to the emperor, strongly advising that an effort should be made to introduce the breed into Europe; but nothing came of it.[1] Mohair yarn was, however, known in Western Europe before this date.

[1] Dr. Hayes says that it was not until the year 1555 that the Angora goat was distinctly made known in Europe through Father Belon, who had travelled in Asia Minor, by a brief but sufficiently characteristic description.

In 1655, Tournefort wrote about the Angora goat and the mohair industry of Turkey in his *Voyage to the Levant*, after having travelled through Asia Minor. He remarks that the Turkish Government "does not suffer the fleeces to be exported, because the people of the country gain their living thereby. The thread of this goat's hair is sold for from 4 livres to 12 or 15 livres the oke.[1] The workmen of Angora use this thread of goat's hair without any mixture, whereas at Brussels they are obliged to mix thread made of wool; for what reason I know not. In England they use up this hair in their periwigs, but it cannot be spun." It thus appears that, by the middle of the seventeenth century, mohair yarn was spun into textures at Brussels, and no doubt at some other European cities. Mohair goods were, however, not known in England until early in the eighteenth century, although, as Tournefort shows, the yarn was worked up into periwigs there at least fifty years earlier.

As a knowledge of the beautiful fibre grew in Europe, and the splendid camlets imported from Angora came more into use, the demand for mohair goods increased, and the supply of yarn was scarcely adequate to the demand. Recognising, as it thought, the importance of preserving its monopoly in mohair goods, the Turkish Government had made it a capital offence to export "tiftik" (as the unspun fleece is called in Turkey); and mohair was only allowed to be exported when spun into yarn or woven into

---

[1] A livre is a franc, and is equal to 10·69 pence. An oke is 2¾ lb.

fabrics. The Levant Trading Company was formed about the middle of the eighteenth century, with headquarters at Smyrna, one part of its business being to secure mohair yarn. It purchased and exported to Europe the yarn spun in Angora. In course of time, as the trade grew, a number of Englishmen and Dutchmen were sent out by the Company to superintend the spinning of the yarn. These men had eventually to leave, as the Turks became restless, and their lives were in danger. Some of them had taken Greek wives: these women with their children remained in Angora, where their descendants are to be found to-day. There still exists a record of these people in the old Armenian Church at Vank, two miles outside Angora, where two tombstones, inscribed in Latin, bear the names of a Mrs. Van Lennep and a Mr. Black, who died there about 1774.

There is fortunately an account of the process of spinning the mohair yarn in Angora, and of the weaving of mohair textures from this yarn. Captain Conolly, whom Thomas Southey (*On Colonial Wools*, 1848) describes as the highest authority on this particular subject which could be quoted, wrote a paper in 1839, read before the Asiatic Society in 1840. He says that after the goats have completed their first year they are clipped annually in the spring, in April or May. The females' hair is considered better than the males', but both are mixed together for the market, with the occasional exception of the two-year-old ewe's fleece, which is kept with the picked hair of other white goats (of which, perhaps, 5 lb. may be chosen from 1000) for the native manufacture of the most delicate articles. In 1839 an oke of good common tiftik was selling in the Angora bazaar for about 1s. 8½d., while the finest picked hair of the same growth was realising 2s. 8d. When the tiftik fleeces have been shorn in spring, women separate the clean hair from the dirty, and the latter only is washed, after which the whole is mixed together and sent to market to the various villages of the mohair area, Angora receiving the largest supply. In these various villages the mohair is spun into yarn.

The tiftik is bought by the women of the labouring families, who, after pulling portions loose with their fingers, pass them successively through a large- and a fine-toothed iron comb, and spin all that they thus card into skeins of yarn called "iplik"[1] of which six qualities are made.[2] Conolly's paper proceeds : "The women of Angora moisten their carded goats' hair with much spittle before they draw it from the distaff, and they assert that the quality of the thread much depends upon this ; nay, more, that in the melon season their yarn is incomparably better, as eating this fruit imparts a mucilaginous quality to the saliva. 'Divide,' they say, 'a quantity of tiftik into two parts ; let the same person spin one half in winter, and the other in the melon season, and you will

---

[1] The common Turkish word for all thread.

[2] Conolly says : "An oke of Nos. 1 and 2 now (1839) fetches in the Angora bazaar from 24 to 25 piastres, and the like weight of Nos. 3 to 6 from 38 to 40 piastres. (A piastre is about 2¼d.) Threads of the first three numbers have been usually sent to France, Holland and Germany ; those of the last three qualities to England."

plainly see an important difference.' In winter, they added, the thread cannot be spun so fine as in summer, as, owing to the state of the atmosphere in the cold season, it becomes more harsh (crisp)."

The yarn thus spun in the various villages is forwarded to the looms at Angora, which has

Photo. W. Roe] [Graaff Reinet.
Young Angora Goat Rams, bred by John Rex and the late J. B. Evans, from the Reitfontein Stud Flock (now dispersed).

always been the chief, if not the only, town in which tiftik has been manufactured into cloth.

The yarn then passes into the weaver's hands, but before he uses it, it is well saturated with a gelatinous liquor called "chirish," made from a root like a radish, which comes to Angora from the neighbourhood of Koniah. This root is dried and pounded, mixed with water, and well shaken in a bag. Then the liquor is strained off, and small skeins are steeped in it, while large hanks are watered by the mouth, when they have been spread out, according to the following process, as witnessed by Conolly : " We found the workmen before sunrise on a level space by the banks of the Angora stream. Upon a centre and two cross-trees was rather loosely stretched a double web of yarn seventy feet by seven, which was kept extended and separate by sliding cross-sticks. Two men walked up and down the sides of this frame at the same time, nearly opposite to each other, holding bowls of chirish liquor made into a thin yellow mucilage ; of this they continually squirted, or rather blew out, mouthfuls in alternate showers all over the web, while others followed them to press the threads together for a moment, and then to change their position relative to each other, by means of the sliding cross-bars mentioned, so that all might be equally moistened, as well as to rebind any threads that had given from the tension. The chirish liquor had a sweetish and not unpleasant taste, but the squirters complained that it totally destroyed their teeth, and showed bare gums in proof. They distributed their jets with singular dexterity, in broad casts of the minutest drops, and expressed doubts whether, considering the clammy nature of the liquor used, any watering pot could be made to do their work as well, and save them from its inconvenient effects. This operation is repeated several times. The work is always commenced in the cool of the morning, so that it may be completed ere the heat of the sun can operate to dry the thread quickly. A long web, like the one described, having been sufficiently moistened, its threads are divided into breadths of the sizes ordered; the weaver sends his comb that one end of a portion may be fitted into it, and carries the rest away, rolled upon a stick, to be drawn out as his work advances.

"The women of Angora knit gloves and socks with the tiftik yarn, working them both furry and plain, and making some socks of the latter sort so fine as to cost 100 piastres (20s.) the pair. The surplus of this yarn they sell to native weavers of stuffs. The weaver seeks threads of equal thickness, and takes the skeins that he matches back to the women spinners, who reel them into one thread, assisting this operation with chirish mucilage. The connected thread being returned to the weaver in large hanks, he, with a hard wheel, winds off small portions through a pan of water on to bits of reed cut to fit his shuttle."

Southey said he saw some of the articles made at Angora, which Conolly sent to the Asiatic Society—gloves, so ingeniously wrought that it puzzled the manufacturers at Leicester to find out where the workmanship began or ended; and children's socks so skilfully made that the manufacture quite puzzled some of the English hosiers.

"The clothes woven from tiftik," says Conolly, "are of two kinds, 'shalli' and 'sof,' or twilled and plain cloth, and the manufacture of these is confined to men. The weaver sits with nearly half his body in a small pit, at the bottom of which he works two or four treadles with his feet, according as he wishes to make plain or twilled cloth. Part of his loom is fixed to the floor before him, and the rest is suspended over it from the ceiling. He contracts to work a piece of 30 'piks,' or rather more than 21 yards, for a sum which varies, according to the texture required, from 15 to 100 piastres; and, by working steadily, he may finish a piece of this regular measure in six days.

"These stuffs are dyed at Angora. Indigo and cochineal, with tartar, nitric, and sulphuric acids, were mentioned as articles exported from Constantinople and Smyrna. Yellow berry [1] grows to perfection in the neighbourhood, and some spoke of a grass yielding the same colour as indigenous to the soil. Coffee colour, a favourite one among the Turks, they obtain by mixing cochineal with the rind of the green walnut. They remarked that cloth made of dyed thread keeps its colour till it falls to pieces, while that which is dyed in pieces fades with comparative quickness."

Such was the state of the industry when Angora was the great manufacturing centre for mohair goods. In her palmiest days, there were in Angora about 1200 looms at work, sending out 20,000 pieces of stuff annually to Europe, in addition to yarn.[2]

---

[1] Consul Cumberbatch, in his 1895 report, referring to this berry, says: "The yellow berry, the fruit of a species of buckthorn (*Rhamnus Infectorius*), having been formerly an article of export of great value for dyeing purposes, much labour and expense were at one time bestowed on its culture, but the universal use of cochineal dyes has reduced its demand to less than one-fourth, and its value to one-tenth, of what it realised twenty-five years ago, so that the cost of gathering the berry is barely covered. Cesare is the principal centre where it is grown."

[2] Another authority gives the figures as 1800 looms and 35,000 pieces of stuff.

The year 1820 is a memorable one in the annals of Turkey, for it was in that year that there occurs the first authentic record of an export of unmanufactured mohair from Asia Minor to Europe. It is probable that before this, small quantities of mohair had been occasionally exported; but in 1820 it is first recorded that a "few bales" were shipped at Constantinople for Europe. The raw fibre, however, was so little understood, and so little appreciated, there being no skilled workmen, and no machinery to spin it into thread, that it only realised 10d. per lb. But after that date the European demand for the raw mohair rapidly increased; and the ordinary price, says Conolly in 1839, was 18d. per lb. for many years, though it had fluctuated from 14d. to 27d. Up to the date of the Greek Revolution, it would seem that there was but little demand for the raw material in Europe; until then, the manufacturing trade of Angora flourished with practically unimpaired vigour. The citizens of Angora, says Conolly, take the Greek Revolution "as a point from which to date their decline, remarking that, before that period, there was a prohibition against the export of tiftik from Turkey, except when wrought up in the form of iplik, or home-spun thread, so that the interests of the native spinners and weavers were protected against the machinery of Europe". The Turks are no doubt correct in fixing upon this event from which to date the decline of the manufacturing industry of Angora, for, owing to British influence, the Turkish Government was induced at that time to admit machine-made fabrics from Europe, and to permit, as a regular thing,[1] the export of unmanufactured mohair. The introduction of European stuffs into Turkey caused a decreased native demand for shalli and sof, for the Turkish grandees, who used to wear full summer robes of these stuffs, gradually adopted an European style of dress. But though this change of costume, as Conolly says, doubtless had some effect upon the Angora manufactures, they were probably chiefly injured by the introduction of cheap French and English merinos into the Turkish bazaars.

In 1835 mohair spinning was begun in England at the suggestion of Thomas Southey, and a large European demand was quickly created, for the raw material was already being spun on the Continent, and soon European machinery produced a better yarn than that hand-spun at Angora and at a cheaper price. In 1836, Titus Salt purchased his first bales of alpaca, soon followed by purchases of mohair, and began vigorously to develop collaterally the manufacturing industry in these two products.

Owing to these various causes—change of fashion among the Turkish grandees, the introduction into the Turkish bazaars of cheap French and English merinos, the large and growing demand in Europe for raw mohair, and the superiority and cheapness of machine-spun yarn—" the value of Angora shawl

---

[1] It would seem as if, before this date, although a certain amount of raw mohair was exported from Turkey, the exportation was not a recognised industry, even after the strict prohibition against it was no longer enforced, but that, at this date, its exportation became a regular and recognised industry on a large scale.

stuffs declined so quickly and so completely," says Conolly, "as to entail great loss upon the wholesale and retail merchants who dealt in them, and little short of ruin upon the weavers, hand-spinners, dyers and others who were connected with the manufacture at Angora itself".

The year 1839 was another notable one in the history of the Angora mohair industry, for in that year the exportation of yarn spun in Angora ceased, from that time forward only unmanufactured mohair being exported.

	Date.	Bales Yarn.	Bales Tiftik.
Constantinople,	1836	538	3841
	1837	8	2261
	1838	21	5528
	1839	—	5679 (about)
Smyrna,	1839	—	1250 (about)
Total Turkish export,	1839	—	6929

Weight of bale = 180 lb.

In 1839, says Conolly, as the European manufacturers found it more convenient to make their own thread by machinery, the demand for (Angora) home-spun thread had practically ceased, and its value in Turkey had fallen one-half. Yarn was then no longer spun in the various villages, as their hair was exported in the raw state; and Angora itself had so declined that there were perhaps fifty looms employed (in manufacturing fabrics for local consumption) where, in its palmy days, 1200 were employed in weaving largely for export.

Thus came about the decline and collapse of

the manufacturing industry of Angora. The inhabitants of Angora felt it keenly, but, on the whole, it cannot be doubted that the change was beneficial to Turkey. As Conolly said: "Though the city has suffered, the province must gain largely by the change, if the Sultan can be made sufficiently aware of his own interest to treat it fairly".

In 1839 the export from the whole of Turkey was about 1,247,000 lb. In 1895 the export was about 11,000,000 lb. This is a result which could never have been obtained under the old conditions. The manufacturing trade of Angora, which was at best but small, has indeed been ruined; but the gain to the pastoral industry, and to the whole community, has far more than compensated for it.[1]

For a long time after mohair had been imported regularly into England, no distinction seems to have been made at the ports of entry between it and similar products, such as cashmere, alpaca, etc.; they appear to have been lumped together. According to Southey it was not till 1843 that there is a separate account of mohair, or "goats' wool," imported into the United Kingdom, when the amount was 575,523 lb. It was then but little known in England, and was for some time used for the list ends of woollen goods, and did not command much attention.

[1] In the early days of the mohair export trade of Angora the hair used to be conveyed in bales on camels' and horses' backs, those carried by camels weighing about 275 lb., those by horses (the great majority) about 165 lb., the average weight being about 180 lb. Now there is a railway from Angora to Constantinople.

In 1844 the imports into England were 1,290,771 lb., of which 97,529 lb. were re-exported to Germany, Holland, Belgium, France and the United States of America.

In 1846 she received 1,287,320 lb., of which 48,093 lb. were re-exported. From 1845 to 1846 mohair was realising from 1s. 3d. to 1s. 8d. per lb. These figures show that England had already thus early obtained, practically, the monopoly of the mohair export from Turkey ; and the fact that she was working up nearly all she received at home shows how rapidly her manufacturing trade had developed. Yet even later than this it may be gathered that mohair fabrics, at any rate of superfine texture, were not well known in England, for in 1851 the jurors of the great exhibition reported : "There are also goods composed of mohair with cotton warps and silk warps. All are characterised by peculiar lustre and brilliancy, equal in many cases to silk ; they are also remarkable for regularity of texture, softness, and fineness. It may be confidently stated that similar goods have never before been produced."

In 1853 the total Turkish export was 2,916,509 lb., and in 1858 it was 3,312,012 lb., at 3s. per lb. ; that is, the yield had almost trebled since 1839.

In 1853 Titus Salt erected his works at Bradford, now among the largest mohair works in the world. In 1836 "a young man, wandering about the docks at Liverpool, was attracted by a quantity of long-fibred, frowsy stuff, the like of which he had never seen, and the use of which nobody seemed to know. It had come from South America, 300 bales of it, and had been lying in the warehouse for months without a purchaser, and food for rats. The next day he returned and offered 1s. 6d. per lb. for the whole lot, an offer which was accepted with alacrity. The stuff was alpaca, and the young man afterwards became Sir Titus Salt."[1] The manufacture of alpaca goods drew attention to mohair, and, as has been mentioned, the trade in the two was developed collaterally. The mohair trade, in consequence, received a great impetus, and grew rapidly, especially after Salt's mills were started, till at the present day mohair has quite outdistanced its rivals, and of all lustre fibres is undisputed king. Salt, who perhaps more than any other man really brought this about, will always occupy a prominent and honourable place in the records of the mohair industry.

In 1838 a few Angoras had been imported to the Cape, more as a hobby evidently than with the hope of developing an industry here which was to surpass that of Turkey; but at the date at which we have now arrived (1853), only their bastard progeny, much deteriorated, survived. In 1856 Mosenthal imported thirty, desiring to develop the industry here. About the same time, it seems to have become apparent to the English manufacturers that Turkey could not supply the rapidly increasing demands of the trade fast enough. Most prominent among these men was Titus Salt, who eventually decided to attempt to increase the supply of mohair by developing the industry at the Cape. In furtherance of this idea, in 1857 he sent

[1] *Bulletin of the National Association of Wool Manufacturers*, Boston, December, 1895.

out some Angoras to the late Hon. Dr. White, with whom he entered into partnership in the venture.

These two years, 1856 and 1857, are most memorable dates, not only in the annals of the Cape, but in those of the world's mohair trade. It will be remembered that, at this time, Turkey had an absolute monopoly in mohair. This monopoly was not to continue much longer. In 1857 there appears the first recorded export of Cape mohair into England, the amount being 870 lb., valued at £10. Ten years later the export was 50,832 lb., valued at £1963. But Turkey's monopoly was practically uninterfered with till 1874, when, after averaging an export of about 650,000 lb. a year for four years, the Cape appeared with the proud record of 1,036,570 lb., which seems to have been about one-fifth of Turkey's export in the same year. From this date the Cape has been Turkey's rival, rapidly gaining on her, until to-day her output is about equal to that of Turkey, and her hair but little inferior. The Cape seems destined at no distant date to take the premier position. America has never been a serious competitor with Turkey, her average yield at the present day being only about 500,000 lb.

In 1862 the Hon. Israel Diehl was sent by the United States Government to Turkey, to report on its Angora goats and mohair trade, with a view to the further development of those industries in the States. His report was presented in 1863. The following is a *résumé* of a portion of a paper by him, which appeared in the *U.S.A. Department of Agriculture's Report* for 1867.

He found the natives of Angora still engaged

to a small extent in manufacturing goods from mohair for local trade in practically the same primitive manner, and with the same primitive appliances to which their ancestors had been accustomed. He says the fleece was first taken to a running stream, where it was washed by hand and trampled under foot in the water. It was then spread upon the sand to dry and bleach, after which it was assorted according to fineness, length and purity. It was then hackled on a simple, old-fashioned hackle, consisting of a few dozen long iron nails driven through a board. After hackling, the fleece was placed in rolls and spun into yarn, mostly by the women and children. For this purpose a common distaff was used, or a stick from 12 to 18 inches in length, with cross pieces, rendering it about equivalent to a large spool. It was then ready for the loom, which was of the simplest and rudest construction, and of the same unvarying type that had been used by countless generations. These looms cost from about 21s. to £5 10s. each, some of them being ornamented with rude carving. The ordinary expense of a loom was given at £4 6s. 8d. per month. A number of these looms were strung along the sides of a house, some houses containing as many as twenty. The process of weaving was necessarily tedious and expensive. It was proposed to import some of the Turkish workmen to America, but it was found that, while they asked higher wages than the workmen of England and France, they accomplished less.

The years in which mohair reached its highest prices were from 1858 to 1876. During these nineteen years mohair was never below 3s. per lb., except for a little while in 1865, when it fell to 2s. 9d., and quickly jumped back to 3s. 2d.; in 1868, when it dropped to 2s. 3d., and came back to 3s. 5d.; and in 1874, when it ranged from 2s. 9d. to 3s. 9d.; it was generally between 3s. 3d. and 3s. 9d., and actually went up to 4s. 1d. in 1870 (the highest it has ever been), and 3s. 10½d. in 1875. This was a period of unexampled prosperity and activity in both the Angora industry and the mohair manufacturing trade. The number of Angora goats rapidly increased, the area which they occupied was greatly extended, a large number were exported to the Cape, and the whole industry was in a ferment, which continued until about 1880.

For some years, as has been indicated, mohair had been greatly gaining in favour of the fancy trade, and had become an article of much importance. In 1867 it became most fashionable for ladies' dresses, and everything on the spot and to arrive was bought beforehand for consumption in England. The *U.S.A. Agricultural Department's Report* for this year remarked that the demand for mohair was permanent and increasing, and would continue to increase until met by a vastly more copious production; and that, as the stereotyped character of the Asiatic industry gave no reasonable hope of an enlargement of the supply from that quarter, England and the other continental manufacturers were looking to the Cape, Australia, the States, and South America for an increased production to meet their necessities; and, it adds, the value of the entire interest would be enormously enhanced by the opening of an adequate and permanent source of supply.

The mohair was exported mostly to England

(to some extent to France), where it was spun into yarn, and then distributed over Europe for manufacture into cloth. In 1867 it was said that at Roubaix, in France, 140,000 lb. were worked up per week during the season. In consequence of the abnormal demand for mohair, there was much trade jealousy. "For very transparent motives," remarks the *U.S.A. Report* of 1867, "the process of spinning has been represented by those in the interests of the monopoly as very expensive and difficult, nay, even a profound secret, known only to those now engaged in the business." It was complained that the extraordinary demand at that time was partly due to the attempt of the English monopolists to absorb the entire production of Asia Minor, by sending agents over the whole country to secure the clip as soon as it was shorn; further, that the English agents kept up fictitious prices in Asia Minor to discourage operations by outside parties. To this end, it was said, quotations in Asia Minor were, in some cases, kept fully equal to those in England, leaving no margin for export or import duties, cost of transportation, profits, etc., while the mass of the clip was quietly taken, at very reduced prices, from the shearers, who were kept blissfully ignorant of the telegraphic or newspaper prices' current reports!

However this may be, it is certain that England did eventually obtain, practically, a monopoly of the trade, and her position is now rendered secure by the fact that the Cape, one of her colonies, produces as large a quantity of mohair as Asia Minor does, and will soon produce more than half the world's supply.

The long period of high prices and phenomenal prosperity came to an end in 1880. There had been warnings of the coming collapse; for some time, all-wool French cashmere goods had been steadily advancing. In 1875 mohair sold at 3s. 10½d. per lb. It took its first downward plunge,

Photo. Arthur Green]   [Port Elizabeth.

Two-tooth Angora Goat Ram, property of S. and E. Hobson, Fair View, Aberdeen Road; bred by W. C. Hobson, Martyn's Ford, Jansenville. As photographed in 1897. This ram took :—
    1st prize for single ram, Agricultural Show, Graaff Reinet.
       "   "   "   "   "   Port Elizabeth.
    1st prize and champion single ram,   Grahamstown.

from which it has never recovered, from 1876 to 1877, when it dropped from 3s. 7d. to 2s. 6½d. In 1879 it dropped to 1s. 6d., which was lower by 6d. than it had been since 1856; and things wore a very unhopeful appearance. But in 1880, in a manner peculiar to this product, it jumped back at a bound to 2s. 9d. This was, however, an expiring effort, for in the same year it subsided to 1s. 9d., and at about this figure it remained till 1884, when it dropped down and down, touching 1s. 2d. in 1885, and 11½d. in 1886, or 6½d. lower than it had been in 1879. With sundry fluctuations, it remained at a little over 1s. (except when in 1889 it touched 1s. 9d. and at once fell again) till 1895, when, at one bound, it sprang up to 2s. 7d. It was, however, in 1880 that the final and disastrous fall took place, when the all-wool French cashmere goods supplanted mohair textures in fashion.

The Turks became alarmed at the great fall in price of mohair and the decline of their staple industry, and attributed it to the fact that their Government had allowed and was allowing so large a number of Angora goats to be exported, especially to the Cape—a blind disregard of facts, as the *Bulletin* observes, as overproduction has never been an element in depressing the price of mohair; the world's supply being so small, prices depend absolutely on the caprice of fashion. However, the Turks clamoured and appealed, until in 1880 the Sultan issued a prohibitory edict, absolutely forbidding the exportation of any more Angoras. But, even from their point of view, this was too late, for, as we have seen, the industry was firmly established at the Cape, and growing at an extraordinarily rapid rate.

Through the kindness of Messrs. Thomas & Cook, of London, I am able to give figures showing the yearly importation of Turkish mohair into England from 1875 to 1889, inclusive. As England obtains practically all the Turkish hair, the figures may be taken as closely indicative of the annual clip, but rather under than over the exact amount. Turkish mohair comes to England in bags weighing about 170 lb. each.

1875	-	-	31,300 bags weighing	5,321,000	lb.
1876	-	-	26,000 ,,	,,	4,420,000 ,,
1877	-	-	35,200 ,,	,,	5,984,000 ,,
1878	-	-	27,300 ,,	,,	4,641,000 ,,
1879	-	-	34,300 ,,	,,	5,831,000 ,,
1880	-	-	48,500 ,,	,,	8,245,000 ,,
1881	-	-	24,834 ,,	,,	4,221,780 ,,
1882	-	-	53,325 ,,	,,	9,065,250 ,,
1883	-	-	42,688 ,,	,,	7,256,960 ,,
1884	-	-	53,058 ,,	,,	9,019,860 ,,
1885	-	-	37,492 ,,	,,	6,373,640 ,,
1886	-	-	57,796 ,,	,,	9,825,320 ,,
1887	-	-	33,015 ,,	,,	5,612,550 ,,
1888	-	-	44,171 ,,	,,	7,509,070 ,,
1889	-	-	52,024 ,,	,,	8,844,080 ,,

From 1890 onwards the amounts were as follows :—[1]

1890	-	-	-	4,120,220	lb.
1891	-	-	-	6,496,115	,,
1892	-	-	-	7,774,541	,,
1893	-	-	-	8,005,887	,,
1894	-	-	-	6,889,165	,,
1895	-	-	-	11,000,000	,,
1896	-	-	-	4,900,000	,,

The average value per annum of the mohair for the five years 1890 to 1894, inclusive, was £365,593. In the case of the Cape Colony it was £403,068 per annum over the same period. Messrs. Thomas & Cook estimate the clip of

---

[1] These figures have been obtained from Messrs. Thomas & Cook, Mr. W. R. Payne (manager to Mr. J. K. Cilley, New York), and from the *Bulletin* for December, 1895.

Turkish mohair (all of which, practically, goes to England) at about 7,650,000 lb. per annum, but the yearly fluctuations are remarkable. For instance, the 1895 yield was over 4,000,000 lb. *more* than that of 1894, while that of 1896 was over 6,000,000 lb. *less* than that of 1895.

The yearly clip of Turkish mohair appears to be fairly regular in amount, but the yearly imports to England vary greatly. The reason for these great fluctuations, according to Messrs. Thomas & Cook, is that the article is used to a certain extent as a kind of investment by the local dealers and others in Turkey. It is not unusual for those dealers to carry from 10,000 to 25,000 bags (170 lb. per bag) from one year to another according to the circumstances of the market. They form their own opinions of the prospects of the market from such information as they can gather, and, if they take a favourable view, they hold very tenaciously. For instance, at the beginning of the present year (1897) they held over between 3,400,000 lb. and 4,250,000 lb. of the old clip; but, when political troubles assumed an acute form, they became very eager sellers, irrespective of the conditions of the trade in England.

Mr. George Gatheral, in a letter to me, dated Constantinople, 24th April, 1897, adds some further interesting details. "The mohair clip of Asia Minor," he says, "has been for generations a kind of investment, and the entire stock of the staple is never thoroughly cleared out. We have a familiar proverb among the native dealers that Asia Minor is like an old flour sack, no matter how much you beat or shake it, you will always shake some dust out. The term 'clip exhausted' can never be really true, no matter how high the price may go.

"To begin with the peasant. When the clip opens, he is pressed for money to pay his annual goat tax, but if the price be low, he will borrow money at interest and hold a portion of his clip for better prices later on. There are always money-lenders ready to advance on the security of the clip.

"Formerly, mohair was the only thing the peasant could treat in this way; at present, with the railway to Angora, he can sell his wheat for export and keep all his clip of mohair, if he likes, for an improvement in prices. So that if prices are low, not more than half of the clip will be sold at clip time.

"Then you must come to the small capitalist, dealer or even shopkeeper. They all invest their surplus money in Mohair. The country is insecure, it is unsafe to have money. Mohair is bulky and cannot be stolen easily; on the other hand it is valuable as compared to its bulk and can always be sold at some price or other. So, for all that very large class, mohair is an investment, and, what between peasants and dealers, the bulk of the clip can be held by natives if they think the price low, irrespective of the ideas of European buyers. The plan adopted by these natives is to buy (say) 1000 okes of mohair; they do not consider their capital so many pounds worth of mohair, but so many pounds weight, and when they see that they can sell their 1000 okes at a price which will leave them a margin to buy another 1000 okes, they sell, replace, sell, replace, carrying always their 1000 okes till the price reaches a high level and then they will clear out.

" You will thus understand how there is always stock held here, and how there is always a surplus left over of one clip if the demand in Europe be weak and prices low. This also explains the reason why, when a demand springs up, prices suddenly rise and go on rising, because so many holders just close their hands at once on what they hold, and it is only by successive advances that goods can be obtained. You will see from lists of shipment that in 1890 a surplus was left over of more than half the clip, and that up to 1895 still surpluses were left over. Then came 1895 with its unprecedented demand, when prices rose from 1s. 2d. to 2s. 6d., which led everybody to sell out old stocks. In 1896 demand slackened, prices kept dropping, and we have now before us a clip and a half, or well on to 70,000 bales." [1]

Average Turkish mohair is worth about 2d. per lb. more than the same quality of Cape hair, but there does not seem to be any marketable difference between the very best from each country.

With regard to the yield from the two countries, Mr. W. R. Payne gives the following figures :—

1894.	Turkish	- -	6,900,000 lb.
	Cape	- -	9,000,000 ,,
			——— 15,900,000 lb.
1895.	Turkish	- -	11,000,000 lb.
	Cape	- -	11,100,000 ,,
			——— 22,100,000 lb.
1896.	Turkish	- -	4,900,000 lb.
	Cape	- -	10,000,000 ,,
			——— 14,900,000 lb.

[1] That is, about 11,900,000 lb.

The *Bulletin* for December, 1895, says that "the present available world's supply of mohair from all sources can be placed at between 18,000,000 lb. and 20,000,000 lb., coming in nearly equal proportions from Turkey in Asia and the Cape, supplemented by about 500,000 grown in the United States". England receives, in the first instance, not only all the South African mohair, but practically all the Turkish mohair which reaches the market, and works it all up in her own mills, except about 1,250,000 which she annually re-exports to the States.

CHAPTER XII.

IMPORTATIONS TO THE CAPE COLONY.

The First Importation.

Before the Angora goat was introduced into the Cape, efforts had been made to import and breed the Cashmere. Up to the middle of the present century, great ignorance prevailed in Europe as to what were known as "wool-bearing" goats. The Cashmere and the Angora were frequently confounded; they were even thought to be identical, and were often referred to as "Cashmere or Angora goats". The Angora goats imported in 1848 into the United States were for a long time known as Cashmeres. Even in circles interested in the trade in goats' hair, it was not generally known from what part of Asia either the Cashmere or the Angora respectively came; and many were the initial difficulties importers had to overcome before they could ascertain where and how to procure such goats as they wanted.

The Cashmere is the nearest relative of the Angora. It is found principally near the regions of perpetual snow, on the cold and dry table-land of Thibet, 12,000 to 16,000 feet above the sea level. More than any other goat it is capable of resisting cold; in fact, great cold is necessary to bring its fleece to perfection. It has a long, heavy, straight fleece of little value, at the roots of which grows a very fine, very soft down, of great value, called " poshm ". The longer the outer fleece, as a rule, the more abundant the undergrowth. The colour of the Cashmere goat varies ; in white animals the undergrowth is white ; in those of any other colour it is usually a shade or two lighter than the outer coat, and is not so highly prized. The undergrowth begins to appear in the autumn, and is shed earlier in the spring than the outer fleece. To collect it, which is a most tedious work, the goats are combed in April (before the long hair begins to be shed), first with a coarse comb, and then with a fine one. Pegler says that the quantity obtained from a good goat is about half a pound. The "poshm" generally reaches the market in an unprepared state, and is there separated by hand from the long hair with which it may be mixed. Yarn for cashmere shawls is spun from only the finest hair, and for the best shawls it is never dyed, each shade being matched to the colour of the pattern required. As indicating the exquisite fineness of this undergrowth, and the beauty of workmanship sometimes devoted to this manufacture by the natives, a correspondent writes to me that the wife of a high Turkish dignitary showed him a shawl which she said had taken over three years to make, and which, though it was about 14 by 16 feet, she drew through a ring which she took from her finger for the purpose.

In 1725, says Mr. D. Hutcheon, C.V.S., the Dutch Company made an effort to establish a breed of Cashmere goats in the Cape Colony. Twenty-four were obtained and sent to the Cape, *ria* India.

Of these, only eight reached their destination, the others dying on the way; and of these eight only one was a ewe, which unfortunately died soon after landing. The seven rams were put to Boer goat ewes and the resulting female progeny cross-mated with their imported sires. Tolerably good hair was obtained from the second cross; but the imported rams died, and, as no others were introduced, the breed, for want of careful selection, deteriorated; the hair became of little value, and the industry was abandoned.[1]

The next importation was of a few Cashmeres which came originally from a flock imported into France by M. Ternaux, an eminent shawl manufacturer. The history of the importation of this flock is almost like a romance.[2] The return of the troops from Egypt under Napoleon made a taste for shawls general in France; and Ternaux, desiring to meet the demand, commissioned an agent to attend the great Russian fair at Novgorod, the general mart for all Asiatic productions. There an Armenian exhibited to him a sample of "poshm," and promised to bring him a large package of it at the next fair. The Armenian kept his word, and brought a bale of 60 lb. The exportation of this article being at that time prohibited, it "became necessary" to smuggle it away. This small quantity duly reached Ternaux's mills, and served as a basis for encouraging experiments. The war of 1807, however, and the momentous events which followed, prevented the enterprise from being then

[1] *Official Handbook of the Cape.*

[2] This story is condensed from Southey, *On Colonial Wools*, 1848.

pushed forward. In 1817 Ternaux, having discovered that this hair was the produce of Thibet "shawl-goats," induced a French captain who was going to Calcutta to procure for him some genuine Thibetan "goat-wool"; and thus was again successful in procuring a supply, though only a few small bales, of this valuable material. This served to stimulate Ternaux to further efforts. In 1819, he and his partner, Joubert, assisted by the Duc de Richelieu and the French Government, procured from among the mountains of Persia and the neighbouring provinces a large number of Cashmere goats, selected with great care, Joubert himself undertaking the journey. The difficulties that Joubert overcame were enormous, especially on his return journey with the goats, when he was obliged to leave 200 behind in the Ural mountains, and for a considerable distance had to journey on with seventeen carts with sick and tired ones in his rear. At length, however, he arrived at the Crimea, where he embarked with 568 goats, 240 being pure-bred, the remainder crossed. They were landed in France in 1819.

It was from this lot that a Mr. Riley procured some which he imported to New South Wales; and from which, in 1835, he sent three to the Cape—one pure ram, one pure ewe, and one crossbred ewe. These goats were purchased by Mr. Korsten, of Port Elizabeth. All I can ascertain further about them is from a letter by Mr. F. W. Reitz in the *Cape Monthly Magazine*, in 1857, who states: "I was told they died of scurvy—a disease which the Cashmeres imported by Ternaux were much troubled with".

This was the last attempt to introduce the Cashmere into the Cape. The failure to establish this breed in South Africa need not, however, be lamented; for, in the first place, the Angora, a much more remunerative animal, and one better suited to the climate, has been introduced; and, in the next, it is almost certain that if the Cashmeres had increased here, they would have lost their one valuable property. Their fine soft undergrowth is a protection which has been developed to shield them from the intense cold of the snow-clad mountains which are their native habitat. In this warm climate their yield of "poshm" would soon have ceased, or so diminished and deteriorated that the goats would have been of but little value.

The first importation of Angoras into the Cape Colony (or South Africa) was made in 1838 by Colonel Henderson, formerly of Bombay, who was a partner in the firm of Dixon & Co. Mr. F. W. Reitz, writing to the *Cape Monthly Magazine* in 1857, states: "Colonel Henderson, in the year 1838, imported, by a very circuitous route, and at very great expense, twelve rams and one ewe of the long-haired Angora into the Caledon district. No published account of these animals was given by Colonel Henderson, who, having embarked a considerable sum in the speculation, could not be expected to be very communicative till he had first tried to reimburse himself for the severe loss he must have suffered. After his death or departure from the Colony, some of these rams, or their get, fell into the hands of Messrs. Vos, Hopley, and others." Mr. Julius Mosenthal, in the same magazine, says these goats came *viâ* India, probably from Arabia to India, and were thence shipped to the Cape. Mr. T. B. Bayly says they came by the route of Bassora and Bombay, and adds that more than one-half of the number died, and that the survivors were distributed among farmers in the vicinity of Cape Town. Mr. Reitz further says that Hendrik Vos and W. Hopley, in communicating the results of their experience of Angora farming to the Swellendam Agricultural Society, stated : " It was supposed that something had been done to the male animals at Angora to render them incapable of propagating, as only one male (which was born on the road) proved perfect ".

For all practical purposes, as far as South African goats were concerned, it may be said that, although fourteen goats were landed, this first importation consisted of two, a ewe and her ram kid ; for the twelve rams which arrived at the same time had all been rendered impotent before leaving Turkey.

Such is the history of the first importation of Angoras to the Cape Colony. It is to be wished that fuller information were obtainable. That little ocean-born ram kid and his dam were the founders of the South African flocks of mohair goats, the forerunners of that great industry which has been so beneficial to this country. The day on which the little fellow leapt ashore, beside his dam, fifty-nine years ago, at Table Bay, is a memorable date in the history of South African pastoral products.

Let us glance at their South African relatives, whose future they were so profoundly to influence.

When the first Europeans landed in the Cape, they found the natives in possession of a short-haired variety of goats, practically indigenous to the country. But no goats are recorded as being in the possession of the colonists till 1691, when the number was 220. These goats, says Mr. Hutcheon, C.V.S., were very inferior to the common goats of South Africa at the present time, which owe their superiority in size and appearance to improvements effected by repeated importations of high-class goats of the common varieties of Europe.

The Boer goat of to-day strikes one as an animal peculiarly South African, as it browses on the arid kopjes of the Great Karoo. It is a large animal with powerful legs, a grand carriage, a bold, free step, and wild, prominent eyes. The coat is short, smooth, and coarse, of almost any colour or combination of colours, frequently being dappled. It is extremely hardy, fattens readily, and carries a large amount of flesh, which, however, is pungent and strong, and unpalatable to a refined taste. But, in up-country districts, in desert-like parts of the Karoo, they are most valuable, for there they are often the only kind of stock fit for slaughter, as they keep fat when other stock are thin or die. In the early days, the Boer goat and the Afrikander sheep were the only small stock possessed by the colonists, and this goat was justly held in high estimation by the old pioneers, for it increases with great rapidity (triplets at a birth being by no means infrequent), and its skin makes very superior leather, as is evidenced by the constant demand in the tanneries of the Colony to-day. The Boer goats have in many parts of the Midlands and the East been ousted by their beautiful rivals, the Angoras; but still their number, according to the 1891 census returns, amounted to 3,444,019 or about 250,000 in excess of the number of Angoras.[1]

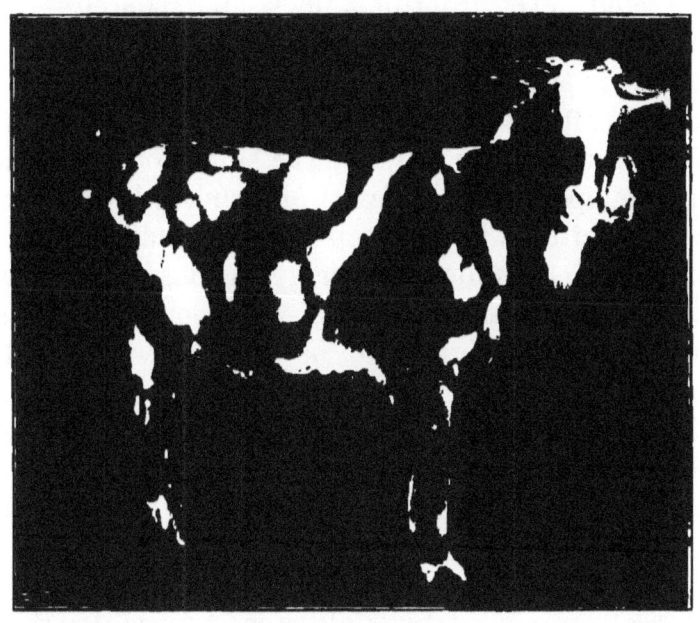

Photo. W. Roe]   [Graaff Reinet.
Boer Goat Kapater.

The greatest numbers are in Calvinia, Carnarvon, Murraysburg and Hay. However, all over the Colony, except along the Frontier, a use is still found for some of them, even where the Angora reigns with the Merino; the kapaters are used as "voer-

[1] Average value, Angora kapater skins, 9*d*. each.
      ,,   ,,   Boer   ,,   ,,   3*s*. to 3*s*. 6*d*. each.
Average weight, prime Angora kapaters, 55 lb. each.
    ,,   ,,   ,,   Boer   ,,   60 lb. to 65 lb. each.
(The Angora skins of course being clipped of their mohair.)
    These weights and values have been kindly furnished by Messrs. Combrinck & Co., Cape Town.

bokken," leaders to flocks of sheep, being trained to the work, and understanding certain words of command. It is an odd spectacle to see a couple of immense gaily-coloured kapaters marching as directed to the front of a flock, and sedately—one almost imagines proudly—leading the way into a kraal or through a gate with the sheep trooping closely after them. It is almost impossible, says Mr. Hutcheon, to estimate the saving of both time and temper which a few well-trained Boer goats will effect on a large sheep farm at times of shearing, dipping, or dosing, when portions of flocks of sheep require to be taken in succession into a small and strange enclosure to be caught; while their services in leading flocks which have to travel long distances, or across rivers, are simply indispensable. He has seen two kapaters lead a flock of 2000 sheep through a good-sized river in lots of 100 or more at a time.

These goats are subject to a very virulent kind of scab, produced by a different acarus to that which affects Angoras. In the early days, when it was not understood how to cope with scab, and when there were no dipping tanks, it was not uncommon in a severe drought for whole flocks to be almost exterminated by this disease.

Such are the Boer goats which have supplied the mothers of nearly all the Cape Angoras. The service they have rendered to the Angora industry of South Africa is almost incalculable. But for the fact that there were several millions of Boer goats, thoroughly accustomed to the country, to furnish innumerable ewes for grading-up purposes, the industry would still have been in its infancy. As it is, instead of increasing our Angoras solely by breeding from a few imported animals, we have been able, within a very few years, to grade up some millions from the good old Boer goat mother-stock, whose progeny, already outnumbering the mohair goats of Turkey and nearly as well bred, now yield more hair than Turkey, of a quality, on the whole, nearly equal to Turkish, and in many instances quite equal to the very best that Turkey can produce.

A number of white ewes of this variety were selected and put to Henderson's ram, which was in-bred to his own progeny by careful selection. The flock thus raised was farmed in the Caledon district, first by Henderson, and then by De Vos; and, later, in the Swellendam district, by Franz van Aardt, from whom it passed to Hopley, in the same district. Owing to the fact that the ram's life was a long one, a flock of considerable excellence was eventually obtained, yielding in some cases hair of splendid quality. Bastard rams were in the meantime sold to various farmers in Caledon, Swellendam, and neighbouring districts, and then further inland. The mohair goat rapidly spread, and, in a few years, there were a great number of bastard Angoras over a large and ever-widening tract of country. The stock thus obtained found its way (says Mosenthal) to the Bokkeveld, the Zwaart Ruggens, the Camdeboo, the Rhenosterberg, and the Winterveld. In the Winterveld, between Hopetown and Richmond, he saw "a flock of bastard Angoras at Mr. Sinclair's farm, amounting to 600 or 700, all white, bearing long hair, but no fresh blood having been imported in the Colony for many years, their wool was coarse and useless ". And he adds : " There are but few farmers in the Eastern Province[1] who do not possess a few goats with some of the Angora blood in them. They are easily distinguished from the pure African goat by their lengthy white hair, and the long curve-

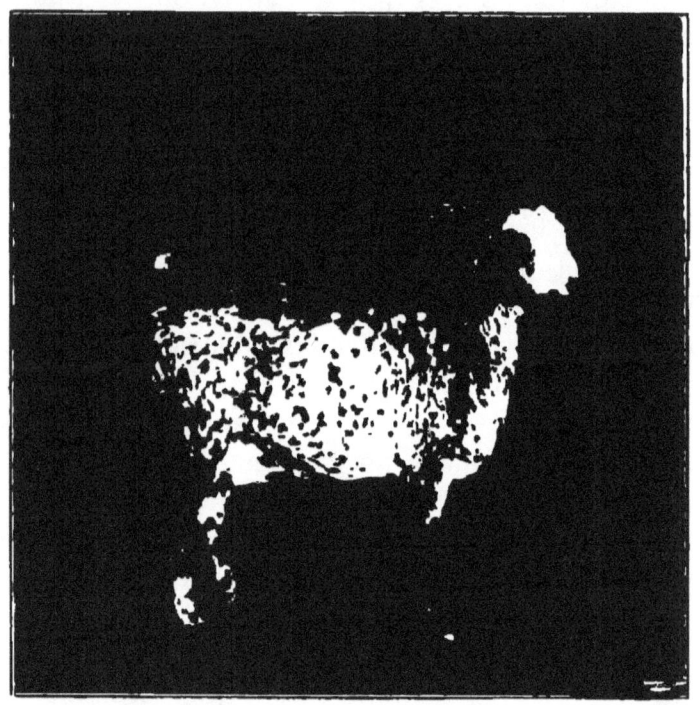

Photo. W. Roe] [Graaff Reinet.
Boer Goat Ewe.

shaped horn. The best bastard Angora wool which I have seen, besides a beautiful sample from Swellendam, was from a small flock belonging to Mr. Hendrik Vos, sen., of Graaff Reinet, which he told me he kept at Mr. Rubidge's farm, Pretorius Kloof. . . . Bastard Angora wool of the third and

[1] Written in 1857.

forth cross has been exported from Swellendam and Caledon, and realised, as Mr. John Barry informed me, 8*d*. per lb. in England."

Mr. A. Buckly, writing in 1893, says that many years ago (I take it to be in the early fifties) he was anxious to try Angoras as a new industry, and bought up all he could obtain in the Eastern Province. "The best I could get," he states, "appeared to be goats one-quarter bred. I made every inquiry as to where I could get good ones; and, hearing the brothers Sinclair, in the Middleburg district, had some good ones, I rode to them in the hopes of getting a supply. But it was a false report, they had none. But they told me of a Dutchman who had a thoroughbred ram. I rode thirty miles to see him, and bought him; but he did not appear more than half-bred. I then heard from Deer and Deitz (of Port Elizabeth) that there were some thoroughbreds in the Western Province. They bought one for me, said to be a thoroughbred ram, from Mr. Barry, father of Judge Barry, but he was not so good as some afterwards imported by Mr. W. R. Thompson." T. B. Bayly, after remarking that Henderson's goats were not remarkably prolific (he does not appear to have known of the impotence of the twelve rams), says that had they been so, still they were too few in number to acquire a permanent hold on our agricultural system; and, as the pure blood was not maintained by subsequent importations, the breed greatly deteriorated.

It is thus evident that, from this one ram and ewe, cross-bred Angoras of different grades had spread far and wide throughout the Colony, from

Cape Town to the Frontier, before ever any other importations were made, and that hair of considerable excellence had been produced. Hair from the progeny of Henderson's goats was actually exported from as far east as Baviaan's River, near Bedford, 6d. per lb. being paid for it in Somerset East in 1857. Indeed, it is remarkable to how great an extent Henderson's importation affected the goat industry of the Colony. The blood of his goats permeated to some extent most of the flocks throughout the country (except perhaps in the far north-west); and, although their progeny had seriously deteriorated in parts, and no pure-bred descendants seem to have existed eighteen years afterwards, yet it is clear that they prepared the way for the more rapid influence of subsequent importations, which were thus enabled to be crossed in the first instance with goats with a considerable infusion of Angora blood in them, instead of having to be put direct to pure Boer goats. The progress of the industry from 1856 (the date of the second importation) was, in consequence, much more rapid and widespread than it would otherwise have been: more rapid, for the reasons just mentioned; more widespread, because the first objections to Angora blood had been overcome and its benefits recognised. The Colony is under a deep debt of gratitude to Colonel Henderson. As to the little ram kid, he must always occupy a place of affection in the thoughts of those engaged in the Angora industry, who recognise the far-reaching and beneficial effects of his impress upon the flocks of the Cape.

The rapid spread of the Angora goat is not accounted for, however, alone by the fact that farmers desired to breed mohair. The infusion of new blood of a distinct variety of goat seems to have had a pronounced beneficial effect upon the constitution of the Boer goats—a fact which perhaps at first, more than mohair considerations, accounts for the extraordinarily rapid and extended spread of the Angora cross. All the early authorities agree that the Angora blood made the Cape goats less subject to cutaneous diseases, and more able to resist scab ; also that the cross-bred progeny arrived earlier at maturity, and yielded a more palatable flesh. For instance, T. B. Bayly, in 1857, states : " Those who tried the cross in former years seem to concur very generally in the opinion that the Angora goat and its progeny are exempt from the skin diseases so common among the goats of the Colony". F. W. Reitz corroborates this and speaks of " the evident improvement which a cross or two with these goats produced on our Cape breed—in their constitution, earlier maturity, weight and carcass, and lesser liability to cutaneous diseases, as evidenced by the flocks of Messrs. Hopley, Van Reenan, T. Myburg, W. Smallberger, and others in the Swellendam district ".

CHAPTER XIII.

IMPORTATIONS TO THE CAPE COLONY (continued).

THE 1856, 1857 AND 1858 IMPORTATIONS.

SEEING the manifest advantages conferred upon the Cape flocks by the importation of the Angora, and the success of the mohair industry, the Swellendam Agricultural Society resolved to make inquiries, and, if possible, to aid in introducing, without delay, fresh blood of the same breed, to improve the cross already obtained, or prevent it from deteriorating. With this object in view, Mr. F. W. Reitz addressed the committee of the Commercial Exchange, London, begging them to obtain the necessary information for the Society. Writing in 1857, he says: "The secretary wrote an immediate answer, dated 21st August, 1848, promising to lay our communication before the committee at their next meeting. But we have never had a word from them since." The Swellendam Agricultural Society, through its treasurer, the late Hon. Dr. White, then corresponded with the secretaries of the Agricultural and Horticultural Societies of Calcutta and Bombay, and later addressed Messrs. Dixon & Co., whose partner Colonel Henderson had been—all without success. A subscription was next set on foot by the Society with a view to offering a reward to the first person who should import a small flock of Angoras, and £70 was subscribed; but, as the Cape of Good Hope Agricultural Society refused to co-operate, and as no similar subscriptions were raised in other districts, this plan was abandoned. Not yet despairing of success, a company was next established, through the instrumentality of the Society, in which shares to the amount of £1200 were taken, the object being to import a flock. A great deal of correspondence followed with, among others, the Colonial Ministers in England and the English Consul-General at Constantinople, but the goats were never obtained. The Russian war was given as a reason for the non-fulfilment of the order. The order, however, was never retracted; and the company's money remained in the hands of the treasurer until the announcement that Mr. J. R. Thomson, of Constantinople, had entered into a private speculation with Messrs. Mosenthal to import Angoras, when the different amounts were refunded to the respective shareholders. This was the last of the praiseworthy efforts of the Swellendam Agricultural Society: from this time, the year 1851, the Society abandoned the project.

Correspondence was ineffective, for so little was then known in the Colony about the mohair goat, either exactly where it could be purchased, or through whom, or by what route imported. But that which the Society had been unable to accomplish was destined to be achieved by the private enterprise and personal adventure of a firm of Port Elizabeth merchants.

The second importation of Angoras into the Colony was made by Messrs. Mosenthal in 1856. The story of how this was accomplished is told by Mr. Julius Mosenthal in the *Cape Monthly Magazine* for 1857. He says that for many years past the benefits of introducing the Angora had been acknowledged by men of experience. This opinion " was corroborated by a public subscription, opened at Swellendam and Caledon, where the principal farmers subscribed from £10 to £20 each, for the purpose of raising a fund towards the importation of Angora goats. The money went home, the Agricultural Societies discussed the matter, but the attempt to obtain the Angoras remained unsuccessful." He says he was assured that millions of " wool-bearing " goats could live and thrive in South Africa, and he was convinced that even " the Ruggens, the Karoo, dry and apparently barren tracts of land," could give food to endless herds of these animals. His narrative continues : " I was informed that South Africa, more than any other country, is especially adapted, in pasturage and climate, to rear the wool goat ; that the African goat, crossed with the Angora, is not liable to scab (*brandziekte*), a disease of which many thousands of Cape goats perish annually ; and I was gradually convinced that the Angora goat ought to be procured. We had at that time some lions and tigers to forward to the Earl of Derby, who, we were informed, possessed Angora goats in his menagerie. We availed ourselves of this opportunity to obtain information from whence and how we could possibly procure the goats. The information we received was such that we foresaw so many obstacles in our way, that we abandoned the idea for a while."

After various other unsuccessful attempts to obtain the goats, from Thibet by way of Nepaul and down the Ganges, and from Persia or Asia Minor by way of Bassora[1] (on the mouth of the Tigris and Euphrates, in the ancient Babylonia), and otherwise, the firm at length decided that one of the partners should go in person to Asia to procure them. So, when peace was declared with Russia, Mr. Julius Mosenthal says his brother Adolph " proceeded to the Orient, having for his object to ascertain whether what we had not been able to accomplish by a port of the south (Bassora), we might perhaps obtain by some northern port". Her Majesty's Government and various other high officials helped him greatly, and he succeeded in obtaining a number of rams and ewes. But, before his journey was completed, cholera broke out in the East, and he had to return to a port on the Black Sea, where he remained with the goats from March to July, 1856, to watch over their safety. " He then succeeded," says Julius Mosenthal, " in shipping them to the Mediterranean, where they had to undergo quarantine, and were ultimately landed in Southampton, from whence they were conveyed to London, and sent grazing in Victoria Park (August, 1856), until they were in a fit condition to be shipped to this Colony. Of these

---

[1] The confusion which existed as to the difference between Angora and Cashmere goats has already been remarked upon.

we have landed thirty in the Cape of Good Hope."[1]

Mosenthal must have purchased a considerable number more than he landed, for Bayly refers to "the loss of so many of the goats," but says that the thirty, "when landed in Cape Town, after long-continued privations and perils by land and sea, were, with the exception of being a little low in flesh, in the best of health, and had no signs of any cutaneous disorder, as might have been expected after their protracted confinement, and so long a continuance of dry and heating food". Bayly further says that Mosenthal's monetary loss must have been considerable, as, in addition to many goats dying before the Cape was reached, the expenses attending their transport from the East to Europe, and thence to the Cape, were heavy.

I do not know how these goats were distributed, or what became of them all, except that Graaff Reinet got a large proportion of them. In March or April of the year 1857 there were sold by public auction, on the Church Square of Graaff Reinet, seven rams and one ewe, the first pure Angoras that had ever been seen in that part of the Colony, which is now the headquarters of the

---

[1] With reference to these goats Mr. Binns writes to me: "I heard, but will not vouch for its truth, that they had been wilfully injured to prevent their being of use as breeders, by some rascally Turks". There is no further evidence, to my knowledge, of their having been so injured. It seems probable that the remembrance of the injuries inflicted on Henderson's goats was still prevalent in Turkey, for Mosenthal's were evidently quite sound.

Angora industry. The names of the purchasers and the prices obtained were as follows:—

		£	s.	d.
1 ram	P. F. Bower	117	0	0
1 ,,	John Meintjes	97	0	0
1 ,,	H. S. Van Blerk	78	0	0
1 ,,	Willem Burger	67	10	0
1 ,,	Isaac de Klerk	100	0	0
1 ,,	George Murray	69	0	0
1 ,,	Jacobus Blom	67	10	0
1 ewe	P. F. Bower	60	0	0
		£656	0	0

The average price was thus £82 each.

Three months later, three more were sold there:—

		£	s.	d.
1 ram	C. J. Rabie	155	0	0
1 ,,	B. J. J. Burger, sen.	37	0	0
1 ,,	Johannes Botha	30	0	0

One month later, two ewes were sold there:—

		£	s.	d.
1 ewe	Willem Burger	60	0	0
1 ,,	Jacobus Blom	50	0	0

And some time later, C. J. Rabie purchased one ewe out of hand for £45.

Thus out of the thirty landed by Mosenthal, Graaff Reinet obtained fourteen, namely, ten rams and four ewes, at an average cost of about £73 15s. 9d. each.

With regard to these goats sold at Graaff Reinet, Bayly, in 1857, says: "It seems, by the Frontier papers, that some disappointment was expressed there, regarding their inferior size; whether they were actually smaller than imported animals of the same breed previously known in that quarter, I have no means of knowing". Bayly is in error in supposing that pure Angoras had ever been seen in Graaff Reinet or in that part of the Colony before. These goats of Mosenthal's were the first pure-bred Angoras ever seen there. This may to some extent be inferred from the farmers' complaints as to their small size. Never having seen the pure animal before, and not knowing that it was somewhat small, they evidently expected it to approach in size those large cross-bred goats from Henderson's flock with which they were familiar.

The next importation was the third, and was made in December, 1857.

It has been shown in a previous chapter how, in consequence of the extraordinary demand for mohair about this time, the English manufacturers saw that the supply from Asia Minor alone would be inadequate to the demand, and began to consider whether the Angora goat could not be acclimatised in other countries. Chief among these manufacturers was Titus Salt, who, after careful study on the subject, imported a number of Angoras into England in conjunction with the Earl of Derby, hoping to domesticate them there. These were probably the goats referred to by Julius Mosenthal as being in the Earl of Derby's menagerie. England, however, did not suit them, and Salt's thoughts turned to other countries.

Meanwhile, the Swellendam Agricultural Society had been making continuous efforts to obtain an importation of Angoras; and the Earl of Derby had been applied to for information by the firm of Mosenthal. Thus Mr. Salt's attention was directed to South Africa, and he got into correspondence with Dr. White, who was treasurer to the Swellendam Agricultural Society. Having heard of the success of Henderson's importation, and of the desire in the Colony to secure more Angoras, he decided to send some out, believing that thus he should carry out his idea of establishing the breed in South Africa, and increase the supply of mohair.

Through the courtesy of Dr. White, who, in 1893, placed certain letters at my disposal, it is clear that this importation was a joint speculation between Mr. Salt and Dr. White; there is an agreement to that effect; and it is also certain that the goats left London for the Cape on the 23rd November, 1857.

That there were a considerable number, rams and ewes, seems likely from the terms of the agreement between Mr. Salt and Dr. White, for it was stipulated that the breed should be kept pure, and that the "wool" should be sent home, and disposed of by Mr. Cook, of Thomas & Cook, to the best advantage of their mutual benefit. Later, Mr. Salt wrote to Dr. White, sanctioning his putting the rams to common ewes, "to create a stock, the wool of which will, no doubt, be of some value in the market".[1] The agreement was for seven years, the division of the flock to take place at the end of that period.

The date is fixed by a letter from Mr. W. White to his brother, the doctor, dated London, 23rd Nov., 1857, in which he says: "If the steamer meets with pretty fair weather she ought

[1] Letter of Mr. W. White to Dr. White.

to be in Table Bay by the end of December, a very nice time for the animals. They are well provided and leave by eleven o'clock to-day."

The *Bulletin* states that they stood the two voyages (from Constantinople to London, and from London to the Cape) remarkably well; and that Dr. White wrote to Mr. Thomas that there was "not the slightest difficulty with them in any way; that, in fact, they might have been born in the country, their condition was so good, while the fleeces showed no falling off in length, lustre, or otherwise".

These goats were located in the district of Swellendam, and (with those of Mosenthal's which were not sent up country) formed the foundation stock of pure-bred Angoras in the Western Province.

A year or two after this, Mr. Ziervogel, of Graaff Reinet, purchased some rams from this pure-bred flock of Dr. White's, and took them up to the Graaff Reinet district. These goats of Ziervogel's, together with Mosenthal's fourteen, formed the foundation stock of pure-bred Angoras in the Midlands.

But, both in the West and in the Midlands, there were numerous cross-bred descendants from Henderson's goats, which greatly facilitated and expedited grading up ordinary flocks, the pure-breds forming nuclei for stud flocks.

The descent of many of the most noted flocks of the Midlands can be traced to Mosenthal's and White's goats, while some go right back, without a break, even to Henderson's.[1]

---

[1] Mr. D. Hutcheon, C.V.S., *Official Handbook of the Cape*, mentions that the Hon. Dr. White, subsequent to this im-

IMPORTATIONS TO THE CAPE COLONY.

The next importation—the fourth—was made by the late firm of W. R. Thompson,[1] of Grahamstown, about 1858 or 1860, and consisted of from thirty to forty goats.

Some of the Angoras were sold soon after their arrival, it would seem. Mr. A. Buckly says he bought half the ewes from Thompson, and the late Frank Holland (who, Mr. Buckly says, was a partner of Thompson's in this transaction) got some; but Thompson kept some and farmed them himself. These goats seem to have been very pure. They were the foundation stock of Angoras in the Eastern districts.

After Thompson's death his estate was realised, and Mr. D. Watson, of Llangollen, Alice, purchased all his goats, which had been kept pure. Mr. Watson does not know what part of Asia they came from; at that time it was kept secret. Their fleeces weighed from 4lb. to 5 lb., the hair being very fine, kempless and without oil; all the kids were pure white (I believe this cannot be said of the progeny of any subsequent importation), and two kids at a birth was a most rare occurrence; the rams were not heavy-bodied, and their horns were small and fine and white (the same remarks applying, of course, with allowances for sex differ-

portation of Angoras, obtained a pair of Alpacas, a male and a female. The latter gave birth to a lamb, but the male killed it. Some time after the female died, being much older than the male, which, becoming distracted at the loss of his partner, wandered away, and was found drowned in a neighbouring river. Thus began and ended the Alpaca industry at the Cape.

[1] Not to be confused with J. R. Thomson, of Constantinople.

ences, to ewes). With the exception that he purchased two rams and three ewes from an importation by Blaine & Co. in 1868 (which, he says, were inferior to Thompson's goats), Mr. Watson kept his flock quite pure till he sold it to Mr. Tom Niland in 1877 or 1878. What eventually became of Mr. Buckly's goats I do not know, but Mr. Niland's and Mr. Holland's flocks have up to the present day been considered among the very best in the Colony. They do not closely resemble other South African flocks, although their peculiar characteristics have been to a considerable extent modified by an infusion of blood of later importations.

Mr. Watson says that he was forced to part with his Angoras because the natives were killing them for the sake of their skins, which must have seemed very novel and beautiful to people who had never seen these white goats with long silky ringlets before. During the kidding season the ewes which kidded during the day were left out at night; and on one occasion fifteen ewes with their kids were left in the veld. On the herdsman going for them in the morning he found all the ewes killed and skinned, and the kids standing beside the dead bodies. Mr. Watson says that W. R. Thompson did more for the Colony than any other merchant in Grahamstown, and that he also shipped the first bale of wool that ever went from the city.

Mr. A. Buckly says that, having bought half of Thompson's imported ewes, he "gave the first impulse to the farming of them by taking the highest prizes for them in the country, sending to England the prize bale, which weighed over 80 lb., and fetched 3s. per lb.". He adds: "By favour of Mr. W. Hume, of Port Elizabeth, I got some of my own mohair manufactured into three different kinds of material, with which all my family were clothed; and no other material in the country could equal it in wear".

The importations to the Cape Colony may, I think, be divided, broadly speaking, into two classes. The first class comprises the four already mentioned, and is more or less representative of the original pure Angora; the second comprises the remainder, from 1868 (the date of the fifth importation) onward, and is representative of the modern Angora. Up to the date of the fourth importation there were yet in Turkey a certain number of pure or almost pure Angoras of the original type, but at this date crossing had become very general, and the two types were becoming confused. The best goats were still, however, considered to be those which approached nearest to the original type. Ten years later the original type had disappeared or gone out of favour, being superseded by the heavier-fleeced modern type; and the idea of what a really first-class Angora goat should be had changed considerably. In 1838, or even in 1858, no ram clipping 14 lb. or ewe clipping $8\frac{1}{2}$ lb. of really good clean hair could have been found.[1] Such heavy fleeces were a later development peculiar to goats of a later period. Consequently the importations of 1838, 1856, 1857 and 1858, may be taken as of one type, and those of 1868 and later of another type. All I can learn of the goats of the first four

---

[1] Mr. Binns remarks that this is undoubtedly correct.

importations goes to show that they bore a much closer resemblance to the original pure Angora than did those of subsequent importations. Bayly's and Mosenthal's conception of what a pure Angora should be, from their description of the goats imported in 1856, shows this; and Bayly says he saw one of Henderson's goats in 1840, and that it exactly resembled Mosenthal's. All the information forthcoming with reference to Dr. White's importation in 1857 bears this contention out, and Mr. Watson's description of Thompson's goats confirms it. Finally, it is what might have been expected from what has been shown with regard to the crossing-out in Turkey.

CHAPTER XIV.

IMPORTATIONS TO THE CAPE COLONY (*continued*).

THE FIFTH AND SUBSEQUENT IMPORTATIONS UP TO 1880.

IMPORTATIONS to the Cape Colony, subsequent to 1858, were as follows :—

1868. Messrs. Blaine & Co., of Port Elizabeth, chartered a sailing vessel, the *Grace Darling*, to load 376 Angora goats[1] at Constantinople, direct for Port Elizabeth. These were purchased by Mr. Binns, in the Ulgaz-Dagh, Merguzeh, Araj, and Cherkesh districts of the province of Kastamouni, and were mostly rams. The vessel met with very bad weather on the voyage, resulting in great mortality among the goats. I do not know how many were landed. A number of these, rams and ewes, were sent to the Zwaart Ruggens to form the nucleus of a thoroughbred flock, in which Messrs. Blaine & Co. were jointly interested with the late Mr. J. B. Evans. The remainder, consisting of fifty-four rams and forty-four ewes, were sold by

---

[1] George Gatheral gives the number as 400. Binns says: "The *Grace Darling* was chartered to convey 400 goats, but, in a fearful storm in the Black Sea, I lost 200 odd in one night; and obtaining extension of charter-time from H. Blaine, of London, I returned to Asia Minor and bought up as many as I could get in the limited time allowed me; thus I could only deliver 376".

auction at Port Elizabeth in December, 1868. Mr. Binns got a letter from Mr. H. Blaine, of London, saying these goats were satisfactory and that the Cape farmers were much pleased with them.

1869. In this year Messrs. Blaine & Co. imported the largest shipment that ever came to South Africa. The steamer *Mary*,[1] chartered direct for Algoa Bay, loaded at Constantinople 806 Angora rams and ewes, of which 720 were landed at Port Elizabeth. These goats were purchased by Mr. Binns, in the Ulgaz-Dagh, Merguzeh, Araj. Cherkesh, and Geredeh districts of the province of Kastamouni, and in the districts of Angora and Beibazar, in the province of Angora. They were sold by public auction at Port Elizabeth in November, 1869, the sale lasting over three days. The total outlay in connection with this importation was £13,000. At the sale there were representatives from Natal and the Orange Free State (where Angora farming had hitherto been comparatively, if not altogether, unknown), as well as from almost every district in the Cape Colony. Mr. Binns says that three experts, Messrs. John Seager, J. R. Thomson, and Gulbenkion, were appointed to examine the goats before they were finally taken over at Constantinople, and gave him a certificate that they were a particularly good lot.

1869. Messrs. A. C. Stewart & Co., of Port Elizabeth, received an importation of 100, consisting of seventy rams and thirty ewes, purchased by John

---

[1] "The *Mary* was to have come with the 806 goats, but the *Melvina*, a similar, but smaller boat, was substituted." (Binns.)

Seager, who had an interest in the venture. Binns says they were purchased in the Ayash, Chorba, and Beibazar districts, that they cost Seager, in the first instance, about £2 15s. each, and that, not being limited to price, he had a free hand and was thus enabled to obtain animals of great excellence. He also says that everything conspired to make this an exceptionally good lot : Seager was interested monetarily ; he was one of the largest buyers of mohair in Turkey, and consequently could bring business pressure to bear on the Turkish flock owners to induce them to sell animals which they would otherwise not have sold ; and the goats were obtained in the very best districts. He adds that this lot contained "the largest proportion of good goats" of all the shipments he was acquainted with. These goats are still spoken of by many leading Angora farmers, and always as something most exceptionally good. Two, at least, of the leading stud flocks, those of Mr. R. Cawood and of Mr. R. Featherstone, are descended almost entirely from the goats of this importation.

1870 (probably : the date may have been 1869). Messrs. J. O. Smith & Co., of Port Elizabeth, received about forty, purchased by Mr. Eutichides, agent at Angora for the late Mr. J. Binns.

1870. By several steamers, in lots of from 200 to 250 at a time, there were shipped 750 rams and ewes—515 to Blaine & Co., the remainder to Goodliffe, Smart & Searle, of Cape Town. They were purchased by Mr. Binns in Ulgaz-Dagh, Merguzeh, Araj, Cherkesh, and Chorba. I know nothing further of Goodliffe, Smart & Searle's lot except that they were landed in Cape Town. Of Blaine

& Co.'s, eighty-seven were lost on the voyage out, and some sixty died after landing; the remainder were in due course sold and dispersed throughout the Colony.[1]

1871. Towards the end of 1870, Mr. Binns delivered 385 Angoras nominally to Mr. Parry of Constantinople. These goats had been selected from his own flocks in Chorba, Ayash, Beibazar, and Ulgaz-Dagh. They arrived in Constantinople in September, 1870. At this point there was a hitch in the negotiations, and as no agreement could be come to about a first lien on the sale of the goats, Mr. Binns decided to pick the very best and ship them himself. From these 385, he selected five rams and 183 ewes, and with these started from Constantinople in the beginning of October, having arranged with Blaine & Co., of Port Elizabeth, for an advance of £2 10s. per head. In the Mediterranean Sea a severe storm was encountered, and twenty-two tons of hay were lost, and twenty-six goats drowned. He landed at Gibraltar with 162 goats. Ten days later the *Good Hope* called and picked up Binns, his Bulgarian shepherd and the 162 goats. After a long and tedious voyage of forty-nine days, they reached the Cape, thirty-nine goats having died on the journey. During the passage one of the stewards had died

---

[1] Binns' version of this lot is different. He says that one John Parry, of Constantinople, having purchased 3000 goats from him, shipped 1200 rams to Blaine & Co., and Goodliffe, Smart & Searle, by the Union Company's steamers, in lots of 100 to 200 at a time. Gatheral says 750 were shipped; 515 were for Blaine, the others were for Goodliffe, Smart & Searle. I can learn nothing further of the other 450 mentioned by Binns.

of small-pox, and, in consequence, the *Good Hope* on reaching the Cape was placed in quarantine. Owing to these protracted delays, the ewes kidded on board ship, and, having only dry food, had not a sufficient supply of milk for the kids, which all died except one. Binns at length landed at Port Elizabeth in March 1871, with 119 ewes, four rams, and one kid, which had proved to him a very expensive lot. He nursed them for three months at Port Elizabeth and Uitenhage; but when the time came to sell, about two-thirds had cast their hair. In the end he left the goats with Blaine & Co., who, I believe, eventually sold them by public auction. There were probably some very choice animals among them. The ill luck which had attended Mr. Binns in this venture did not cease yet. After an absence of twenty-two months at the Cape, he returned to Asia Minor, to find that out of his flocks, numbering altogether about 2000, there remained but 125, the others having been swept off by an epidemic of pleuro-pneumonia.

1871-1873. Gatheral sent some sixty or eighty goats from Angora, in two lots, to the Cape Copper Mining Company.

1873. Gatheral sent sixty goats, twenty rams and forty ewes, purchased in the Angora, Beibazar, and Geredeh districts, to Messrs. Mosenthal, Sons & Co., of Port Elizabeth.

1875. Gatheral sent 110, mostly rams, purchased in the same districts, to the same firm.

1876. Gatheral sent 120, mostly rams, from the same districts, to the same firm.

1877. Gatheral sent 110, mostly rams, from the Beibazar district, to the same firm.

1879. The late Mr. J. B. Evans, a well-known Angora farmer, of Graaff Reinet, proceeded to Asia Minor to purchase goats, accompanied from Angora by the late Mr. Gavin Gatheral. He visited various goat districts, and finally purchased twenty-three rams and seven ewes in Dortdivan, a sub-district of Geredeh, in the province of Kastamouni, about ninety miles north-west of the town of Angora. The district of Geredeh, and its sub-district of Dortdivan, together with the distinguishing characteristics impressed upon the Angoras there by local conditions and other causes, have been dealt with in considerable detail in a previous chapter. It is sufficient to say here that the essential peculiarity of the Geredeh goat (a peculiarity yet more pronounced in the goat of Dortdivan) is a fleece with an abnormal excess of oil, " so surcharged with grease as to seem almost black ".

Mr. Evans is said to have conveyed his goats from Dortdivan to the coast, through deep snow, on mules' backs, each mule carrying two goats; provender for the goats being conveyed in the same manner. Mr. Evans says that the goats as they stood in the docks at London (twenty-seven in number then) cost him £1000, exclusive of his time and trouble in procuring them. One ewe seems to have died during the journey from Dortdivan to the coast, and nine more during the remainder of the journey. Twenty of these goats (seventeen rams and three ewes) were landed at Port Elizabeth in December, 1879, consigned to Messrs. Blaine & Co. They were sold by public auction (Mr. C. A. Neser being the auctioneer) at Graaff Reinet, on 13th March, 1880, as follows :—

1 ram,	1½ years,	to J. B. Evans	-	-	£60
1 ,,	,,	,, Maasdorp Bros.	-	-	140
1 ,,	,,	,, G. Jordaan	-	-	175
1 ,,	,,	,, W. J. Edwards	-	-	400
1 ,,	2 ,,	,, J. H. Featherstone	-	-	40
1 ,,	,,	,, J. Rex	-	-	120
1 ,,	,,	,, C. J. Rabie	-	-	125
1 ,,	,,	,, T. Plewman	-	-	130
1 ,,	,,	,, R. Kingwell	-	-	145
1 ,,	2½ ,,	,, H. van der Merwe	-	-	150
1 ,,	3 ,,	,, J. H. Featherstone	-	-	270
1 ,,	,,	,, T. Plewman	-	-	450
1 ,,	3½ ,,	,, Maasdorp Bros.	-	-	120
1 ,,	,,	,, T. Hartzenberg	-	-	140
1 ,,	,,	,, J. B. Evans	-	-	160
1 ,,	,,	,, W. Rubidge	-	-	240
1 ,,	,,	,, P. J. van Heerden	-	-	395

17 rams; average, £191 15s. 3d.   £3260

1 ewe	-	-	- W. Edwards	-	£70
1 ,,	-	-	- J. H. Featherstone	-	75
1 ,,	-	-	- Minnaar & Retief	-	85

3 ewes; average, £76 13s. 4d.   £230

Mr. Neser says that the two rams which realised £60 and £40 respectively " were sick and looked miserable" on the day of the sale, hence their comparatively low price. £450, £400 and £395 are the highest prices that have ever been paid for Angora rams in South Africa, and the average price of the rams has never been approached. This was, therefore, monetarily, the most successful sale of Angoras ever held in South Africa, however inferior some of the goats may have been. They were well advertised, and, being represented as a new breed, created a great sensation. Goats had been imported from Geredeh earlier than 1879; for instance, in 1869, 1873, 1875 and 1876; and it is certain that oil was quite common in the Angoras of the Cape long before this shipment of Evans's arrived; but it would seem as if nothing quite like some of these goats, with dense fleeces black with oil,[1] had been seen out here before. There have been keen, and at times acrimonious, controversies in the public press as to the effect of these Geredeh goats (and of a similar importation in 1880) upon the flocks of the Colony. It seems to be granted that the effect was very marked where they were used, that they increased the weight of the fleeces of the flocks into which they were introduced (some of the very best stud flocks have none of their blood), but shortened and coarsened the hair. Whatever purpose the Geredeh goat with abnormal excess of oil may have served in the past, he has quite fallen into disrepute with leading stud breeders now, and would meet with severest condemnation if exhibited at any of the leading agricultural shows to-day.

Mr. Evans appears to have purchased these goats more as a speculator than as a breeder, for he sold all except two (which he bought in at the sale for £60 and £160 respectively), includ-

---

[1] "I may state that the first shipment of goats by Mr. J. B. Evans were not all yolky goats, as the goat I bought for £400 was distinctly a non-yolky animal, as well as several others of the same lot. The goat I bought of the last lot for £295 was just of opposite type, large frame well covered all over with long staple, but bad head."—Extract from letter to me by Mr. W. J. Edwards, Klipfontein, Graaff Reinet.

ing the best and highest priced rams and all the ewes.

1880. The prices realised by Evans's goats induced sundry firms to at once set about procuring other importations, and Mr. Evans himself, in conjunction with Messrs. Blaine & Co., ordered another consignment from Geredeh. In this year Mr. Gatheral shipped two lots at Constantinople for Port Elizabeth. On 26th October 200 were despatched as follows : fifty rams, probably mostly from Beibazar, to Messrs. J. Mosenthal & Co. ; sixty rams, from Beibazar, to Messrs. J Mosenthal & Co. ; fifty, namely, forty rams and ten ewes, probably mostly from Beibazar, to Messrs. J. Searight & Co., J. O. Smith & Co., and Holland ; forty, namely, thirty rams and ten ewes, from Geredeh, to Messrs. Blaine & Co., and Evans. And on the 31st October 218 were despatched as follows : 178, namely, 128 rams, fifty ewes, from Geredeh, to Messrs. A. C. Stewart & Co. ; forty, namely, twenty rams, twenty ewes, probably from Beibazar, to Messrs. J. Mosenthal & Co.

The goats were consigned to the firms mentioned ; but other firms and individuals were interested, e.g., J. O. Smith & Co., J. A. Holland, Frank Holland (of Adelaide), H. David & Co. (of Somerset East), and Adler & Co. Mr. Binns, who saw the goats of the first shipment, and examined them on board ship at Constantinople, says that less than one-fifth had a great excess of oil ; the majority being non-oily. Those imported by Evans and Blaine seem to have been, as a lot, the oiliest. The 178 of the second shipment, purchased in Geredeh, were not goats with a great excess of grease, though there may have been some individuals that were. But there is no doubt whatever that, in addition to those imported by Evans and Blaine, many other goats with grease, some with a large amount, were imported in these shipments of 1880, and in other shipments previous to 1879.

[Photo. Arthur Green]   [Port Elizabeth.

Two out of First Prize Pen of three Angora Goat Rams, the one on the right having taken the Champion Prize at the Port Elizabeth Agricultural Show in 1897. Bred and owned by J. Hobson & Sons, Graaff Reinet.

It is well to bear this in mind, for it is still contended in some quarters that oil in South African Angoras was unknown previous to 1879, that it is due solely to the Geredeh, and solely to those Geredehs imported by Mr. Evans in 1879 and 1880. This contention is not only unsupported by facts: it is completely contradicted by them. Oil was known in the Colony previous to 1879; the Geredeh itself was imported as early as 1869; oil has never been singular to the Geredeh; many of our most noted flocks have, as far as is known, no Geredeh blood at all in them, and certainly not a drop of the blood of the two lots of 1879 and 1880.

The two large shipments of 1880 came *viâ* Southampton, and reached Port Elizabeth within a few days of each other, about the middle of December. Pleuro-pneumonia was introduced into the Colony by some of these goats; by Evans's in Graaff Reinet, and by H. David & Co.'s in Bedford.[1]

I have not been able to trace exactly how many reached the Colony, nor how they were all disposed of; but it appears that A. C. Stewart & Co. sold forty-seven at Port Elizabeth on 12th January, 1881, for £3233; that H. David & Co. sold sixty at Somerset East on 26th January for £4707 10s.; that J. B. Evans sold thirty at Graaff Reinet on 26th February for £3172; that J. A. Holland sold forty-eight at Port Elizabeth on 21st January for £1633 10s. 4d. for J. O. Smith & Co.; that Blaine & Co.'s were sold by Kirkwood, Marks & Co. at Port Elizabeth; that a portion of Adler & Co.'s were sold at Port Elizabeth by J. A. Holland; that the market was over-stocked, and J. A. Holland took a lot of those he had in partnership with Adler & Co. to Cradock, where they were sold by George Armstrong; and that another lot of Adler's were sent toward Victoria West.

Details of some of these shipments furnish interesting information.

[1] See Chapter xv.

The forty-eight Angoras imported for joint account of J. O. Smith & Co., J. A. Holland and Frank Holland were purchased, probably in the district of Beibazar, by or through Gavin Gatheral, British vice-consul at Angora, Frank Holland negotiating the purchase from this end. It is evident that Holland gave Gatheral minute and careful instructions to purchase the best class of animals; for, writing to Holland under date 17th July, 1880, Gatheral says: "I am pleased to note you reduce your order one-half, because the goats you require are somewhat of a fancy breed, very difficult to find and still more difficult to buy when found. The Turks know their value just as well as any Cape grazier, and it is only the fearful weight of taxation and the absolute need of ready money that make them part with them to the hated but indispensable Giaur, as they choose to call all Europeans. I think I shall be able to secure forty rams and ten ewes of the 'unique breed,' as they are called, quite equal to those of Evans's;[1] and, as the purchase will be made at a much more favourable season of the year, I have good hopes of improving even on that purchase. I should have preferred if you had decided on having the 'ten-pounders,' as they are easier and more profitable to buy, but as you have decided on having the best, I shall take care that you get full value for your money. I note with care the points you insist on, and shall pay close attention to them in selecting. I have found, in addition to those points you mention, that Cape graziers pay great attention to the belly being well covered with mohair without the

[1] The 1879 lot.

parting division which many otherwise splendid rams undoubtedly have. As such choice rams are generally household pets on the Turkish farms, they have names, and these I shall take note of and send you with the literal translations. Many of them are extremely humorous and appropriate. They have also amulets, pieces of parchment inscribed with verses from the Koran, to prevent them from the 'evil eye'. With a little care these also can be procured, and would, I suppose, be appreciated as curiosities at the Cape."

This consignment consisted of forty rams and ten ewes, purchased at a first cost in Asia Minor of £25 each, or £1250 for the lot.[1] When shipped at Southampton for the Cape (all expenses paid, including agents' commission, in all £480 19s. 1d.) the goats cost £1730 19s. 1d. Two were lost, and the purchase amount and other expenses, together with insurance, amounting to £62 7s. 3d., were refunded. Thus the forty-eight goats shipped at Southampton cost £1668 11s. 10d., or £34 15s. 3d. each. Their total cost landed in Port Elizabeth, per s.s. *Roman*, was £1762 9s. 3d., or £36 14s. 4½d. each. The landing charges are dated 16th December, 1880. Sold in the colony on 21st January, 1881, they netted £1633 10s. 4d., or £34 0s. 7½d. each, entailing a loss to the importers of £128 18s. 10d., or £2 13s. 8¼d. each.

By the same steamer *Roman* there were shipped at Constantinople the thirty rams and ten ewes, pur-

---

[1] Mr. Binns wrote to me as follows with regard to this statement: "It is all nonsense to say that the goats were *purchased* at £25 each, though Gatheral may have obtained that as *his* price for them".

chased in the Geredeh district, consigned to Blaine & Co. and J. B. Evans. These were sent up country to Mr. Evans's farm, near Graaff Reinet. Some of them had contagious pleuro-pneumonia, and caused an outbreak of that disease at Mount Stewart. After some little delay Messrs. A. F. du Toit & Co. sold the lot, consisting then of twenty-two rams and eight ewes, by public auction at Graaff Reineton Saturday, 26th February, 1881. The rams averaged £109 12s. each, and the ewes £95 each. The average for the rams was second only to that obtained by Mr. Evans's 1879 importation; and the average price for ewes is the highest ever obtained. One ram was purchased by Mr. W. J. Edwards for £295, and one by Messrs. Maasdorp Brothers for £250. Seven other rams realised from £115 to £162 10s. each, and the remainder from £55 to £95 each. One ewe was purchased by Mr. Walter Rubidge for £150, one by Mr. J. B. Evans for £140, one by Messrs. Draper & Plewman for £135, while the remaining five realised from £45 to £85 each.

Taking the importations of Angoras to the Cape as a whole, a very large majority of the goats were sold to farmers in the Midlands: Graaff Reinet, Aberdeen, Jansenville, Somerset East, Bedford, Fort Beaufort, Cradock, and Willowmore; and there is no doubt that though, on the whole, they were eagerly bought up, really first-class animals were scarce, and that many, especially in the 1880 importations, were simply worthless mongrels. Nor was there any uniformity to type as to style of hair or quantity of oil. In many cases coloured kids, often quite black, were born, even when the parents were both imported. So evident was the Kurd blood, even in some of the most expensive and most fancied goats, that, in one season, a selected stud flock of Geredeh goats is stated to have thrown nearly fifty *per cent.* of coloured kids, some of them black. Many of the last importations were purely speculative, both on the part of the purchaser in Turkey and the Cape importer. The desire was not so much to introduce first-class animals as to make money on the transactions. In addition to this, extensive crossing with the Kurd goat had been resorted to in Turkey to meet the extraordinary demand for mohair, and Angoras were, more or less, in a state of transition there. The same complaint of red and black kids from imported stock was made in America.

In 1880, as has been shown, there was a sudden and great decline in the price of mohair. The Turkish peasants erroneously attributed this to over-supply, seeing the large numbers of Angoras exported, especially to the Cape. They became alarmed. An agitation was set up, which resulted in 1880 in the issue of an edict by the Sultan absolutely prohibiting the exportation of any more Angoras. It seems clear, however, that, notwithstanding this prohibition, Angoras might have been obtained surreptitiously. But the Cape did not want any more; the market was over-stocked; money had been lost on some of the 1880 importations; and it was evident that, as the price of mohair had so declined, it would not pay to import to the Cape.

So the Cape went steadily on grading up its flocks by careful selection, improving, in many cases, on even the best animals that had been imported.

CHAPTER XV.

IMPORTATIONS TO THE CAPE COLONY (continued).

THE 1895 AND 1896 IMPORTATIONS.

IN 1895, however, the idea of securing another importation began to be discussed in the Colony, and £1000 was placed upon the parliamentary estimates. The leading Angora farmers were agreed that there was considerable risk in importing from Turkey, as the best Cape stud flocks had been brought to so high a state of excellence; it being recognised that importation was no guarantee of purity or excellence, however superior a goat might appear. At a meeting of Angora farmers, it was decided that it would not be safe to import unless experienced men were sent from the Cape to select the animals. Messrs. R. Featherstone and C. G. Lee were chosen for this purpose. Pleuro-pneumonia was also dreaded, and it was recognised that, if any goats were imported, every necessary precaution should be taken to prevent the reintroduction of that deadly disease. Meanwhile, the prohibitory edict of 1880 had been reissued by the Sultan, the idea of allowing any Angoras to leave Turkey meeting with the most strenuous opposition there. But Mr. George Gatheral, of Constantinople, who had been striving for some years for permission to export, was eventually successful in obtaining it, mainly through the influence and untiring efforts of Sir Philip Currie, who had been appointed H.B.M.'s Ambassador at the Sublime Porte.

In a letter to the *Eastern Province Herald*, Port Elizabeth, dated Constantinople, 4th Nov., 1895, Mr. George Gatheral wrote as follows: "In May last, owing to the presence of H.B.M.'s Ambassador, and to a favourable turn in the mind of His Imperial Majesty the Sultan, I obtained an Imperial Concession to export Angora mohair goats, and at the same time the Government stated that it would be the very last granted. As soon as the fleece had sufficiently grown to show the quality of the mohair, namely, early in August, I sent my experienced men to buy the goats, and during two months I had an unceasing conflict to get the animals safely out of the country. Immediately that it became known that goats were to be exported again, an influential meeting of all the mohair merchants and dealers took place in Constantinople, and decided to oppose the effort by every means in their power. They wrote to all their agents up country to represent to the farmers that export of bucks meant mohair coming back to 14d.; that the reason of the late advance was the prohibition of export to the Cape, which had led to the degeneration of the Cape hair. The dealers also brought influence to bear on the Governors-General of the two provinces where purchases were to be made, and through which the animals had to pass, and these Governors did all in their power to prevent purchase. A monster petition, under the auspices of the Angora Governor-General, was drawn up, signed, and addressed to H.I.M. the Sultan, begging His Majesty to save their industry from ruin, and to prohibit export. The Governor, moreover, sent officials to instruct the peasants not to sell any goats. The goats already purchased were to be given back to the peasants, and finally my man was taken off under arrest to the chief town in the district. The Turkish populace were excited, and this arrest saved my man's life. H.B.M.'s Ambassador, however, took the matter up with firmness and promptitude; urgent telegrams were obtained from the Minister of the Interior to the Governors-General, instructing them to remove obstacles and give my men all needful help. This they at last were compelled to do, and, accompanied by an escort, the further purchases were made and the flock protected from brigands and thieves who attempted to seize the animals. After nearly two months, the goats came down just as Constantinople was in a state of terror and massacre, one of my men being knocked down, bayoneted, and left for dead in the street. Finally, the flock which had been selected with so much care and at the serious risk of life, was shipped for Southampton on 16th October last. The flock consists of 115 goats ordered by Messrs. Mosenthal, Sons & Co., and fifty goats ordered by the Right Hon. Cecil Rhodes. The entire shipment is the result of a very careful and painstaking selection by experienced judges and chosen from thousands of the very best flocks in the very best districts of Asia Minor. These animals should please your judges, I think. I have always pleased them hitherto, and these, in my opinion, are the finest that have ever been sent to the Cape."

It will be seen from this letter that these goats

were purchased not only in several districts but in two provinces. The two provinces referred to, and which may be said practically to comprise the mohair area of Asia Minor, are Angora and Kastamouni. It, therefore, seems that the whole mohair area contributed to supply these goats—a conclusion which their entire lack of uniformity would appear to justify. The flock, after a journey of seventeen days, reached Southampton on the 2nd November, and left there per the Bucknall Liner *Manica* on the 5th November, reaching Cape Town on 3rd December, and Port Elizabeth on 6th December, 1895. Very rough weather was experienced from Constantinople to Southampton; and one goat died on the way out, about five days before the vessel arrived in Table Bay; the remainder were in excellent condition, under the care of two Armenians and a Turk. Mr. Rhodes's fifty were landed the day they arrived, and conveyed to Groote Schuur, his residence at Rondebosch, near Cape Town; Messrs. Mosenthal's 114 were landed in Port Elizabeth on 6th December, and at once conveyed direct to the show ground. All were placed in quarantine to guard against their introducing pleuro-pneumonia.

On the whole, the goats were a very inferior lot. There was no uniformity; they were of widely different types and degrees of excellence; individual fleeces were generally uneven, backs often faulty, bellies deficiently covered, breeches generally bad, and kemp astonishingly common. The very choicest were inferior to the best goats of leading Cape breeders, and the great majority fell far short of that standard, many being worthless mongrels, from a stud-breeder's standpoint. As a lot, they showed distinct traces of common blood, and the taint of the Kurd goat was in several instances glaringly visible in blue heads and red legs. There were, however, a few really good animals. Mr. Rhodes, whose goats, on the whole, were said to be inferior to Messrs. Mosenthal's, disposed of his privately. Mosenthal's were sold by public auction, by Mr. J. A. Holland, on Tuesday, the 4th February, 1896. The attendance at the sale was probably the most representative body of Angora goat farmers ever assembled together in South Africa, and among these were men who, it was believed, would have given £1000 for a really exceptionally first-class ram. Many of the goats had cast their hair, but this made no difference to the sale, as they had all been carefully examined in full fleece by intending buyers. When landed, they were infested with hypodermic larvæ of the bot fly, but a certificate was read from the Colonial Veterinary Surgeon certifying that they were clean when put up for sale. All were sold, the ninety-five rams for £4581, or an average of £51 1s. 3d. each; the nineteen ewes for £808 10s., or an average of £42 4s. 8d. each. The highest price paid for a ram was £330 by Messrs. W. Rubidge and G. H. Maasdorp; another realised £230, and was purchased by Mr. W. Miller; one was sold to Mr. P. H. Gericke for £195, and eleven more went at from £105 to £175. The lowest price paid for a ram was £6, and three more went at under £10 each; thirteen between £10 and under £20; and thirty-seven at between £20 and £30. The highest priced ewe was sold to Messrs. Miller

Bros. for £112 10s.; no other realised £100 or over. Miller Bros. bought the next for £80; and the third was bought by Mr. R. Cawood for £65. The lowest priced ewe realised £15.

Eleven months later, Mr. George Gatheral sent another consignment of Angoras to Messrs. A. Mosenthal & Co. They were landed at Port Elizabeth on 6th November, 1896, and consisted of thirty-three rams and thirty ewes,[1] bearing, on the average, about five or six months' growth of hair. After having been quarantined in the Agricultural Society's show-yard for two months, they were sold at public auction there on 13th January, 1897, by Mr. W. Armstrong. The sale was not so well attended as the preceding one. Thirty-three rams were sold for £2035, or an average of £61 13s. 4d. each; and twenty-seven ewes for £1302, or an average of £48 4s. 5d. each. The highest price paid for a ram was £380, by Messrs. G. H. Maasdorp, W. Rubidge, and W. J. Edwards, of Graaff Reinet; the next was sold to Messrs. J. Scholtz & Co., of Aberdeen, for £180; eight went at between £90 and £162; and eighteen went at under £30, the two lowest prices being £11 and £10. The highest price paid for a ewe was £205 by Mr. W. J. Edwards; the next went to Mr. J. H. Featherstone for £157; eleven went at under £30, the lowest price being £12.

(*The Midland News*, Cradock, says it is understood that two of the rams and six of the ewes

---

[1] The consignment, which came per the s.s. *Duke of Westminster*, consisted of thirty-three rams and thirty ewes; but of the ewes only twenty-nine were advertised and only twenty-seven sold. I presume three died.

were purchased for a company, per Mr. P. Heugh, that intended to ship them to Nyassaland, where a determined effort would be made to establish Angora goat farming on the highlands of the Interior.)

£380 is the highest price that has been paid for a ram since 1879, but it is said that the purchasers of this ram were prepared to pay double the amount they gave for him. £205 and £157 are the highest prices ever paid for single ewes in the Cape Colony, and constitute a South African record. As such high prices are paid nowhere else in the world for Angora goats, £450 for a ram and £205 for a ewe (an extraordinary price) may be confidently taken as world's records. It is satisfactory to know that the Colony possesses goats of its own breeding superior to even these high-priced imported rams and ewes.

These goats were, as a whole, similar in type but superior to those of 1895, though there were a number of very inferior animals among them. The ewes were considerably better than the rams, even the best ram being surpassed by several of the ewes. All had kemp; some very little, others a great amount. The favourite ram was an oily goat, somewhat harsh and apparently short in staple; his locks were wide and flat instead of being round and ringy (curled), and his fleece opened up a little too much on the skin. He was of good medium size, beautifully covered, of admirable symmetry, and of refined and thoroughbred appearance all over : an excellent animal. A prominent Angora breeder, and excellent judge, who has hitherto held that the goats imported by Mr. J. B. Evans in 1879 and 1880 were the best that ever came to the country, wrote to me that the 1896 lot were equal to the goats of those two importations, and that one ram (the one above remarked upon, which sold for £380) was superior to any in either of them. The ewes as a whole were good, a few of them being of rare merit and exceeding beauty.

This completes the list of importations to the Cape, as far as my knowledge goes. It is perhaps impossible to say exactly how many Angora goats have been imported; but it is safe to say, in all, they number over 3000. They have come from numerous districts in Asia Minor, and are representative of the general run of Turkish goats. There has been no uniformity among the goats imported; they cannot be said to be representative of any definite type or types. Each animal stands solely on its own individual merits, and not as the representative of any type. In the future there may be certain fixed varieties among Angora goats, as there are to-day among Merino sheep; but at present no such varieties exist. Some very superior animals have been imported; but Mr. Binns says the very best have never left Turkey. A great many mongrels have also been imported, and Angoras are to-day as mixed at the Cape (except the best stud flocks) as they are in Turkey. However, notwithstanding the fact that many thoroughly bad animals have been imported, so inferior as certainly to injure rather than improve even the average Cape flocks; yet, owing to the suitability of the Cape climate and pasture to the Angora goat, and particularly to the superior intelligence of the Cape breeders and their adoption of more modern and scientific methods of breeding, the quality of the best stud flocks has been raised to so high a standard of excellence, that Turkey would probably profit by obtaining new blood from the Cape for use in its very best flocks. On the other hand,

Photo. Arthur Green]　　　　　　　　　[Port Elizabeth.

Full-mouth Angora Goat Ram, bred by R. C. Holmes, Karree Hoek, Pearston, owned by F. C. Bayley, Britstown. Never beaten as a two-tooth (Champion at Grahamstown Agricultural Show, 1895); numerous Second Prizes as a four-tooth; and First Prize as full-mouth at Port Elizabeth Agricultural Show, 1897. As a two-tooth he clipped 9 lb. 1 oz., and as a four-tooth 13 lb. 4 oz. (twelve months' fleece).

considering the inferior type of farmers engaged in the industry in Turkey and the primitive and unscientific methods of breeding in vogue there, further importations to the Cape seem wholly unadvisable, unless under the auspices of the Angora

Goat Breeders' Association, and unless two of the very best judges in the Colony go to Turkey to select the goats. Failing this, the Cape industry will best advance without assistance from Turkey. It but remains for the Cape farmer to have a clear conception of what kind of fleece he desires his goats to produce, and then to work unswervingly towards the realisation of that conception. The breed here is in a most plastic state yet, but the leading breeders are gradually and surely fixing it; and, what is most hopeful, gradually bringing their goats towards uniformity to one type.

CHAPTER XVI.

THE PLEURO-PNEUMONIA EPIDEMIC IN THE CAPE COLONY.

PLEURO-PNEUMONIA, or contagious lung sickness, among goats was introduced into the Colony by some Angoras in a consignment of 200 imported from Turkey. They left Constantinople on 26th October, and came *viâ* Southampton, arriving at Port Elizabeth about the middle of December, 1880. Mr. Binns, who examined these goats on board ship at Constantinople, says he took the numbers of some of the best rams and sent them to Cape friends, warning them, however, that " many of the goats had pneumonia when shipped ".

One lot from this consignment, belonging to the late Mr. J. B. Evans, were sent by rail to Mount Stewart, arriving there on 23rd December, and were placed on Mr. J. H. Cawood's farm, Jackal's Laagte. Within a few days the disease broke out in a flock of 460 belonging to Mr. Cawood, into which the imported goats had been introduced. The goats began to die rapidly, and when about 200 had succumbed, Mr. Cawood killed the remainder. Fortunately, this was the only flock running on that part of the farm. The carcases were buried, and the spread of the disease prevented. One of Mr. Evans's rams was reported to have died at Mount Stewart, and several more after their arrival at his farm; but the disease was not conveyed to any other parts on his farm or elsewhere.

This outbreak was hushed up; and the facts might never have been forthcoming, but that later, when compensation was being paid to the Bedford farmers whose goats had been killed by order of the Government, Mr. Cawood put in his claim. Then the facts became generally known, and Mr. Cawood got £300 compensation.

The other outbreak was of a much more serious nature. It was caused by a goat from the same shipment, and began in the Bedford district about a month later than that at Mount Stewart. Messrs. H. David & Co., a firm of merchants in Somerset East, were interested monetarily in a number of the goats of this shipment. Their goats were conveyed from Port Elizabeth by rail to Cookhouse, arriving there on 22nd December, and thence by ox-waggon to Somerset East, where they were sold at public auction on 26th January, 1881. At this sale, a Mr. van Niekerk bought a ram which he took to his farm, Brakfontein. The disease, conveyed by this ram, broke out there on 29th January. Next it appeared on the farm of Mr. Botha, near Goba Drift, and soon on many other farms in the Bedford district. As it spread with great rapidity and deadly effect, Mr. D. Hutcheon, the Colonial Veterinary Surgeon, was sent up to investigate. He at once tried the effects of inoculation; in a few weeks, 30,000 had been treated; but the ewes, which were then in kid, aborted, and the kids were found affected with a modified form of the disease. Some farmers tried to rear such kids as were not premature, but they communicated the disease to the flocks.

The number of flocks affected and not inoculated was nineteen, containing 7500 goats, of which 5000 died of the disease.

The number of flocks inoculated after the disease had appeared in them was twelve, containing 12,550 goats, of which 4380 died.

The number of flocks inoculated previous to any appearance of the disease, but in which the disease subsequently broke out, was thirty-five, containing 21,500 goats, of which 2860 died.

The number of flocks inoculated that were free from the disease when inoculated, and in which the disease never appeared, was eighteen, containing 9950 goats.

Thus about 12,340 Angoras perished, exclusive of kids (computed at not less than 20,000), which either died from the disease or were lost by abortion.

The total number of goats inoculated was 44,000, the total number inoculated a second time was 20,000, and the total number inoculated a third time was 1600, making a total inoculation of 65,600.

It will be seen from the above figures that inoculation was fairly successful as regards the minimising of the death-rate; but Mr. Hutcheon soon saw that the disease would never be eradicated by inoculation, and that, unless it were eradicated at once, it would obtain a permanent hold on South African goats and become endemic in the country. There was only one way to eradicate it, namely, by killing all infected flocks. This Mr. Hutcheon advised, and the Government promptly acted on his recommendation. Two prominent farmers were associated with him to decide what goats were to be killed and to fix the rates of remuneration. This commission of three, which was granted a free hand, set to work at once, and so vigorously and thoroughly did they fulfil their important duty that in a short time they completely succeeded in stamping out the disease. This was practically accomplished in January, 1882, just a year after the outbreak; only one flock on the farm of Mr. S. Painter, where the disease appeared again, had to be dealt with (and was promptly and successfully dealt with) after that date.

There were killed :—

	£	s.	d.
3514 goats, average compensation value 12s. 3½d. each	2158	2	0
2311 kids, average compensation value 5s. 7¾d. each	653	1	6
17 rams, average compensation value 55s. 10½d. each	47	10	0
5842	£2858	13	6

The total amount paid out by Government to farmers as compensation was £3178 13s. 6d., as follows :—

	£	s.	d.
Paid to Bedford farmers for 5842 goats killed	2858	13	6
Paid to Bedford farmers as compensation for 320 goatskins	20	0	0
Paid to Mr. J. H. Cawood, of Mount Stewart, for 460 goats	300	0	0
	£3178	13	6

This amount, however, does not represent the whole cost of fighting with and eradicating the disease;

there were other expenses, connected, for instance, with the actual work; but the total cost to the country was under £4000—a mere trifle when it is remembered that the Angora goat industry was saved and a deadly disease absolutely exterminated from the country. The total number of goats lost through the disease was about 38,200.

The country has not yet forgotten, and never will forget, what it owes to Mr. Hutcheon, though, since the perilous days when he saved the goat industry, he has so served the Colony as to endear himself to every man who takes an intelligent interest in its pastoral and agricultural development.

Pleuro-pneumonia is indigenous to Asia Minor, being most common and dangerous in low-lying and damp situations. It does not exist always in a severe form, but at times it assumes an epidemic character and a most virulent and deadly form, sweeping the Angoras off by hundreds of thousands. There is no record of its having appeared out of the country to which it is indigenous except in the outbreak in the Cape Colony. On its appearance here it was quite unknown to veterinary science, so Mr. Hutcheon had to break new ground. It is a contagious disease, closely analogous to pleuro-pneumonia in horned cattle, and if it had not been promptly stamped out would have obtained a general hold on the Angoras of this country, and have needed ceaseless combating, just as lung sickness in cattle does. In time, like other diseases which are so deadly on their first introduction to a new country, it would probably have assumed a milder form; but it needs no argument to prove that Mr.

Hutcheon did the country an inestimable service in eradicating it at once.

The disease in the Colony was in a most virulent form; every goat in every flock in which it appeared was attacked, and the mortality, running sometimes as high as 80 per cent., averaged about 60 per cent. The death-rate was highest among those first attacked in any flock, probably because they were peculiarly susceptible, and lowest among those last attacked. It is a disease conveyed by direct contagion, and not an infectious one. The germs are not conveyed great distances by the wind. The course it runs may be divided into two periods: first, a period of incubation or latency, from seven to ten days; second, in full strength, from ten to thirteen days, the exact course depending on the susceptibility of the animal.

It is remarkable how long the disease was latent in the imported goats. Some of them were observed to have it when the consignment left Constantinople in the last week of October. It did not break out during the voyage, nor was it in the first instance observed among the imported goats in the Colony. In both outbreaks it appeared among Colonial flocks as soon as the imported goats were put to them; at Mount Stewart at the end of December and in Bedford a month later—two and three months after the shipment left Turkey. The fact that it did not break out during the voyage, and until Colonial flocks became infected, may perhaps be accounted for on the supposition that some of the imported goats, having had the disease in Turkey, retained diseased lungs; as is sometimes the case with horned cattle here that have recovered from lung sickness, and yet are capable of infecting healthy cattle because their lungs remain more or less locally injured and diseased for a long time. With regard to others, it would seem that they had either had the disease and recovered, or that, coming from a country where it is always prevalent to some extent, often in a mild form, they were not very susceptible. If the report be true that, *after* the Mount Stewart outbreak, several of Mr. Evans's imported rams, which had so far been healthy, contracted the disease and died, the above supposition would seem to have strong support; it would seem to prove that such animals had somehow secured an immunity *in Turkey;* but that the disease, having been conveyed to the Cape flocks, had acquired a virulency so potent that the immunity they had hitherto enjoyed was not capable of being sustained. But, whatever the explanation, it is certain that those goats brought the disease from Turkey. South Africa should guard itself well against its reintroduction.

The facts given in this chapter have been obtained almost entirely from the Reports of the Colonial Veterinary Surgeon for 1881 and 1882.

CHAPTER XVII.

THE MOHAIR AND ANGORA GOAT INDUSTRIES OF THE CAPE COLONY.

Though Angora goats were imported into the colony in 1838, no official record of any export of mohair appears until 1857. It is certain, however, that, soon after 1838, mohair was sent from the Cape to England, and was exported in small quantities, more or less regularly, before any official records were made. Thomas Southey (*On Colonial Wools*, 1848) says that before mohair (or, in fact, any lustre goods) appeared in the official returns of imports into Great Britain, it used to come in wool bales with wool and was passed as such. There seems to be no doubt that such mohair as was exported from the Cape to England previous to 1857 was sent in this manner. Writing in 1857, both Mosenthal and Bayly mention that Cape mohair, both of good quality and also bastard hair, had been sold in England at a remunerative price. This is what might have been expected, for a very large proportion of the Colonial flocks had received an infusion of Angora blood more or less strong from Henderson's importation in 1838, before the second and third importations (in 1856 and 1857). In 1857, before the new blood had penetrated so far, Mr. J. W. Stevens, of Cradock, bought two bales full in Somerset East at 6d. per lb. This hair had been grown by Mr. Izak de Klerk, near Baviaan's River Drift, in the Bedford district, who, in consequence of some prominence as an Angora farmer, was locally known as Izak Bok-Boer. It was taken into Somerset East by buck-waggon, loosely wrapped up in a buck-sail. Mr. Stevens had ten canvas bags made to hold it, and then shipped it to London,

Photo. W. Roe]　　　　　　　　　　　　[Graaff Reinet.

Angora Goat Ewes, bred and owned by G. H. Maasdorp, Winterhoek, Graaff Reinet.

where it realised 1s. per lb. As mohair was then selling in Bradford at 2s. 6d. per lb. this sample was evidently very inferior. It was a common practice in the early days (the sixties) in the Midlands for the buyer to offer the farmer so much a bale, unweighed (£90 was a frequent offer), to take the lot.

The following returns, showing the quantity and value of mohair exported from the Colony from 1857 to 1897, have been kindly supplied to me by the Customs department:—

Year.	Quantity.	Value.
	Lb.	£
1857	870	10
1858	—	—
1859	602	3
1860	385	12
1861	784	61
1862	1,036	54
1863	1,354	73
1864	8,104	608
1865	6,992	368
1866	21,165	986
1867	50,832	1,963
1868	102,570	4,030
1869	260,932	14,746
1870	403,153	26,673
1871	536,292	43,059
1872	876,861	58,823
1873	765,719	45,913
1874	1,036,570	107,139
1875	1,147,453	133,180
1876	1,323,039	113,967
1877	1,433,774	116,382
1878	1,358,395	108,353
1879	2,288,116	130,775
1880	2,590,232	206,471
1881	4,146,128	262,660
1882	3,776,657	253,128
1883	4,443,971	271,804
1884	4,329,355	239,573
1885	5,251,301	204,018
1886	5,421,006	232,134
1887	7,153,730	268,446
1888	9,598,768	305,362
1889	9,442,213	351,544
1890	9,235,249	337,239
1891	9,953,548	355,426
1892	10,516,837	373,810
1893	9,457,278	527,619
1894	10,003,173	421,248
1895	11,090,449	710,867
1896	10,001,028	572,230
1897	12,583,601	676,644

The Cape Colony now yields about one-half of the world's supply of mohair, or about the same quantity that Turkey yields.

The remarkable fluctuations in price disclosed in the above list are due solely to the caprice of fashion; the scarcely less remarkable fluctuations in quantity from year to year are due to an increased or diminished supply according as the price rises or falls; and to the effect of bad seasons, when clips are light, large numbers of goats die, and few kids are reared. For instance, in 1881, before the effect of the great fall in price in the preceding year could be fully felt, the yield was 4,146,128 lb., while the next year, when the fall had reacted on the Angora industry, the yield had actually decreased to 3,776,657 lb. On the other hand, the 1887 and 1888 clips were grown in good seasons, and in each year the yield showed an increase of about 200,000 lb. over the preceding year; whereas there was severe drought in 1888 and 1889, and consequently the 1889 clip was actually less than that of 1888, and the 1890 clip less than that of 1889. In both these years, 1888 and 1889, a large number of Angoras perished from the drought and inclement weather, especially in 1889, when a couple of days' cold rain in September, when the goats were bare, killed in the Somerset East and Cradock districts alone upwards of 20,000. With regard to the year 1896, the Collector of Customs in his Report to the Cape Parliament says: " The falling off in Angora hair, both in quantity and value, is to be deplored, evidencing as it does a diminished production consequent upon the reduction of our flocks owing to drought, and a fall in price in the European market of this staple article".[1]

The following is a return of the number and value of goat skins (both Angora and Boer goats) exported from the Colony for ten years:—

Year.	Skins.	Declared Value.
		£
1885	1,202,120	103,209
1886	1,113,023	104,894
1887	1,051,312	99,923
1888	1,340,685	109,068
1889	1,530,799	123,789
1890	1,597,733	142,425
1891	1,577,479	130,454
1892	1,726,528	132,717
1893	1,693,031	131,843
1894	1,619,385 (weighing 5,164,409 lb.)	111,825

In computing the number of goats in the Colony it is safest to be guided by the returns of the Census of 1891; for, though other statistics have been taken since, they are not as reliable as those of the Census.

[1] Through the kindness of the Collector of Customs, I am enabled, while revising the proof sheets, to give the figures for 1897, inserted at the last moment in the above table. It will be seen that the amount of mohair exported exceeds that of the highest previous export for one year by 1,500,000 lb.

MOHAIR AND ANGORA INDUSTRIES OF CAPE COLONY.

Angoras in the Cape Colony, according to the 1875 Census	877,988
Increase within the Colony as constituted in 1875, up to the 1891 Census	2,161,925
Angoras in the Colony as constituted in 1875, according to the 1891 Census	3,039,925
Angoras in Griqualand West (annexed in 1880), according to the 1891 Census	52,714
Angoras in the Transkei (since 1875), according to the 1891 Census	91,379
Grand total of Angora goats, 1891 Census	3,184,018
Other (Boer) goats in the Cape Colony, according to the 1875 Census	2,187,214
Increase within the Colony as constituted in 1875, up to the 1891 Census	395,502
Boer goats in the Colony as constituted in 1875, according to the 1891 Census	2,584,716
Boer goats in Griqualand West (annexed in 1880), according to the 1891 Census	295,632
Boer goats in the Transkei (since 1875), according to the 1891 Census	563,671
Grand total of Boer goats, 1891 Census	3,444,019

Thus, in 1875, there were in the colony as then constituted 877,988 Angoras and 2,187,214 Boer goats, a total of 3,695,202 goats. In 1891 there were, within the same area, 3,039,925 Angoras and 2,584,716 Boer goats, a total of 5,624,641 goats; showing an increase of 2,161,937 Angoras, and of only 397,502 Boer goats. These figures indicate how rapidly the Boer goat is being superseded by his more beautiful and more remunerative rival. In 1891, within the whole colony as then constituted, there were 3,184,018

Angoras and 3,444,019 Boer goats: a grand total of 6,628,037 goats.[1]

It will thus be seen that, whereas in 1875 there were 1,309,226 more Boer goats than Angoras, in 1891 that majority had been reduced to 260,000. It is almost certain that to-day (1897) the Angoras are considerably the more numerous; and it cannot be long before the Angora almost entirely absorbs the old pioneer goat, just as the Merino sheep is absorbing the old fat-tailed Afrikander.

Confining the statistics to the 1891 Census Returns: of the Angoras, the European or white population owned 2,073,601, the Fingoes and Kafirs, 213,774, and other coloured races 96,643; of the Boer goats, the white population owned 2,167,215, the Fingoes and Kafirs 932,832, and other coloured races 343,972. There were 2·09 Angoras and 2·26 Boer goats to each person (white and coloured); there were 7·62 Angoras to each white person, and 0·27 to each coloured person; there were 5·75 Boer goats to each white person, and 1·11 to each coloured person; and there were 14·39 Angoras and 15·56 Boer goats per square mile of the whole Colony.

The four districts which contained the most Angoras were:—

---

[1] For the sake of comparison, it may be stated that, according to the Census Returns of 1891, there were in that year 13,631,011 woolled sheep, and 3,075,095 other (Afrikander) sheep in the Cape Colony: a grand total of 16,706,106 sheep. The woolled sheep yielded 56,038,659 lb. of wool.

	Goats.	Yielding lb. mohair.
Somerset East	429,258	888,006
Cradock	292,895	681,670
Jansenville	285,277	718,653
Willowmore	251,380	491,411

Thus, the Angoras of Jansenville yielded about $2\frac{1}{2}$ lb. each; those of Cradock about $2\frac{1}{3}$ lb.; those of Somerset East about $2\frac{1}{7}$; and those of Willowmore nearly 2 lb. each. The Customs Returns for 1891 show that 9,953,548 lb. mohair were exported, which would give a yield of a little more than $3\frac{1}{8}$ lb. per goat; but the 1891 Census gives the amount as 6,833,558 lb., which gives a yield of about 1 lb. less per goat. As the Customs Returns (though they include Free State mohair, a small quantity) are undoubtedly more correct on this point than those of the Census, it will be safe to reckon that the goats of the four districts mentioned clipped about 1 lb. each heavier than the Census Returns indicate (that is, Jansenville $3\frac{1}{2}$ lb. and so on).

The four districts containing the most Boer goats were :—

Calvinia	227,993
Carnarvon	199,646
Murraysburg	186,637
Hay	140,856

There were some statistics taken for the year ending 31st May, 1894, which I give, because they furnish some details not specified in the 1891 Census Returns. These statistics, however, are not believed to be at all reliable, and so must only be accepted in a general way.

According to the returns for the agricultural year ending 31st May, 1894, there were in the whole Colony only 2,619,708 Angoras, and 2,303,640 other (Boer) goats: a grand total of 4,923,348, or an actual decrease from 1891 of 1,704,689 goats (564,310 Angoras, and 1,145,379 Boer goats). During that year goats died or were lost as follows:—

From scab and poverty	203,409
,, worm	72,581
,, *klaauw* and *tong-ziekte* (including foot-and-mouth disease)[1]	7418
,, 'cnenta[2]	40,879
,, gall sickness	49,523
,, any other disease	64,868
,, destroyed, stolen or lost	78,802
,, exposure or drought	349,587
Total	867,067

There was an actual decrease (according to the Statistical Register, from which these figures are taken) of 707,607 on the grand total of the preceding year, 1893 (namely, 191,498 Angoras and 516,109 other goats).

[1] *Klaauw* and *tong-ziekte*, foot-and-tongue sickness.
[2] 'Cnenta, a poisonous plant; the most obvious indication of a goat having eaten it is paralysis of the hind quarters.

CHAPTER XVIII.

THE ANGORA GOAT AND MOHAIR INDUSTRIES OF THE UNITED STATES OF AMERICA.[1]

THE first importation of Angora goats into America was made in 1848. During the administration of President Polk, says Colonel Richard Peters, the Sultan of Turkey requested that a suitable person might be sent to that country to conduct some experiments in the culture of cotton. Dr. James B. Davis, of South Carolina, was selected to perform this important service. On his return to the States in 1848 the Sultan, desiring to show his appreciation of the courtesy of the President of the United States, caused nine of the choicest goats of Angora to be selected for presentation to Dr. Davis. Of these, eight seem to have reached America—two rams and six ewes. They were kept by Dr. Davis on his farm near Columbia, South Carolina, and seem to have been of a particularly excellent quality. It may not unreasonably be supposed that the conditions under which they were acquired furnished a guarantee of their excellence, a supposition borne out by the opinion generally held of them in

---

[1] I wish to thank Mr. W. G. Hughes, Hastings, Kendall Co., Texas, for the information he has supplied personally, and for assisting me in obtaining much of the information contained in this chapter.

America as compared with subsequent importations; for instance, Colonel R. Peters, who owned goats from six different importations, and who was in his day perhaps the most competent authority in America on this subject, says they were superior in many respects to subsequent importations.

These goats were the foundation stock of the Angora industry in America. Dr. Davis seems to have sold some of these goats as soon as landed.

In 1854 Colonel R. Peters visited the farm of Dr. Davis. At that time the doctor had nine pure Angoras, two rams and seven ewes; and in addition he had one "pure-bred Thibet ewe," several half-bred between the Thibets and the Angoras, and quite a number of ewes graded between the Angoras and the common short-haired goats of the States. The "Thibet" goats I take to have been of the Cashmere type, more or less pure. A good deal of ignorance prevailed at that time (as has been pointed out in the chapters on the Cape Colony) as to what constituted an Angora and what a Cashmere; so much so that even Dr. Davis thought his pure Angoras were Cashmeres, whereas, according to the unquestionable evidence of Colonel Peters (fully corroborated by later knowledge), they were undoubtedly Angoras of a very superior class. Colonel Peters purchased the nine pure Angoras in 1854 at $1000 each, and also several of the "Thibet Angoras". The fact that the real Angoras and the "Thibet Angoras" (Cashmeres) were inter-bred, perhaps accounts, to some extent, for the undergrowth about which Mr. Hoerle speculated in his letter to the *Texas Live Stock Journal* (see Chap. viii.). Colonel Peters removed these valuable goats to his farm, Atlanta, Georgia, and, breeding them there with great care and intelligence, became the father of the Angora industry of America.

In 1861 Colonel Peters sent two sixteen months old pure Angora rams to Mr. William M. Landrum, Joaquin Co., California. These were the first pure Angoras to enter California. A month or two later Mr. Landrum exhibited them at the State Fair, and was awarded a special premium—a large silver goblet—for the introduction of the "Angora or Cashmere goat". One of these young rams died from snake-bite after siring only about thirty kids, but the other attained great notoriety, being known along the Pacific coast as "Billy Atlanta," after the name of his breeder's farm in Georgia, and as the "King of the Cashmere goats". He was accidentally killed when ten years old, after siring about 2000 kids. Colonel Peters, his breeder, says with pardonable pride: "He won the sweepstake prize against all competition at every fair to that preceding his death, his numerous descendants are scattered all along the Pacific coast, and his blood courses in the veins of one-half the Angora flocks, pure-bred and grades, in that part of the Union, estimated (in 1882) to approach 70,000 head".

While on the subject of Colonel Peters's flock, it may be mentioned that, in 1868, he sent twenty-five choice-bred goats into California, seventeen of which were purchased by Messrs. Landrum, Butterfield & Son; and that, in 1872, Messrs. Landrum & Rogers acquired the larger portion of his pure-bred flock and removed them into the same state.

California is surpassed in the number of its Angoras at the present day by Texas alone, the largest individual owner being Mr. C. P. Bailey, of San José, who owns about 10,000 out of some 59,000 in that state. Mr. Bailey is probably the largest owner of Angoras in America, and is a breeder of some of its best goats, as evidenced by the premier position of his exhibits at the Chicago Exposition in 1892.

I have had insuperable difficulty in obtaining accurate information as to subsequent importations; but state what I have been able to gather, in the hope that it may reach the eyes of those who are better informed on this point than myself, but whom my very limited knowledge of America has prevented my coming into touch with, and that thus my data may be supplemented and corrected where necessary, the matter being of much interest to all Angora farmers.

The following list is compiled chiefly from information obtained for me by Mr. W. G. Hughes from Mr. Wm. M. Landrum, Brownsville; and to a less extent from Dr. John L. Hayes's book. The goats all came from Turkey.

1856 or 1857 (the second importation). R. Peters and C. S. Brown imported about six or eight to Atlanta, Ga.

1864. W. W. Chenery, of Boston, and of Belmont, Mass., imported a lot. Forty were shipped, but they had scab, and some died on the voyage and the rest after being landed.

1866. W. W. Chenery imported twenty.

1867. W. W. Chenery imported twenty more.

The first choice of ten were for Wm. M. Landrum. Gray and Gilmore, and Flint, also obtained goats from this lot. Dr. Hayes says that, in 1868, Chenery had about eighty to ninety pure Angoras on his farm at Belmont.

1869. Israel S. Diehl and Charles S. Brown received 135 out of 150 shipped to their order. Two of the choicest were for Wm. M. Landrum, one of which, a "hornless Kastamboul" ram, which clipped 10 lb. at six months' growth of fleece, became widely celebrated. In 1870, Diehl and Brown sent most of their goats to California, sixty arriving there and being acquired by Messrs. Landrum, Butterfield & Son.

1870. Mr. A. Eutichides, a Greek, shipped 175 from his father's flocks in Turkey. Many of these died on the voyage and after landing, from scab with which they were infected when shipped. The survivors, which proved to be only grades, were sent to California, and sold by auction at the State Fair. Ewes realised $14, and rams $10 each, these prices being the current rates for fourth-grade American-bred Angoras.

1874. Wm. Hall and John M. Harris imported nine, three of which were of a very high standard of excellence, the remainder not being of good quality.

1875 or 1876. An English captain brought two to Galveston, and sold them to Parish, of San Antonio, Texas. These were of exceptionally superior quality.

1876. John M. Harris visited Angora, and purchased twelve yearlings, two rams and ten ewes, which, with their increase on the way, cost him, at the time of their landing in America, over $500 each.[1]

1879. Colonel R. Peters imported "three Geredeh Angoras," through Charles W. Jenks, of Boston. Peters says "the party who furnished them" inaccurately represented them as a "new breed" (the same thing occurred in the same year in the Cape Colony), and adds that they were in no respect superior to thoroughbred Angoras in his own flock.

In 1880, the Sultan's edict, prohibiting the further exportation of Angora goats from Turkey, was published.

I have not been able to hear of any further importations from Turkey.

Some, if not all, of Chenery's goats seem to have been selected by Gavin Gatheral, British Vice-Consul at Angora; and a general consensus of opinion appears to allow that, as a whole, the best goats were those imported by Chenery, some of them being animals of very great merit.

The total number imported into America would seem to be about 400.

Some Angoras have on two occasions been imported into America from the Cape Colony: one consignment of six[2] from the flocks of the late J. B. Evans, of Graaff Reinet, in 1886; the other, of two rams, from the flocks of R. Cawood, Ganna Hoek, Cradock, in 1893. Mr. Evans's are said to

---

[1] I am not sure whether the goats referred to in this paragraph and in the 1874 paragraph are not the same lot. Harris *did* visit Angora in 1876.

[2] Mr. Henry Fink, of Leon Springs, Bexar Co., Texas, says the number was four, two rams and two ewes.

ANGORA AND MOHAIR INDUSTRIES OF UNITED STATES. 241

have been "a fine lot," and Mr. Cawood's were spoken of in the highest terms by Mr. C. P. Bailey, the importer, who said they had finer and heavier fleeces than his own goats.

On several occasions a number of Angoras have been imported into the Cape Colony from the United States, in every case disastrously for the American importer. The Cape farmers would not

Photo. W. Roe]   [Graaff Reinet.
Angora Goat Ewes, bred and owned by Guard Hobson.

have them at any price, considering them inferior and quite inadmissible as stud animals. The same fate met even a small consignment of Mr. C. P. Bailey's Chicago prize goats, which he had sent out in the hope of establishing a market here for his rams. Five rams reached the Cape Colony, and could not find a purchaser. I saw these goats, which, at the request of the Port Elizabeth agent, Mr. Cawood was allowing to run on his farm,

16

Ganna Hoek. The Cape farmers were undoubtedly wise in refusing to purchase or even use them.

Returns showing the exact number of Angoras in the States do not seem obtainable, but Mr. William L. Black, in his pamphlet, gives the following estimate:—

Texas	75,000
California	59,000
New Mexico	52,000
Oregon	15,000
Nevada	11,500
Idaho	8,000
Wyoming	7,000
Arizona	5,700
Missouri	5,200
Utah	2,000
Montana	1,500
Kansas	1,200
Indian Territory	900
Georgia	750
Kentucky	500
Pennsylvania	400
Illinois	300
Tennessee	250
South Carolina	200
North Carolina	200
Colorado	200
Mississippi	150
Louisiana	150
Connecticut	150
Alabama	75
Arkansas	75
Florida	75
Iowa	75
Virginia	75
Nebraska	50
Washington	50
West Virginia	50
Total	247,775

These 247,775 goats are, however, by no means all of good quality. Mr. W. R. Payne, manager to Mr. J. L. Cilley, of New York, who, from the fact of his handling so much of the clip from all parts of the United States, is excellently qualified to express an opinion, thinks that "the number of really good shearing animals showing a fleece of the mohair characteristics, curl, lustre and weight, would not exceed half that number, or say 100,000 head that would clip a 4 to 5 lb. fleece".

This opinion is borne out by an estimate of the U.S.A. clip of mohair, computed by several authorities at from 500,000 to 600,000 lb. per annum, or not much more than 2 lb. per head per annum, whereas a fairly good and even flock of Angoras should yield, as Mr. Payne fairly estimates, about 4 lb. to 5 lb. each per annum.

America, however, has a considerable manufacturing industry in mohair; and as her own yield is not sufficient for her manufacturing requirements she imports, almost exclusively from England, what she requires in excess of her home production. This amount has averaged for the past five years about 1,250,000 lb. per annum. For the year ending May, 1896, however, she imported nearly 3,000,000 lb., but this was during the abnormal demand created by a fashionable craze for mohair dress goods, a demand which proved to be but temporary. The average annual importation of mohair may thus be taken at about 1,250,000 lb., which, added to her home production, supplies her mills with nearly 2,000,000 lb. to work up yearly.

Mr. Payne says that the mohair industry of the States is on the increase, but the product is not improving in quality or length of staple, a good deal of what Cilley receives being still "poor, low, short cross-bred stuff"; and he adds that the country greatly needs further importations of pure-bred first-class Angora goats.

In the States, the Angora industry being comparatively in its infancy, and the number of Angoras small in proportion to the population of the country (which is about 75,000,000), the skins of these beautiful goats are in great demand, the sale of specially prepared skins being an important and remunerative part of the industry. This is a state of things which strikes the Cape farmer as strange, when in his own country the Angoras are to the white population in the ratio of about $7\frac{1}{2}$ to 1. At the Cape the skins are so common that they are not valued as articles of adornment or for rug-making purposes, and are hardly used at all, being exported roughly dried, no firm or individual making a business of preparing them; but in America the contrary is the case. Mr. Wm. L. Black, general manager to the Fort McKavett Tanning Company, Menard, Co. Texas, in his pamphlet, says he was "first attracted to the Angora goat as being a most excellent substitute for the wild fur-bearing animals so rapidly becoming extinct"; and he proceeds to show how widespread is the use to which the skin of the Angora may be applied:—

"The buffalo, which has supplied buggy and carriage robes for so many centuries, has been exterminated, and nearly all other kinds of fur are very rare and expensive.

"The demand for this class of product has

always been enormous, and a glance at any fur dealer's price list will convince any one that the fur industry is one of great promise. There is no domestic animal that can supply this great demand of the human family better than the Angora goat, inasmuch as the skins can be taken in such a variety of stages.

"For instance, when the hair is of one month's growth it can hardly be distinguished from the Astrachan, if dyed black; or it can be taken at an earlier period of growth and be made to represent the polar or black bear, according to the character of the dyes used.

"It may not be known that nearly all the buggy robes that are now sold as wild animal fur are nothing more than goat skins dyed; and perhaps young ladies who admire the so-called *real monkey skin* muffs and cloaks, will be surprised to learn that they are only straight-haired goat skins dyed black.

"One of the most profitable uses that the Angora skin is put to is in making lace trimming, which commands a price per yard equivalent to $15 for a single hide.

"Another use is in making floor rugs, and coverings for the backs of sofas and arm-chairs. The beautiful lustre of the curly hair is brought out in a most effective manner by the reflection of gaslight, and nearly all housekeepers who have not already got them are anxious to possess some.

"The supply of this class of rugs is very limited; and the price, until very recently, was very high; $10 and $12 being often paid for choice skins.

"The present marked value of Angora skins, in a raw state, is about $2 each, for well-haired skins; and if it were not for the enormous importation of foreign skins, particularly Chinese, which are brought here by the thousands of bales, owing to there being no import duty on them, the price for our home product would be much higher.

"It may be well, perhaps, to state that the Chinese goat skin does not compare in fineness with the Angora, yet they are used extensively for cheap buggy robes and rugs, which naturally depreciates the selling value of the better article."[1]

It seems to be generally agreed that very large portions of the States are well adapted to Angora goats, an opinion formed from actual experience over a number of years. This being the case, it is difficult to account for the fact that the industry has progressed so slowly, especially when one considers that the hair is so valuable, the skins in such great demand, the flesh prized as a food, and the tallow (12 lb. from a full-grown goat) considered as good as any that reaches the Chicago market. It is still more incomprehensible when one considers that there are large portions of the country suitable to goats and not suitable to sheep, so that in such parts the Angora and the Merino do not come into competition (as is the case in Australia). In 1868 Dr. Hayes was most sanguine as to the rapid progress of the industry, but in 1882 he acknowledged that it had so far proved a failure. To-day there seems to an outsider no reason why the industry should not make almost

[1] *History of the Angora Goat or Mohair Industry*, a fifteen-page pamphlet by W. L. Black, Texas, 1895.

as rapid progress as it has made in South Africa; but although those interested in the industry are agreed that it is highly remunerative, there does not seem any greater likelihood of its going ahead now than there was in 1868. There is, of course, some adequate reason for this, but I cannot ascertain what that reason is.

The U.S.A. Government seems to have *no statistics* relative to the subject treated of in this chapter.

CHAPTER XIX.

THE ANGORA GOAT AND MOHAIR INDUSTRIES OF AUSTRALIA.

It was, I believe, from the Cape Colony that Australia obtained some of her first Merino sheep; and it is indirectly due to the same country that she was induced to experiment with the Angora. Her phenomenal success in the one is not more pronounced than her failure in the other. In the sheep industry, Australia has completely eclipsed the Cape, but in the Angora industry, South Africa is not only immeasurably ahead of Australia, but seems certain, in the near future, to be unrivalled, perhaps unapproached, by any country in the world.

The pioneer of the Angora industry in Australia was Mr. Sechel, a Melbourne merchant, who, having heard how the mohair goats had increased and thriven at the Cape, decided to introduce them into Victoria. In 1856 he imported seven, which were purchased at Broussa and came *viâ* Constantinople and London to Melbourne. This was the first importation into Australia. These goats were acquired by the Zoological and Acclimatisation Society of Victoria, and were kept in the Society's grounds in the Royal Park in Melbourne.[1]

---

[1] About six or seven years later, some Cashmere goats were imported into Victoria; but this industry seems to have

The second importation of Angoras was in 1866. The Acclimatisation Society of Victoria, in return for some specimens of the fauna of Australia (including a wombat), was presented by the Imperial Acclimatisation Society of France with "twelve pure-bred Angoras of a very high class". These were added to the little lot already in the Society's grounds in the Royal Park. But, as the flock was still too small to be of any practical use to the colony in general, the Society voted £600 to defray the expenses of another importation; and a Mr. McCullough, a gentleman who had taken great interest in the introduction of the Cashmere and the Angora, added a similar amount for the purchase of a number on his own account. In 1865 a special agent, acquainted with the qualities of the Angora, was sent to Asia Minor from London to select and purchase as many pure Angoras as the funds at his command would permit. The goats were obtained in the neighbourhood of Broussa, driven to Smyrna, and shipped *viâ* London for Melbourne, where they arrived early in 1866, after a tedious voyage of 127 days, with a loss of only two on the voyage. Mr. McCullough sold his moiety to the Society. The number landed was ninety-three in all, and they cost the Society an average of £16 each. These were also added to the little flock

been abandoned; for, in 1866, the Annual Report of the Acclimatisation Society states that the attempt to acclimatise the Cashmere had proved a failure. (In 1832, Mr. Alexander Riley, of Raby, imported some Cashmeres—obtained from the Ternaux importation into France—into New South Wales. I know nothing further of this importation except that in 1835 Mr. Riley exported three to the Cape Colony, which were sold for £150. See Chapter xi.)

in the Royal Park. Here they were carefully bred; and, from time to time, sales were made by the Society of pure rams and ewes, with the object of introducing the breed into different parts of the country; but the Society wisely retained the choicest of both sexes, and, by careful breeding, was successful in producing animals superior to those imported. It was found, however, that they did not thrive well at the Royal Park.[1] So it was decided to sell some and move the others to a more suitable part. Before selling, the flock was carefully culled by Mr. Jonathan Shaw, an experienced and skilful classer of Merino sheep; the choicest goats were taken out and retained by the Society; the remainder were sold. The price at which they were sold, £5 5s. each, though much less than their actual value, was fixed at that amount with a view to securing their widespread distribution over the country, and to place them within reach of settlers of limited means. In every instance the result was failure. Some were exported to other Australian colonies, where for a time, in some instances, they did better; but, ultimately, the result was the same, failure in every instance; except in the case of South Australia, where the experiment met with a slight measure of success.

The choice goats retained, about fifty in number ("a magnificent flock," says Wilson), were sent by railway to Ballarat, and were driven by easy stages to Longerenong, a station of Wilson's on

---

[1] So the director of the Society states, writing in 1896. Sir Samuel Wilson, in 1873, says that the limited pastures at the Royal Park were insufficient for the increasing numbers of the flock.

Photo. Arthur Green [Port Elizabeth.

J. Hobson with the Champion Angora Ram of the Port Elizabeth Agricultural Show in 1897. Bred and owned by J. Hobson & Sons.

the Wimmera, where they arrived about the middle of December, 1870. They passed into the possession, or were placed under the care, of the late Sir (then Mr.) Samuel Wilson, Vice-President of the Zoological and Acclimatisation Society of Victoria.

In 1873, when Wilson published his pamphlet, *The Angora Goat*, this flock numbered 114, and consisted of forty rams and seventy-four ewes. The rams averaged 3 lb. $2\frac{1}{2}$ oz., and the ewes 2 lb. $4\frac{1}{4}$ oz., or an average all round of 2 lb. 9 oz. each. The best ram clipped 7 lb., $14\frac{1}{2}$ oz., one year and five days' growth of fleece. The hair seems to have been spout-washed. Very little progress was made with the flock from 1873 onward. Writing of these goats in December, 1896, the Director of the Acclimatisation Society states: "They were afterwards removed to another property of Mr. Samuel Wilson's at Mount Bute and Ercildoune; and here a small number remain—I don't know how many, but I don't think there are more than 100 or 200". And he adds: "Practically the attempt to introduce the Angora goat into Victoria, after many years' trial, has proved a failure".

In 1869 Mr. Price Maurice imported ten "pure Angoras" into South Australia from Asia Minor, and made further importations in 1871, 1872 and 1873—in all, sixteen rams and 168 ewes. They are all said to have come "from Angora," but this does not seem likely to be correct, for Mr. Maurice named his station "Kastamboul," after the capital of the Province of Kastamouni. It is stated that each goat cost £20 in transit alone. In 1895 they were said to have numbered about 2000, and were described as small animals on short legs, with very lustrous fleeces hanging in ringlets, with a fine soft undergrowth; the average weight of fleeces of twelve months' growth being about 5 lb. each, the heaviest running as high as 10 lb.

It is impossible to ascertain at present how many Angoras there are in Australia, or even how many there are in any one of the colonies, or what quantity of mohair is produced; for, as the head of the Department of Trades and Customs of Victoria states: "There is no information whatever in the statistics of this or any of the other colonies in regard to Angora goats, the reason being that the animals are not exported or produced for trade purposes. A very few have been introduced for experimental purposes, but I have been unable to hear of any in Victoria except a flock of about 200 at Mount Bute;" and he adds that "probably there are not 2000 goats in the whole of Australasia".

Practically, it would seem the Angora industry does not exist in Australasia. That country does not appear to be suitable for the mohair goat. Mr. Albert A. C. Le Souef, Director of the Zoological and Acclimatisation Society of Victoria, says: "In my opinion the reason the experiment has failed is that the lands of Victoria and of most parts of Australia are unsuited to the habits of Angora goats. The Karoo in South Africa where they thrive is a perfectly different country to anything we have in Australia: it is dry and arid, and covered with small shrubs and plants, which are evidently suited to the habits of the animal in question. In this dry tract of country there are also numbers of stony hills, in which the goats delight. The one answer I can give to Mr. Schreiner's questions is that, practically, there are no Angora goats in Australia. Our sheep and cattle thrive splendidly, but Angora goats do not."

The following table, furnished by the Government Statist of Victoria, fully confirms the above statements :—

IMPORTS AND EXPORTS OF MOHAIR FROM VICTORIA FROM 1886 TO 1895.

Year.	Imports.		Exports.	
	Quantity.	Value.	Quantity.	Value.
	Lb.	£	Lb.	£
1887	—	—	925	77
1888	—	—	410	48
1889	896	42	820	85
1890	1176	59	820	96

There is no mention of "Angora wool" in the returns for other years than those specified.

When it is remembered that the first importation of Angoras into Australia was contemporaneous with Mosenthal's first importation to the Cape Colony in 1856, and that the first regular export of mohair from the Cape began in 1857 (valued at £10), it is startling to compare the figures of the above table with those of the Cape for the same year. In 1890 the Cape exported 9,235,249 lb. mohair, valued at £337,239, and 12,583,601 lb., valued at £676,644, in 1897.

Apart from the suitability or otherwise of Australia to Angora goat farming, the failure to establish the industry there is amply accounted for by the fact that Australia is so perfectly adapted to sheep; so that the question is, after all, not so much whether the Angora will thrive and pay, but whether it will thrive and pay better than the Merino. Goats and sheep never do equally well on the some veld; that which is peculiarly adapted to the one never suiting the other nearly so well.

Photo. W. Roe] [Graaff Reinet.

Angora Goat Ewes, twenty months old, each carrying a fleece of thirteen months' growth; the fleece of the ewe to the left weighing 10 lb. 1 oz., that of the other 9 lb. 9 oz. Bred and owned by C. G. Lee, Klipplaat.

Australia is essentially a sheep country; and so, though the Angora may thrive fairly well in parts, it is so outclassed by the Merino that it does not pay to farm it. If the goat is ever farmed there, it will probably be exclusively in parts not suited to the sheep, if such parts exist to any extent and are at the same time suited to the goat. It seems clear, however, that Australia does not suit goats well, a conclusion one would expect from what one has heard of the nature of the veld there. Australia appears to have no veld in any way resembling those parts of South Africa so essentially suited to the goat, which are, at the same time, not nearly so well, or not at all, suited to the sheep. A proof of the unsuitableness of Australia to the goat, or of the unprofitableness of farming it, or of the absence of tracts of country suited to it and unsuited to the sheep, would seem in some measure to be indicated by the fact that the common goat is not farmed there.

The facts contained in this chapter have been mainly obtained from Sir Samuel Wilson's booklet on *The Angora Goat*, published in 1873; and from information which Mr. Turner, Prime Minister of Victoria, was kind enough to procure for me from the heads of various departments of the Government service of that colony, and from the Director of the Zoological and Acclimatisation Society of Victoria.

PAPER ON THE OSTRICH.

THE OSTRICH.

(Reprinted from *The Zoologist* for March, 1897.)

THE ostrich, *Struthio camelus*, has been observed with interest from very early times; it has frequently been the subject of remark by African travellers; and it has been domesticated and farmed in the Cape Colony for some thirty years. Yet it is remarkable how little is known about it in scientific circles, and how many misconceptions still prevail as to its nature and habits.[1]

[1] This article is founded on personal observations made during nine years of uninterrupted ostrich-farming in the Karoo of the Cape Colony, and during travels about the country generally. The number of ostriches which were under my care during this period ranged from about 250 to 450. Some of the birds were the progeny of wild birds, brought down as chicks from further up-country. Every year eight special breeding pairs were camped off, each pair in a separate small camp; but the other birds ran in large camps, the extent of the farm being 4600 morgen (about two acres to the morgen). In these large camps, some of which are a couple of miles in diameter, numbers of birds of both sexes run in what is practically a wild state, seldom interfered with in any way, except when rounded up to be plucked or to be fed in a drought. I know, from personal observation when purchasing wild chicks from the nest, and from numerous inquiries, that the habits of birds thus farmed differ in no way from those of native wild birds, except perhaps that monogamy is more difficult. The whole of the Cape Colony is the native habitat of the ostrich; there are feral ostriches in many parts, and wild birds in some of the up-country districts.

How many Species are there?

I have not been able to ascertain whether the question as to the number of species of ostrich has yet been settled. Some writers maintain there are two species; others that there are three. Professor Newton (article "Ostrich," *Encyclopædia Britannica*), after briefly reviewing the evidence, says the question "has been for some years agitated without leading to a satisfactory solution".

The reasons given for classifying the ostrich into three species are :—

That in the North African bird, *Struthio camelus*, the skin of the unfeathered parts is flesh-coloured; in the South African, *Struthio australis*, bluish, except at the angle of the gape, which is flesh-coloured; and in the bird of the Somali country, *Struthio mybdophanes*, leaden-coloured.

It is further maintained that the eggs of the northern ostrich are larger than those of the southern, and have a perfectly smooth surface, while those of the southern are punctured or pitted; also that the northern bird is the smaller, and the cock not so jet-black. Mr. Bartlett adds, as another distinguishing character, that in the southern ostrich the scales of the tarsi and toes, unlike the skin of the other unfeathered parts, are flesh-coloured.

If the question has not been settled, a short description of the South African ostrich may help towards its solution; if it has been, the description may nevertheless convey some useful information to such as are interested in it.

Colour of the Plumage.

Chicks when first hatched, and for some weeks after, have the wings and upper part of the body covered with a mottled dark and white coat of small feathers, ending in solid spiked points, almost like miniature porcupine quills; the lower part with a soft yellow down. The neck is marked longitudinally with wide dark stripes on a lighter ground, and the head with spots of the same colour. Some broods are much darker than others. They soon acquire a plumage varying from ash-colour to brown, the feathers retaining their spiked points for some time. At an age, generally from about twelve to eighteen months, chicks begin to moult their youthful plumage of narrow pointed feathers, and gradually acquire those of the adult bird, possessing them in their entirety, at the latest, when about four years old. Up to the time when the change begins, the sexes are not distinguishable; but after the moult the cocks acquire a black and the hens a drab plumage, the hen's differing from that of a big chick not so much in colour as in the shape and quality of the feathers. The cocks do not change abruptly from their youthful drab to adult black, but pass through what is generally designated by the Dutch word, the *bont* (variegated) stage. Black, brown, and drab feathers are indiscriminately mingled all over the body, the plumes and tails being black-and-white. The same stage is gone through by the hens, but is not nearly so conspicuous, the difference in the colour of the feathers being less marked. At about four years all have their adult plumage;

but both among cocks and hens there is a great diversity in colour in different individuals and in different parts of the country. In all cocks the plumes ("whites") are white, but in hens these feathers ("feminas") vary from white to drab. The "tails" correspond in colour with the "whites" and "feminas," respectively. In both sexes, variations in body-colour are conspicuous. Some cocks are a glittering jet-black, while others are a rusty-brown; a few have odd white feathers dotted about the body; occasionally the secondary wing-feathers are white, or often fringed with white; and I knew of one which was thickly flecked with white over the whole body. In some cocks all the feathers, "whites" excepted, are beautifully curled, almost as though artificially; while in others they have not the slightest indication of curl. These individual variations are in some cases accentuated by differences of climate. Towards the coast the rusty-brown tint (more pronounced than up-country) is often found, while the glittering jet-black, so characteristic of Karoo birds, is comparatively uncommon. On the authority of an ostrich farmer of great experience, who has hundreds of birds on both Karoo and coast farms, Karoo birds produce, on the whole, the best "blacks," coast birds the best "whites". The first essential of black feathers is that they shall be glittering and glossy, and this condition the dry air of the Karoo seems to favour; a white feather must, other characteristics being equal, be soft, with a limp quill, and this seems to be most frequently produced by the damp coast breezes. Hens also vary in body-colour to an equal extent, though, in their case, the differences are not very conspicuous, the colours not being so strongly contrasted. They range from a dark rich brown to light brown, grey, or ash. I have had several hens with each feather ("feminas" excepted) barred across with white at about a quarter of its length from the tip, and one which had the perfect black plumage of a cock.

Colour of the Unfeathered Parts.

The colour of the unfeathered parts of chicks is yellow, which gradually changes to flesh-colour, and, as the adult stage is reached, either remains flesh-coloured, though of not so pronounced a tint, or changes to bluish or leaden—nearly always bluish. Variations not only in colour, but in texture, thickness, and strength of the skin,[1] are both great and frequent. The colour of the neck varies also, in both sexes, from dark—nearly black in the case of the cock and deep brown in the hen—to almost white. The colour of the eye even varies; generally it is brown, but grey is not unknown.

Colour of the Tarsi and Toes.

Chicks[2] may be divided into two lots, of about equal number, by the colour of the scales of the tarsi and toes. Some have light brown scales, others dark brown. There is no grading from one tint to the other; the line of demarcation is clear

---

[1] Ostriches are all branded on the leg, just as cattle are.

[2] The term chick is often used for a bird of as much as **even three years old.**

and unmistakable. The dark-scaled are by some farmers said to be cocks, the light-scaled hens. My attention was only drawn to this peculiarity shortly before retiring from ostrich-farming; I cannot therefore express a decided opinion, not having had an opportunity of testing whether the statement is correct.

At any rate, the scales of the hens invariably remain brown, but those of the cocks change to flesh-colour, varying from nearly white to brilliant crimson. Cocks' legs do not often lose all trace of the crimson tint, though its intensity varies with the seasons, being brightest in a fat bird in the height of his sexual vigour in the breeding season, and faintest when a bird is in a low condition in the winter. It also varies in individual birds, and with their condition, and becomes pale during the period of sitting. During the non-breeding season the coloration, more or less faded, is nearly always confined to the scales of the tarsi; but in all cocks that "come on" during the breeding season it is seldom, if ever, so confined; the tarsi themselves, the toes, and the beak, to a greater or less extent, also becoming affected. Some cocks are then most brilliantly coloured; not only do the toes and the whole of the tarsi become a brilliant crimson, but the upper part of the leg (called by Cape ostrich farmers the "thigh") for half its length, nearly the whole of the head, especially the beak, ears, and around the eyes, are of the same gaudy tint. A vicious cock in full plumage is then a beautiful and imposing creature; the glittering glossy black is strikingly contrasted with the spotless white of his waving plumes, and the bright crimson of his head and legs ; and as, with springy steps, he advances to battle, angrily lashing his wings across his raised body, with tail and neck

Kodak] The Author.
Vicious Cock Ostrich ; Krantz Plaats, Cradock.

erect, and flashing eyes, he is not only a beautiful, but a grand, and, to many a man, a terrifying object.

No corresponding changes take place in the

hen; neither does she become vicious, except when she has chicks.

The Egg; and Size of Ostriches.

As to the alleged difference in the shell of the eggs of the northern and southern ostriches, it may be sufficient to remark that the eggs of the southern bird vary frequently and greatly in respect of size, shape, and shell; some are quite a third larger than others; some are almost spherical, others oblong; and the shells vary from being deeply and thickly pitted to smooth and polished.

Differences in the sizes of ostriches are equally marked; there is no uniformity. Some birds are very much larger than others; they also differ considerably in shape.

Only one Species.

It will thus be seen that all the differences on which the arguments for classifying the ostrich into three species are founded, are commonly present among the ostriches of the Cape Colony—that is, of South Africa generally; for a great many of the Cape ostriches are the progeny of birds brought down from "The Interior"—the Kalahari Desert, Damaraland, and beyond. There is, I think, little doubt that all South African ostriches are of one species; individual variations, accentuated by local differences of food and climate, are quite sufficient to account for all supposed varieties. I do not think that, on the evidence which I have been able to gather, there is any justification for maintaining that there is more than one species of ostrich.

THE OSTRICH.

The Egg and Flesh of the Ostrich.

The ostrich hen lays every other day during the breeding season, and the egg weighs about three pounds; it is a tasty and nutritious food however prepared, very rich, and excellent for making pastry and cakes. It is generally computed to be equal to two dozen fowls' eggs; but this must be on account of its superior richness, for, from personal experiment, the empty shell of a fairly large one exactly held the contents of eighteen fowls' eggs. It takes about forty minutes to boil an ostrich egg hard. The period of incubation is about six weeks. The flesh of the chick, if well prepared, is excellent, but that of an old bird is tough and insipid. The ostrich is, however, never killed for food, and is very rarely eaten, except by native servants.

Its Breast-bone and Powers of Kicking.

The breast-bone of the ostrich is of great thickness and strength, and of course keelless. Its lower edge has a hard pad, which must be useful to this heavy, long-legged bird when it bumps down to the recumbent position. It is obvious that the great weight and speed of the ostrich, and its liability to collide against objects on the ground over which, when frightened, it takes its headlong indiscriminate way, would need that it be protected in front. Its thick convex sternum, almost devoid of flesh, is a most effective safeguard. As an instance of this, I have seen an ostrich, at great speed, run against and snap a No. 6 fencing-wire, striking it with its breast; in the same way I have seen a sneeze-wood pole (a very tough wood used in wire-fencing), four inches in diameter at its thinnest end, broken just where it emerged from the ground; and a chick about eighteen months old run against a loose badly-built stone wall two feet in thickness, and break a gap through it—all these without injury to the birds. The shape and strength of the breast-bone is also a protection to fighting cocks, for the most powerfully delivered kicks nearly always strike there, doing but little harm.

During the breeding season cocks frequently fight, but, unless they kick at each other through a wire-fence (when a broken leg frequently occurs), not often with fatal results. The kick is forward with a downward tendency, and the long nail with which the larger toe is armed often cuts and tears severely. The force of the kick is great; a man goes down before it like a nine-pin. I have seen two cocks charge at each other, the larger of the two, at the first kick, being hurled several yards on to the broad of his back, while the kicker recoiled into a sitting posture; and I possessed a cock which kicked a hole through a sheet of corrugated iron, behind which a man had taken refuge. They can kick as high as a man's face; I have, on horseback, had a hole kicked through my riding breeches above the knee, and have known a boy kicked out of the saddle. Deaths from ostrich kicks are by no means unknown. A really vicious cock seems to fear nothing, unless it be a dog that will attack him. The most striking instance of their fearlessness which I have heard was told me by a railway guard. The goods train he was in charge of was one day rattling at full speed down a steep gradient. A vicious cock saw it coming, and at once got on to the line between the rails, and advanced fearlessly to fight the monster. As the screeching engine approached, he rushed at it from straight in front, hissing angrily, and kicked. He was cut to pieces the next moment.

Leaping and Swimming.

The old idea that an ostrich can leap only over a very low fence, or across none but the narrowest sluit (gully), is incorrect. It is true that perfectly tame birds, grazed within well-defined boundaries, may often be kept there with very insecure fences when they are thoroughly accustomed to recognise such as boundaries; but they will, when startled (never deliberately), sometimes go over a six-strand wire fence nearly five feet high, putting one foot at random on one of the middle wires, and then capsizing over. They will go over a stone wall in the same manner, if too high for them to step upon, often landing upon their feet; and I have seen a cock take a standing jump with both feet on to the top of a wall five feet high, beyond which were his chicks. When accustomed to run in cut-up veld they become very clever at leaping across sluits. They do not stride over, but, coming almost to a standstill at the edge of each sluit, jump with both feet, generally alighting on one foot and striding on at once with the other, like a good steeplechaser.

Even as a chick the ostrich is a powerful swimmer. I have known several birds swim some distance down the Great Fish River when it was running fairly strong, and have heard, on what seems trustworthy evidence, of a cock that was carried a long way down the same river when it was running nearly level with its precipitous banks in the stormy season; he was some hours in the water before he could get out, but emerged unhurt.

Waltzing and Rolling.

All ostriches, adults as well as chicks, have a strange habit known as " waltzing ". When chicks are let out from a kraal in the early morning they will often start away at a great pace. After running for a few hundred yards they will all stop, and, with raised wings, spin round rapidly for some time, often until quite giddy, when a broken leg occasionally occurs. Adult birds, when running in large camps, will often, if the veld is good, do the same, especially if startled in the fresh of the early morning. A troop of birds waltzing, in full plumage, is a remarkably pretty sight.

Vicious cocks " roll " when challenging to fight, or when wooing the hen. The cock will suddenly bump down on to his "knees" (the ankle-joint), open his wings, making a straight line across his breast, and then swing them alternately backward and forward (keeping the line straight) as if on a pivot, each wing as it comes forward being raised while that going backward is depressed. The neck is lowered until the head is on a level with the back, and the head and neck swing from side to side with the wings, the back of the head striking with a loud click against the ribs, first on the one side and then on the other. The click is produced by the skin of the neck, which then bulges loosely just under the beak, and for some distance downward. While rolling, the cock does not rest his body upon the ground, or even touch the ground with it, but sits straight up on his "knees" (ankle-joints), the shin bones being perpendicular to the ground and forming right angles with the tarsi; every feather over the whole body is on end, and

Kodak] [The Author.
Ostrich Cock "rolling"; Krantz Plaats, Cradock.

the plumes are open, like a large white fan. At such a time the bird sees very imperfectly, if at all; in fact, he seems so preoccupied that, if pursued, one may often escape unnoticed. I have even walked up to a rolling cock and seized him by the neck, much to his surprise. Just before rolling, a cock, especially if courting the hen, will often run slowly and daintily on the points of his toes, with neck slightly inflated, upright and rigid, the tail half-drooped, and all his body feathers fluffed up; the wings raised and expanded, the inside edges touching the sides of the neck for nearly the whole of its length, and the plumes showing separately, like an open fan, flat to the front, on each side of his head. In no other attitude is the splendid beauty of his plumage displayed to such advantage. I have occasionally seen a hen roll, but always in a stupid, amateurish manner, the action of the neck especially being very feeble and incorrect, while there is no bulging under the beak, and no click.

The Cry of the Ostrich.

The cry of the ostrich is very correctly described as a " boom ". (The word in use among all ostrich farmers at the Cape is the Dutch verb " brom "; in English, an ostrich " broms," or is " bromming ".) This cry is confined to the cock. It is uttered spontaneously sometimes, especially at night; but generally it is a challenge to another cock to fight, or a note of courting to the hen. It can only be uttered while the bird is standing still. It is a peculiar muffled round sound, very difficult to locate exactly, and conveys the impression that, if it had free vent, it would become a loud roar. It can be heard a considerable distance. It is made by the bird calling, without allowing any air to escape. Each cry consists of three " booms," two short followed by one long, the bird just catching its breath after each note. As no air escapes, the neck becomes greatly inflated during each " boom," in the third to a remarkable extent. This cry may be repeatedly uttered. At night it sounds weird and wild. A faint yet close imitation may be produced by a person closing his lips tight, and attempting to utter two rather short " boos " with an interval of about a second after each, and then one long one, allow-

Kodak]   [The Author.

Ostrich Cock " bromming "—at end of third note of cry ; Krantz Plaats, Cradock.

ing the breath to come into the mouth, but not to escape. The cheeks will become distended just as the neck of the ostrich does.

There are other sounds common to both sexes— an angry hiss, a subdued guttural gurgle (uttered occasionally when much frightened), and a short, sharp note, generally an alarm signal. There is also the penetrating plaintive call of chicks of all ages, a liquid, tremulous, treble cry.

How it Feeds, and what it will Swallow.

The ostrich feeds in a peculiar manner. It tosses the food into a sack in the upper part of the neck, and then swallows it. I have seen a bird toss fully a quart of mealies (Indian corn) into this sack before swallowing; and it is no uncommon thing to see two "swallows" travelling down the neck at the same time with a clear interval between them; or to see one of them (if large and of loose food, *e.g.*, grain) slide back into the sack after being swallowed, if the bird lowers its head to continue feeding before the food has travelled some considerable distance down the neck. The food travels slowly, and performs a complete circuit of the neck before reaching the crop. Crushed bones are greedily eaten; if too large a piece should stick in the neck, it is a simple matter to cut it out and sew the place up again. The wound, as a rule, heals quickly, and causes but little inconvenience.

As is well known, ostriches will swallow almost anything small enough to pass down the neck. I have either known them swallow, or have heard of them swallowing, on evidence which I believe, such things as oranges, small tortoises, fowl and turkey chickens, and kittens. I found a cock in my dining-room on one occasion rapidly demolishing, one after another, the contents of a box of luscious peaches. Some friends were playing tennis with only one ball. A rather vigorous drive sent it beyond the tennis-ground, close to an ostrich hen; she at once swallowed it with evident relish, and brought the game to a sudden end. A cock swallowed several yards of fencing-wire in short pieces, and about half a dozen brass cartridges. These were found in his crop, and had killed him. He had followed the fencers, swallowing the ends of the wires as filed off. An ostrich's crop always contains a large quantity of smooth stones, many of them brightly coloured.

How the Ostrich Runs.

Considerable misconception prevails as to the manner in which the ostrich runs. It seems to be still generally held that, when running, it spreads out its wings, and, aided by them, skims lightly over the ground. This is not correct.

When a bird really settles itself to run it holds its head lower than usual, and a little forward, with a deep loop in the neck. The neck vibrates sinuously, but the head remains steady, thus enabling the bird, even at top speed, to look around with unshaken glance in any direction. The wings lie along the sides about on a level with, or a little higher than, the back, and are held loosely just free of the plunging "thigh". There is no attempt to hold them extended, or to derive any assistance from them as organs of flight. Indeed, I doubt whether the conformation of the wings permits them being held out to any extent with the edge to the front; and the front edge is thickly and heavily covered with long feathers (which are regularly plucked for the market). In fact, it may be said that the wings assume just that position along the sides which the wind would force them into when the ostrich is running at a great pace; their position is exactly that which offers least resistance to the wind as it cuts past.

When ostriches are startled, as by a dog; when they start away to run, or when not very hard pressed, they will often run, and very rapidly, for some distance, with their wings raised nearly upright on each side of the neck, flat to the front; just as, under similar conditions, springbucks will run with the white fan on their backs raised, frequently "pronking".[1] When the ostrich runs thus, with its wings raised, it generally moves with a high, springy, bounding step, never with the long, raking stride of the bird that, hard pressed, is fleeing for its life. Raised wings are undoubtedly an obstacle to the greatest pace. So the springbuck, when he stretches himself out to run his fastest, shuts down his fan, as the attitude which enables him to expand it prevents his attaining to his greatest pace. When an ostrich after a long run is very tired, its wings sometimes droop; this is due to exhaustion; they are never, by a running bird exerting itself to the utmost, held out away from the sides to lighten its weight or to increase its pace. But they appear to be of great service in turning, enabling the bird to double abruptly even when going at top speed.

[1] "Pronking" is the (Dutch) word used to denote the habit these antelopes have of leaping to a great height into the air, the attitude (which expands the white fan) being almost exactly that of a bucking horse.

Nidification, Sexual Relations and Parental Habits.

Greater misconception seems to prevail with regard to the nidification, sexual relations and parental habits of the ostrich than upon any other really important points connected with it.

The best comment upon the various authorities will perhaps be a simple statement of what I know to be the facts.

The Nest.

As the breeding season approaches, a cock and hen will pair, and, having selected a site congenial to their inclinations, proceed to make a nest. I believe that in all cases, in the first instance, one cock and one hen, having paired, select the site and make the nest.

In a camp, no matter how large, where there are many birds and many nests, choice of position is restricted. They like to have their nests far apart; it is exceedingly difficult for a pair to select a spot which shall escape the observation of other birds. Want of space probably accounts for the fact that many sites are unwisely chosen. Generally a stony or sandy rise, however slight, is selected, often beside and partly sheltered by a small bush. The sites being selected, each cock is supreme over all other cocks at his nest and in its immediate neighbourhood.

The nest is simply a hollow depression, more or less deep according to the nature of the soil. It is made by the pair together. The cock goes down on to his breast, scraping or kicking the sand out backward with his feet, cutting the earth with his long and powerful nails. The hen stands by, often fluttering and clicking her wings, and helps by picking up the sand with her beak and dropping it irregularly near the edge of the growing depression.

Laying and Sitting.

When satisfied with their work (and they are easily satisfied, often too easily) the hen begins to lay an egg in the nest every other day. During the laying period the nest is often unattended, and is not slept on at night. A nest in which only one hen is laying contains on the average about fifteen eggs; but she often begins to sit before she has laid her full complement. Sometimes she will lay four or five after beginning to sit, though not often so many; sometimes only one or two; while sometimes she will lay her full complement. The hen generally begins the sitting; she will occasionally sit for one or two days and nights before the cock takes his turn. Now and then, however, the cock will be first to sit; but in such a case he will probably leave the nest for some hours during the day.

When sitting assumes its regular course, the hen sits from 8 or 9 A.M. to about 4 P.M., and the cock from 4 P.M. to about 8 or 9 A.M. The bird whose turn it is to be on the nest keeps its seat until the other arrives to relieve it, when they at once change places. Soon after beginning to sit, the cock loses his sexual vigour and inclinations, and ceases his attentions to the hen.

It is quite incorrect to say that the cock alone sits, or that during the day the eggs are left to the heat of the sun. The cock and hen sit alternately, regularly and steadily, night and day, during the whole period of incubation. Apart from incubation, it is necessary that the eggs should be covered during the day as a protection, in many parts, against small carnivora and monkeys; against the inclemencies of the weather, such as the frequent and violent hail and rain storms which sweep over the country; and against the great heat, which in the summer is almost tropical.[1] The heat from the direct rays of the sun striking upon unprotected eggs, when, after incubation, development has once set in, is so great that it would kill the chicks. Sand

[1] I was, on one occasion, struck by the remarkable behaviour of a sitting hen on a terribly hot still day. I found her sitting, with raised body, over the nest; that is, she had her feet and tarsi along the ground among the eggs as usual, but her body did not rest upon them; she had raised it above them and was sitting on her "knees" (like a rolling cock), and a free current of air passed between her body and the eggs; her wings were held a little away from the body and slightly drooped, the feathers over the whole body being on end, admitting the air to every part; her neck and head were raised up in the normal manner of a non-sitting bird, and she was panting with beak slightly open. This attitude is not uncommon among ostriches in very hot weather: they can remain in it for a considerable time; but I have not seen it assumed by a sitting bird on the nest on any other occasion. One result of the hen assuming this attitude was that all the eggs were completely in the shadow cast by her body and wings; but, although this was one of its effects, I should think she assumed it to cool herself because she was so intolerably hot in the scorching sun on the baking ground in the still air; but the incident is remarkable (apart from the question of whether there was any deliberate intention of cooling the eggs—which I doubt) as indicating the importance she attached to the nest being covered and protected while she was responsible.

thus exposed becomes so hot that even a hardened hand can scarcely endure it. On an average summer's day I tested the heat of the sand, keeping the thermometer in the shade, and found it to be 150° Fahr. The maximum temperature allowed to eggs in an incubator is 104° Fahr., though a few degrees more, if not maintained too long, are not greatly injurious; but if the thermometer stands at 150° Fahr. for some hours daily, chicks will not incubate. However, argument is quite unnecessary; the hen sits on the eggs every day—of this there is no doubt whatever; they are not left to the heat of the sun; if they were, no chicks would ever result; they are covered by the birds during the whole period of incubation.

Times of Sitting well Apportioned.

There are several interesting points connected with the process of sitting. For instance, the time is admirably arranged to allow each bird to feed. The ostrich is a peculiar feeder; in the first place he walks rapidly on and on as he feeds, pecking a few leaves here and a few there in his stride, seldom halting unless he finds some plant particularly to his liking, and then only for a minute or two. In the next place, he is not an indiscriminate feeder, but carefully selects what he likes. This, as a rule, consists of plants, which, owing to the nature of the country, are few and far between. He does not, however, go systematically in search of them, but strides straight on, eating those in his way. Thus he travels long distances while feeding, and requires several consecutive hours if he is to obtain a satisfactory meal. The hen has about four or five hours to feed in the early morning before she goes on the nest; and the cock has seven or eight consecutive hours through the day, after which the hen again has three or four hours in the evening, before she returns to sleep near the nest. Generally, the hen has a somewhat longer time to feed than the cock, but her time is broken into two portions, and she cannot wander so far in search of food as he can, and thus has not the same opportunity of getting on to new ground, where food may be more abundant, from not having been visited so often, for the ostrich is a destructive feeder, eating out the plants he likes when he has not a sufficiently large run. In compensation, the hen occupies the nest only half as long as the cock, which, however, has his feeding time unbroken, and half his time on the nest at night. It will thus be seen that, not counting the hours at night when both are sleeping (the cock on the nest), the duties of incubation are very evenly divided.

Protective Coloration.

The colour of each is admirably adapted to the time spent on the nest, and furnishes interesting examples of protective coloration. It is scarcely possible to conceive a more effective disguise than the sober brownish grey of the hen for day sitting, and the black of the cock for night. When on the nest, the ostrich lays its head, neck, and tail flat along the ground; its naked "thighs" are covered by the wings, the plumes lying close together on the earth almost hidden against the bird's body.

Thus only the low, long-curved body projects above the surrounding level. The cock, at night, is, of course, almost perfectly hidden; while the hen, at day-time, closely resembles a stone, bush, ant-heap, or any little inequality of the veld. One is surprised to see how close such a large bird can lie to the ground, and how even an ostrich farmer may almost walk over a sitting hen in full daylight without seeing her. The cock is simply indistinguishable at night, except to a practised eye, and then only at a few yards' distance. It may be urged that the black of the cock is not a protection in the morning or afternoon during daylight. This is not quite correct. In the very early morning, or in the afternoon towards sundown, it is most difficult to distinguish him; and it is but for two or three hours altogether that he is in the broad daylight, that being the only time in the whole twenty-four hours when the nest is not protected in a singularly effective manner by the colour of the sitting bird. Even then, unless one is close to the nest, his low-lying, long-curved, motionless form blends so closely with the ground and surrounding objects as to be much more difficult to discover than an inexperienced person could believe.

THE LITTLE EMBANKMENT AROUND THE NEST.

As sitting continues, a little embankment is gradually raised around the nest, where the nature of the soil permits. This is not in the original plan of the nest, but is made during the incubation of the eggs. The sitting bird, while on the nest, sometimes pecks the sand up with its beak nearly as far from the nest as it can reach, and drops it around the body. A little embankment is thus gradually formed, and often, just outside, a shallow irregular trench, from which the soil has been taken. The formation of both is aided by a peculiar habit of the birds. When the bird on the nest is much excited (as by the approach of other birds or people), it snaps up the sand spasmodically without rising from the nest, and without lifting its head more than a few inches from the ground. The bank is raised by such sand as falls inward, and the trench is deepened.

The original nest, as has been pointed out, is merely a shallow depression, the earth scraped out being mostly scattered far and wide by the vigorous kicks of the cock. As sitting continues the depression is very liable to silt up again; this is aided by the bird scraping in sand now and then when working the outside eggs in under the body, and by the way it seats itself on the nest. It squats at the edge, and then gradually, in a sliding manner, works itself in, until it covers the eggs, dragging in sand during the process, and thus silting up the nest. The ostrich, being a large, heavy, long-legged bird, when about to squat, bumps with a hard jerk on to its "knees," and then gently lets its body down to the ground. So, when getting on to a nest, it carefully places its feet among the eggs, bumps down with its "knees" outside the nest, clear of the eggs, and then works itself in till the nest is covered. If this method were not pursued the eggs would be broken by the sudden and violent impact with the "knees" as the bird bumps down.

Now the use of the bank, and the reason for its gradual, continuous formation after sitting begins, are apparent; the nest is thus kept hollow. Without it the nest would be liable to silt up and the eggs roll away. That this is its use seems to be clearly shown by the fact that the nest, though hollow, is at times slightly raised above the original level. The embankment, lying close to the bird's body, also serves to carry off some of the rain that falls on the bird, as well as to partly prevent running water entering the nest.

Guarding the Nest.

The cock is very vicious and pugnacious, and will attack any bird or any person approaching the nest; at times he will chase and kick at bucks, jackals, porcupines, and other animals. If, however, a person gets right up to the nest, especially if he kneels or sits beside it, the cock seldom kicks, but puts his head down to the ground, snaps his beak spasmodically, hissing violently meanwhile, and tremulously flutters his wings (which click loudly at the largest joint) in impotent excitement and distress. But if one is only a few yards off he will kick and fight most determinedly. The reason seems obvious; if he kicks at the nest he will almost certainly break the eggs.

The hen is not vicious, and does not fight, except when she has chicks; then the habits of the cock and hen change to some extent; the cock generally runs away with the chicks (he will fight if necessary), while the hen advances to do battle.

Eggs outside the Nest.

Often, during incubation, an egg or two will be found lying outside the nest. Most authorities maintain that the birds put them out designedly, and that such eggs are used as food for the newly-hatched chicks, being broken for this purpose by the parent birds.

There is no truth in either contention. These eggs are rolled out accidentally, and if replaced will not be rejected, as I know from having frequently marked and replaced them by way of experiment. They may be quite fresh, in some stage of incubation, or rotten. There is no truth whatever in the statement that the newly-hatched chicks are fed upon them; but I have seen chicks a few days old greedily eating the dung of their parents, which often, after sitting, is in the form of small pellets. In the earlier days of ostrich-farming I have seen little incubator-hatched chicks supplied with soft cow-dung and beaten-up ostrich egg, but nothing of the sort is done now; they are fed with succulent green food, which is enough for all purposes. If left to Nature, and allowed to run with their parents, they thrive perhaps better than under any other conditions; only they become very wild, and are liable to be killed by hawks, jackals, and other animals.

The Hatching of the Chicks.

If an egg should be broken in the nest, the old birds eat it, shell and all, as they will often do when the first chick or two hatch out. This habit has no doubt given rise to the erroneous belief, expressed by one of the authorities, that the cock breaks the chicks out—cracking the shell with his breast, shaking the chick loose, and then swallowing the membrane! The chicks hatch out unaided, and though no doubt the movements of the parent on the eggs do occasionally help to free a chick which has already pecked through and cracked the shell (as I have seen), there is no design in these movements, and no need for help.

If sitting begins after the hen has laid her full complement of eggs, naturally all fertile eggs will have sufficient time to hatch. Even if she lays one or two after beginning to sit, still all may hatch, for often one bird will remain on the nest during the day (and of course at night) with such chicks as cannot yet stand or walk, while the other feeds close at hand with the stronger ones. Thus the full time for sitting may be, and often is, exceeded by some days, and all the sound eggs may hatch. But if the hen has laid, say, four or five after beginning to sit, it is probable that several will be left in the nest, containing large living chicks (which die in the shell), for the birds will not continue sitting for more than three or four days after the first chicks appear.

Newly-hatched Chicks.

As the time for the eggs to hatch out draws near, the birds become much excited, probably from hearing the chicks crying in the shell, or pecking at it to break themselves out (both sounds being very distinct); the excitement increases as the chicks appear.

When first hatched the chicks are perfectly helpless; the back of the head and adjoining portion of the neck are greatly swollen and out of shape, as are the legs, especially the tarsi and toes, which are puffed and jelly-like, and of a transparent-looking, pinkish yellow. The eyes have a cloudy, expressionless appearance. For some hours they cannot even hold up their heads; they cannot stand firmly until at least twenty-four hours old, nor get about at all until another day older, and then only in a very rickety manner, tumbling over every few steps; nor are they quick and steady on their legs until the swelling has quite subsided. They do not seem to have much consciousness for about the first twenty-four hours, but when once they have found their legs they soon become exceedingly wild unless handled, and rapidly attain to a remarkable speed. For about the first day they eat nothing; after this they may be seen, when the sunshine is warm, sitting on the edge of the nest, just free of the parent, pecking feebly and uncertainly at small objects on the ground, or at anything within their reach. The stronger ones will gradually wander a short distance from the nest with the parent that is not sitting, and eventually all will leave it, being tended by both cock and hen.

Parents and Chicks.

When defending the nest the cock carries himself splendidly, with erect straight neck, his attitude being most imposing and defiant. But when the hen (or the cock) is advancing to protect the chicks, she comes with a rapid, shuffling stride, with lowered head, hissing violently, and with wings fluttering at right angles to the body, flat to the front, and almost touching the ground. Often both cock and hen will run away with the chicks; but if the enemy is close the chicks, especially when very young, will scatter in all directions, and squat separately. Even when older they will squat, if hard pressed. Sometimes, to mislead the pursuer, the parents will feign injury, gradually leading him away from the little chicks. I have seen a cock fall, as if with a broken leg, several times within 200 yards.

When startled the parents emit a short sound of one note, which is a signal of alarm. When the danger is past the chicks (which when squatting lie perfectly still, blending closely with the ground, and are most difficult to discover) arise, and run about in all directions, calling with their penetrating bubbling cry. The old birds return to the neighbourhood where the little ones scattered, and gather them together again. They do not call, but their height, and their keen sight and hearing, enable them readily to find the crying, moving specks. The chicks, too, are very quick at seeing and running to their parents.

The parents know their own chicks, except when quite small, and will kick and peck at others, often killing them. Adult non-breeding birds also do this, as do large chicks to very small ones.

Is the Ostrich Polygamous?

I have not been able to discover any diversity of opinion as to the polygamy of the ostrich;[1] but I do not hesitate to state that the arguments in favour of its monogamy are stronger than those which support the accepted conclusion.

The argument for polygamy is based almost entirely on the fact (an incontestable one) that several hens frequently lay in one and the same nest.

Let us examine this fact and endeavour to ascertain what it implies.

One cock and one hen (not one cock and several hens), having paired, select a spot, and together make the nest. When the spot is well selected, in some secluded place not easily discovered, and where other birds are not in the habit of coming, I have known many cases, in camps containing from 80 to 100 birds of both sexes, where the pair have kept the nest exclusively. Such a nest, unless destroyed by rains or wild animals, is almost certain to yield a large proportion of chicks. This cannot, perhaps, be said of a nest under any other conditions. If, during the laying of the eggs, or after the pair have begun to sit, other hens lay in the nest or sit on it, the yield of chicks will not be so great; there will never, as far as my experience goes, be a good yield; often there are no chicks at all. The pair frequently abandon the nest. A good yield of chicks, in proportion to the eggs laid, is seldom obtained from any nest in which

---

[1] Since writing this, I find that Livingstone appears to have thought the ostrich monogamous.

more than one hen lays or broods; with two hens, a good yield may be got in proportion to the eggs actually sat upon; when there are more than two hens, a few chicks *may* hatch out, but in the great majority of cases there will be none. The chance of obtaining any yield at all lessens as the number of hens increases; with four or more hens it is almost safe to say that chicks *never* result.

Yet it is undeniable that in a camp where many ostriches run, nests are generally shared by several hens, usually by more than two. I have known six or eight to share one nest, and have found a nest with 150 eggs in and about it, many with from fifty to seventy; but it is very exceptional—in fact, almost unknown—for such nests to yield chicks. If it were natural for several hens to share one nest, chicks should result.

Why several Hens often Share one Nest.

Now, how is it, if the ostrich is not polygamous, that several hens often share the same nest?

The following considerations may not quite solve the question, but serve, I think, to help towards its solution.

In a troop of young birds the sexes are about evenly balanced, and, presumably, in the wild state this balance is not much disturbed. But there probably is a preponderance of hens even in the wild state, for in the breeding season the cocks fight among themselves, occasionally with fatal results. In domestication the preponderance of hens is no doubt greater, for cocks are not only killed by kicking at each other through wire fences, thus breaking their legs, but also not infrequently by people they attack. In domestication neither all cocks nor all hens come into season; but as the cocks that are killed are among the most vigorous and mettlesome, the proportion of hens that come into season is greater than that of cocks.

Unattached Hens.

When a cock is ready to breed, he pairs with one hen, and with her makes the nest. If they escape the intrusion of other hens this state of monogamy continues, and chicks result; if they do not, polygamy will probably take place, almost always with disastrous consequences to the nest.

Now, there are other hens in season, and, being in excess of the cocks (which have already paired), they are unattached, having no cocks to mate with or make a nest for them.[1] They surrender to any cock, and are thus fertilised. So excited and overwrought are they that tame hens will often squat on the approach of a man. Such hens generally attach themselves to the cock whose attentions they have attracted (often by intruding on his nest and remaining in the immediate neighbourhood), and lay regularly, at any rate for a time, in his nest. If they cannot lay in the nest because it is already occupied, they will not go at once to another nest, but will deposit their eggs just outside the nest; but if there are many hens to one nest so much bother ensues that some of them be-

[1] Only one case of a hen unaided making a nest has come under my observation.

take themselves to other nests. Others lay in any nest indiscriminately, and are a great nuisance to the farmer. Some keep to one nest until they have laid about a sitting, and then begin to brood; but in such hens the brooding fit does not generally last long, as they can only get on the nest occasionally, and are much disturbed by other hens. Each nest is owned by one cock, but I do not think that generally the hens of his nest are fertilised exclusively by him: sometimes I know they are not. Other hens in season seem to wander about in an unsettled condition, chancing to attract the attentions of any cock and laying indiscriminately in any nest; or they drop their eggs at random about the veld, this habit no doubt helping to give rise to the old Biblical belief, persisting to the present day, that the ostrich leaves her eggs in the sand to hatch by the heat of the sun.

Herein, I think, to a great extent lies the true explanation of the so-called association of several hens with one cock, giving rise to the idea of polygamy. The cock is polygamous, it would seem, not so much from any free choice of his own as because the hens are forced upon him.

Large Chicks Mistaken for Hens.

I think that travellers have often mistaken large chicks for hens. Thus, when they see a cock and some half-dozen drab ostriches together at a nest or in the veld, they at once class them as cock and hens, and say they are polygamous birds, while it is more than likely that the lot consists of one pair with large chicks. I have often seen a large chick mistaken for an adult hen by men of considerable experience as ostrich farmers. Such chicks are not easily distinguished from hens except at close quarters by an experienced man. Andersson seems to have made this mistake, and even to have supposed that a large chick was an ostrich of a different species. It must be remembered that ostriches are some years in reaching maturity, often not attaining their complete adult plumage till four years old. If little chicks (another year's brood) accompanied the pair with large chicks, one would be even more likely to draw a false inference.

Why no Chicks Result.

When several hens lay in the same nest it frequently happens that two wish to lay at the same time. In this case, as a rule, one will lay in the nest, the other on the bare ground outside. Sometimes, however, two hens may be seen on the nest at once. Presently some of the hens will begin to sit (the cock alone sitting at night). One occupies the nest, the other broody hens lying or standing about close at hand, thus betraying its presence. When she arises, whichever of the other hens is quickest, perhaps a laying hen, takes her place. Under these conditions a great many eggs are broken both before sitting begins and afterwards. The hens do not sit by turns; there is no plan in their proceedings at all.

The laying of eggs goes on from day to day by some of the hens even after others have ceased. The consequence of this is that *the same lot* of eggs are never in the nest together for more than a few days at a time. (This I have frequently proved by marking the eggs.) Some are rolled out, new ones are laid, or old ones are rolled in, for the nest becomes trampled almost out of shape by the traffic about it. Thus there are no chicks; the eggs become broken or addled, and the nest is eventually abandoned. Under such conditions it not infrequently happens that the cock (and perhaps some of the hens) abandons the nest in disgust before the full period of incubation is completed. This he never does if he has only one hen and is undisturbed by other birds.

It must also be noted that chicks are attended by one cock and one hen, and that the pair will kick any birds, chicks or adults, that approach them; also that it is a common rule among ostrich farmers to camp off special breeding birds in pairs.

Every authority that I have consulted holds that the ostrich is polygamous, but the evidence against polygamy is very strong: a pair make the nest; the hen lays all her eggs (a full sitting) in that nest; the hatching of the eggs and the care of the chicks are shared equally by cock and hen; the cock loses his sexual vigour and ceases his attentions to the hen, soon after beginning to sit; and one hen to a nest yields the best results.

Evidences for Monogamy stronger than for Polygamy.

I do not, however, think it can be maintained that the monogamy of the ostrich is proved absolutely, but I decidedly think that the arguments in its favour are much stronger than those in support of polygamy. That there is a thoroughly organised polygamy I do not believe. It may perhaps be said that the present state of the relation between the sexes is not quite organised; but if monogamy is not yet firmly established, I hold, at least, that the tendency is that way, and am certain that monogamy is the state most suitable to the propagation of the species, though, under certain conditions, polygamy may be resorted to.

Curious and Exceptional Relations.

Finally, it must be allowed that, while all the facts at my command point strongly to the conclusion that the ostrich is not only often monogamous, but that monogamy is the only condition perfectly favourable to the successful hatching and rearing of young; and that all the arguments in favour of polygamy break down on examination: yet the fact remains that there are a large number of curious and exceptional circumstances connected with the nidification, sexual relations, and parental habits of ostriches that I am not yet exactly able to account for, either on the supposition of fully organised monogamy or polygamy. It is possible that when a larger number of careful observations have been made, and the ostrich, both in its wild state and under domesticated conditions, has been scientifically studied, we shall find certain curious and exceptional conditions governing the nidification and sexual relations of these birds. And it is much to be desired that those especially who have opportunities of studying the ostrich in its wild state, or of obtaining exact information from those who have had these opportunities, should carefully collect all facts, as this matter is one of much scientific interest.

www.ingramcontent.com/pod-product-compliance
Lightning Source LLC
Chambersburg PA
CBHW022054230426
43672CB00008B/1174